OXFORD SHAKESPEARE TOPICS

Published and Forthcoming Titles Include:

Oxford Shakespeare Topics

GENERAL EDITORS: PETER HOLLAND,

AND STANLEY WELLS

Shakespeare and East Asia

ALEXA ALICE JOUBIN

OXFORD

UNIVERSITY PRESS

OXFORD
UNIVERSITY PRESS

Great Clarendon Street, Oxford, OX2 6DP,
United Kingdom

Oxford University Press is a department of the University of Oxford.
It furthers the University's objective of excellence in research, scholarship,
and education by publishing worldwide. Oxford is a registered trade mark of
Oxford University Press in the UK and in certain other countries

First Edition published in 2021

Impression: 1

Published in the United States of America by Oxford University Press
198 Madison Avenue, New York, NY 10016, United States of America

British Library Cataloguing in Publication Data
Data available

Library of Congress Control Number: 2020950684

ISBN 978–0–19–870356–3 (hbk.)
ISBN 978–0–19–870357–0 (pbk.)

DOI: 10.1093/oso/9780198703563.001.0001

Printed and bound by
CPI Group (UK) Ltd, Croydon, CR0 4YY

For Basile

Contents

Contents

x *Contents*

    Plays: *Hamlet*, *King Lear*, *Othello*, *Romeo and Juliet*

    Media and Genres: Singaporean film and theatre
    multilingual theatre, British East Asian theatre,
    American film

    Directors: Ong Keng Sen, Chee Kong Cheah,
    David Tse, Baz Luhrmann

Epilogue   187

    Plays: *Macbeth*, *The Tempest*, *Hamlet*

List of Illustrations

A Note on the Text

Shakespearean quotations, unless otherwise noted, are from Wells and Taylor et al., eds., *Complete Works of William Shakespeare, Second Edition* (Oxford University Press, 2005). All translations are mine unless otherwise noted.

East Asian names appear in the order of family name followed by given name, in respect of East Asian customs, except when they are more familiar inverted (for instance, internationally known playwrights or scholars who publish in English). This book adopts the *pinyin* romanization system for Chinese, Revised Romanization of Korean, and Revised Hepburn for Japanese except when names or phrases are commonly known in a different form. World Englishes such as Singlish are preserved to reflect original spelling and sentence structure. Historical or official names are also preserved (e.g., Canton and Peking University).

Videos, photos, transcriptions, scripts, and critical notes for selected films and productions are available online at *MIT Global Shakespeares* (globalshakespeares.org), an open-access digital performance archive cofounded and coedited by Peter S. Donaldson and Alexa Alice Joubin.

Readers are also invited to consult the glossary, chronology, chapter notes, and further readings.

Prologue

The Cultural Meanings of Shakespeare and Asia Today

Performance is a doubly acted affair that is shaped not only by the characters but also by the actors. Actors embody characters across history and culture. Adaptations, meanwhile, are strangers at home. They defamiliarize canonical works and everyday utterances while offering something recognizable through a new language and form.

When Viola, disguised as page boy Cesario, and finding herself pursued by the lovelorn Olivia, declares that "I am the man . . . she were better love a dream" in *Twelfth Night* (2.2.25–26), she speaks with double irony as a doubly cross-dressed boy actor on the early modern English stage (such as Nathan Field, 1587–1619) and as an adult male actor (Johnny Flynn) in Mark Rylance's all-male production at the Globe Theatre in London in 2012 (dir. Tim Carroll). In Yukio Ninagawa's 2005 Kabuki *Twelfth Night*, Onoe Kikunosuke V brought a new perspective to the notion of gender fluidity when he played in rapid succession Viola, her twin brother Sebastian, and her alter ego Cesario. As an *otokoyaku* (actress specializing in male roles) in the all-female Takarazuka musical production (dir. Kimura Shinji, 1999) derived from *shōjo* (teen girl) mangas, Yamato Yuga's Viola would embody enticing gender fluidity when speaking Japanese, a language that often elides the subject. Since the genre of Takarazuka is an all-female production, Viola's Cesario would not be the only cross-dressing character. *Otokoyaku* actresses present the "sensitive masculinity" of idealized male characters for a predominantly female audience.[1] In addition to making the right choice of employing the familiar or the polite register, based on the relation between the

Shakespeare and East Asia. Alexa Alice Joubin, Oxford University Press (2021). © Alexa Alice Joubin.

speaker and the addressee, male and female speakers of Japanese are restricted by the gender-specific first-person pronouns available to them. The gender dynamics in *Twelfth Night* worked well for Takarazuka, which is known for its romantic, extravagant musicals.[2] Similarly, gendered code-switching creates semantic ambiguity in Kei Otozuki's double performance of both twins, Viola and Sebastian. Having played exclusively male roles in the Takarazuka Revue until her retirement in 2012, Kei brings a unique perspective to her roles in *Twelfth Night*, the second Shakespeare production in Japanese, with a Japanese cast, directed by John Caird, honorary associate director of the Royal Shakespeare Company (Nissay Theatre, Tokyo, March 2015).[3] It was a rare opportunity to see an actress specializing in male roles play Viola, Cesario, and Sebastian.

In general, syntactical differences create linguistic and cultural opportunities in articulating anew Orsino's comments about love from a masculinist perspective and Viola's apology for a woman's love when in disguise (2.4.78–125)—or the exchange between Oliver and Rosalind in disguise as Ganymede on her "lacking a man's heart" when she swoons, nearly giving herself away in *As You Like It* (4.3.164–76). These are but a few examples of how the phenomenon of global Shakespeare reshapes academia, festivals, and theatre circuits. Touring Shakespeare performances and globally circulated films have become a staple at international festivals, allowing audiences to appreciate the vitality of world cinema and theatre.

Since the nineteenth century, stage and film directors have mounted hundreds of adaptations of Shakespeare drawn on East Asian motifs and styles and performed in Japanese, Korean, Mandarin Chinese, Cantonese, Taiwanese, English, Singlish, Hokkien, and a wide range of dialects. Some of the works have originated outside Asia, whereas others have toured from Asia to the West to critical acclaim. They have been recognized as among the most innovative in the world. The first Asian-language performances of Shakespeare took place at different points in history within comparable contexts of modernization: 1885 in Japan, 1913 in China, 1925 in Korea, and 1949 in Taiwan.[4] Performing Shakespeare in Asian styles has constituted an act of defamiliarization for audiences at home and abroad. By the late twentieth century, Shakespeare had become one of the most frequently performed playwrights in East Asia.

Hamlet has been a popular play for political appropriation. Notably, Chinese director Lin Zhaohua staged his production of *Hamlet* (*Hamulaite*) in the wake of the student demonstration in Tian'anmen Square and the Chinese government's crackdown on the democratic movement in Beijing, which culminated in the massacre on June 4, 1989. Lin's *Hamlet* (1989, 1990, 1994), set in contemporary China, used three actors to play the titular character (among other roles) in order to demarcate different stages of psychological development of the prince. The director extrapolated something extraordinary from Hamlet's "To be or not to be" soliloquy (3.1.58–92; delivered alternately and collectively by the three actors) to drive home the message that, in his postsocialist society, "everyone is Hamlet," and Hamlet is one of us. The production paid tribute to the student protestors' boldness in awakening China to the vision of a democratic, civil society. To view the full production (1995 version), visit the page curated by Alexa Alice Joubin on the *MIT Global Shakespeares*: global shakespeares.mit.edu/hamulaite-lin-zhaohua-1995/

Two centuries of Asian interpretations of Shakespeare's plays such as *Hamlet* and *Macbeth* are now making a world of difference in how we experience Shakespeare. Akira Kurosawa's *Throne of Blood* (based on *Macbeth*, Toho Studios, 1957; starring Toshirô Mifune) and *Ran* (based on *King Lear*, Herald Ace and Nippon Herald Films, 1985)— while now canonical in the study of Shakespeare—are far from the earliest or the only Shakespeare films from East Asia. There are several notable early twentieth-century silent film adaptations. Around the time that Asta Nielsen's gender-bending *Hamlet* (dir. Svend Gade and Heinz Schall, 1921) was filmed, silent-film adaptations of *The Merchant of Venice* (*Nü lüshi* [*Woman Lawyer*], also known as *Rouquan* [*Bond of Flesh*], dir. Qiu Yixiang, Tianyi Film, 1927; starring Hu Die [aka Butterfly Hu] as Portia) and *The Two Gentlemen of Verona* (*Yi jian mei* [*A Spray of Plum Blossoms*], dir. Bu Wancang, Lianhua Film, 1931; starring Ruan Lingyu as Julia [Hu Zhuli]) were being made in Shanghai and marketed to the European expatriate and Chinese diasporic communities there and in Canton (today's Guangzhou) and Southeast Asia. An explosion of bold and imaginative interpretations of Shakespeare's plays has occurred since the 1990s, many of which aim to attract audiences in multiple locations around the world. The beginning of the new millennium was for Asian Shakespeares as the 1990s were for Anglo-American Shakespeare on film.

This book traces shared and unique patterns in post-1950s appropriations of Asian and Western motifs across theatrical and cinematic genres. These visions of otherness are located in East Asia, the USA, the UK, and other cultures. The Czech-based artist Nori Sawa combined Japanese Bunraku and Czech puppets in his widely toured solo marionette theatre adaptations of *Macbeth* (1999), *Romeo and Juliet* (2000), and *King Lear* (2004). The culturally hybrid approach to performance has been a signature in his international career since 1992.[5] A Bunraku puppet represents Ariel in Julie Taymor's 1986 Off-Broadway production of *The Tempest* for the Classic Stage Company in New York City.[6] The puppet's head floated above the stage working its magic in various scenes. Prospero freed both the spirit and the puppeteer in the final scene, fusing fiction with reality. Similar to Sawa, Taymor brought together classical Japanese theatre and the Italian *commedia dell'arte* in a visual feast. Kenneth Branagh's Japanesque film *As You Like It* (BBC and HBO, 2006) attempts some form of cultural ventriloquism through its use of film and imaginary locations: Wakehurst Place dressed up with a Zen garden, shrine gate, and trappings of a nineteenth-century Japan torn between samurai and European merchants. The intercultural fusion is reflected by Rosalin's and Celia's Victorian dresses during the sumo match between Orlando and Charles (Fig. 1). Sitting behind them, Duke Frederick dons dark samurai armor. Both *As You Like It* and the dream of Japan are deployed ornamentally in the filmmaker's signature visual romanticism (e.g., Orlando's love letters in Japanese *kanji*).[7] These are but a few examples of hybrid Asian-Western aesthetics. More recently, South Korean director Chan-wook Park's American debut film *Stoker* (Fox Searchlight, 2013) features India Stoker (Mia Wasikowska) as a female Hamlet figure. Well known for his eclectic, Korean-language revenge thriller *Oldboy* (CJ Entertainment, 2003), Park ventures into English-language filmmaking with *Stoker*, which is not explicitly marketed as an Asian adaptation of *Hamlet* but is recognized by many reviewers as a film with Freudian-inflected, Hamletian elements.[8]

How do Anglophone directors such as Taymor and Branagh use imaginaries of Asia differently from directors based in Asia, such as

Fig. Prol. 1 Branagh's *As You Like It*. Rosalin (Bryce Dallas Howard), Celia (Romola Garai), and Duke Frederick (Brian Blessed) at the sumo match between Orlando (David Oyelowo) and Charles (Nobuyuki Takano).

the larger-than-life cherry tree in the widely toured production of *Macbeth* (1980) directed by Yukio Ninagawa? Conversely, what cultural logic governs the circulation and reception of works by East Asian directors, such as *Stoker* by Park, Nori Sawa's puppet theatre, and *Throne of Blood* by Kurosawa? Why do critics repeatedly use the adjective "Shakespearean" to describe the genre fluidity of South Korean director Bong Joon-ho's quadruple Academy Award-winning *Parasite* (Barunson E&A, 2019), which features a unique tonal blend of tragic, comic, lyrical, and horror elements?[9] More so than Kurosawa's films, Bong's Korean-language film has transcended what he called "the one-inch-tall barrier of subtitles" to reach large, international audiences.[10] How do the crossovers between theatricalization and cinematic conventions enrich performances? Directors see the copresence of Shakespearean and non-Western motifs as a unique opportunity, and they use select cultural elements drawn from disparate genres, such as conventionalized gender presentations and Chinese martial arts sequences, as common denominators and bonding agents between different periods and cultural locations. The artists' racial identities can sometimes incriminate them in ethnic selling out or cultural imperialism. In other contexts, however, their cultural origins and locations exonerate them from cultural appropriation.

Directors—regardless of their cultural affiliations—working with Asian motifs often have to contend with their regionally marked cultural identity. Their works are compelled to respond to the competing demands to inhabit simultaneously the local and the global, to be innovative but conservative enough to be palatable, to represent Asia on the world market, and to be the conveyor of an Anglophone West to Asian audiences and vice versa.

This book is titled *Shakespeare and East Asia*, rather than *Shakespeare in East Asia*, to signal the interplay between the two condensed cultural signifiers and to emphasize a shift away from the linear, one-way-street model of tracing the transplantation of a British "giant" into a colonial cultural context. This false dichotomy between the native and the foreign can be broken down when we consider global Shakespeare performances in the context of cross-media and cross-cultural citations, the cultural vibration linking productions in different cultures. Adaptations reference or echo one another, across cultures and genres, in addition to the Shakespearean pretext.

Asian interpretations of Shakespeare matter to Western readers because of their impact on American and European performance cultures, as exemplified by the worldwide recognition of the works of Akira Kurosawa, Ong Keng Sen, and Oh Tae-suk. The pairing of a Western playwright with a set of Asian performance practices provides historically necessary and heuristically illuminating cases of filmmaking and theatre making.[11] The clashes and confluences of Asia and Shakespeare give a "local habitation" to the "airy nothing" of globalization (*A Midsummer Night's Dream*, 5.1.17–18). Asian Shakespeares are sufficiently complex and coherent as a system of signification to interface global cultural studies. For instance, through Asian Shakespeares metacritical inquiries may be launched into how Shakespeare and Asia have been used as cultural signifiers in competing narratives about gender, race, and nation. Further, non-Anglophone interpretations of Shakespeares matter to readers because the expansion of English studies is currently occurring "outside the discipline's traditional Anglophone . . . base." In his study of literary prestige, James English has called for scholars "at the presumptive center of things to begin paying more attention to the forms our discipline is taking at [those] sites of rapid expansion."[12]

Compulsory Realpolitik

Performance creates varied pathways to dramatic and cultural meanings across history, but polity-driven historiography has constructed linear, synchronic narratives that have been flattened by national profiling, a tendency to characterize a non-Western artwork based on stereotypes of its nation of origin and to regard, for example, South Korean adaptations of Shakespeare as political allegories of the postwar tensions on the Korean Peninsula. The problem here is one of *compulsory realpolitik*—the conviction that the best way to understand non-Western works is by interpreting their engagement with pragmatic politics. This approach may impose intentionality upon directors and imply that their works are of interest solely because of their testimonial value. The approach runs the risk of turning global Shakespeares into "mere curiosities or colonial remnants."[13]

As a cultural institution, Shakespeare registers a broad spectrum of values and practices that rivals the complexity of the freighted notion of Asia. Consider, for example, the divergent Shakespeares paradoxically branded by the Globe Theatre in London,[14] by the American Shakespeare Center and Blackfriars Playhouse in Staunton, Virginia, and by a slew of such institutions as the Panasonic Globe in Tokyo (1988–2002) and replicas of the first (1599) and second (1614) Globe theatres being planned for Beijing, Stratford (Connecticut), and Rio de Janeiro.[15] Likewise, the dissemination of knowledge of Asian styles of performance has been fraught with the politics of recognition and branding. Early examples include Madame Sadayakko's (1871–1946) quintessentially Japanese performances in the United States and Europe[16] and Mei Lanfang's (1894–1961) transformation of *jingju* (Beijing opera) into *guoju* (national opera) and a form of "tactical Orientalism" in Moscow (where Bertolt Brecht was inspired to create his theory of the alienation effect), in Washington, DC, and eventually on Broadway.[17] As Fredric Jameson puts it in his working definition, globalization has become "an untotalizable totality which intensified binary relations between its parts."[18]

The first phase of sustained study of global Shakespeare performance unfolded over the past two decades and has brought national political histories to bear on the story of Shakespeare in global contexts. There are detailed histories of national Shakespeares in which "Shakespeare in India" is shorthand for postcolonial, political merits of adaptations of Shakespeare that serve as a tool for resisting Western hegemony. South Korean Shakespeares would be seen as allegories of the divide between North and South Korea, while mainland Chinese works on world tours would be thought to contain attenuated allusions to the Cultural Revolution. Anglophone Shakespeares are assumed to have broad theoretical applicability and aesthetic merits, whereas foreign Shakespeares—even when they focus on artistic innovation on a personal rather than an epic level—are compelled to prove their political worth. Critics are on the lookout for potentially subversive political messages in these works, which are compulsorily characterized as allegories of geopolitical issues.

There are a number of implications of this approach, which isolates performances in their perceived cultural origins. It could miss the rich intertexts between performance traditions; most adaptations borrow from more than one culture. It could subsume local history under Shakespeare criticism or vice versa. It could also imply that works from the Global South or Asia, assumed to be operating as national allegories, are valuable only for their political messages rather than their aesthetic merits, leading to research questions driven by polity—for example, "Why are there so many global Shakespearean adaptations in cultures with no love for Great Britain?"[19] Last, but not least, the fetishization of political merits could unduly emphasize global Shakespeares' alleged deviation from Anglophone practices and, in turn, instrumentalize global Shakespeares for the purpose of diversifying the scholarship and curricula in the United Kingdom, the United States, and Canada.[20] Though there are valuable monographs on national Shakespeares, the same cannot be said of performances across genres that interface with more than one culture or region.[21]

National profiling—the tendency to bracket, for example, "Shakespeare in Japan" in isolation from other cultural influences—is a symptom of the aforementioned assumption that performances in the United Kingdom, the United States, and Canada are normative and aesthetically universal, whereas Shakespeare in Japan bears location-specific, often political, meanings—its aesthetic meanings are either indecipherable or uninteresting. As Rey Chow observes, despite "the current facade of welcoming non-Western 'others' into putatively . . . cross-cultural exchanges," there is still "a continual tendency to . . . ghettoize non-Western cultures . . . by way of ethnic, national labels."[22] Due to the current structure of academia and hierarchies of cultural prestige, Asianists have always been obliged to know their Sophocles, Shakespeare, Molière, Ibsen, and Anglo-European critical theories, though scholars of Shakespeare and European literature tend to regard knowledge of Asian writers and directors as the responsibility of those who specialize in the subfields.

As a result, works by nonwhite authors are imagined to fix their intellectual content "by way of a national, ethnic, or cultural location."[23] Western, white examples are assumed to be more effective in their explanatory power, while African, Asian, and Latin American materials are recruited to serve as the exceptional particular. Henry Louis Gates Jr. makes a similar observation in his call for developing a "black theory" specifically for the interpretation of African American literature to counter the tendency not to see aesthetic merit in black literature. He writes that "black literature and its criticism . . . have been put to uses that were not primarily aesthetic; rather, they have formed part of a larger discourse on the nature of the black, and of his or her role in the order of things."[24]

Equally problematic is the tendency to regard the global and the local as politically expedient, diametrically opposed categories of difference in an often-unarticulated agenda to preserve a literary elite. The global is imagined to be "whatever the United States"—and by extension Great Britain—"is not."[25] In reference to the success of Haruki Murakami's and Orhan Pamuk's novels in translation on the Western literary market, Tim Parks coined the phrase "the dull new global novel" to describe what some critics believe to be a neutral style of writing that lends itself to translation.[26] In this view, these novels do not tend to contain culturally specific references or complex linguistic features of their local languages. They use Western motifs to cater to the taste of Western readers. Karolina Watroba has critiqued this line of argument about works that are "eminently translatable" due to their transparency by pointing out that critics of this type of works assign low aesthetic value to them in the first place: "An undercurrent of elitism is revealed in an ostensibly materialist argument: 'the local' and 'the global' start to sound like code words for 'highbrow' and 'lowbrow.'"[27]

Asian Shakespeares give us a category that we can use to develop a site-specific critical vocabulary to address the epistemological foundation of histories of cultural globalization. They provide historical materials to bear on the tension between cultural homogenization and heterogenization in global communities.[28] This is not to say that studies of Shakespeare in performance should be eclipsed to give way to Asian film and theatre history just because Asia as a whole matters politically and economically in what the journalistic discourse bills as an "Asian century." The approach would risk creating new forms of Cold War-speak and epistemological Orientalism.[29] "Asiacentricity" is as problematic as "Eurocentricity."[30] As Rossella Ferrari writes, scholarship should treat Asian performing arts as "active producers of original epistemologies rather than merely as providers of ethnographies and derivative adaptations."[31] The story of Asian performance is not and should not always be political, though the Western media often gravitate toward stories of political dissidents. Stories of political oppression must be told, but dichotomized views do not get us very far.[32]

While Asia may, in Gayatri Chakravorty Spivak's words, be an "impossible interpellation" due to its inherent diversity and incongruity,[33] and Shakespeare a repository of endless recursive mimesis and theatrical repetition, each of these cultural conglomerates can be configured both to operate as a local canon and simultaneously to project a self-image in new contexts of signification, which is particularly true at international festivals and in touring productions. The critical tendency to prioritize realpolitik in non-Western works leads to blind spots in our understanding of the logic and significance of Asian Shakespeares.

The Postnational Space

Granted, some directors do tap into realpolitik to conceive and market their works. Artists and festival organizers have used Shakespeare and Asia as geopolitical and visual markers in past decades to propagate their worldviews. Many artists rely on international spectators to disseminate their decidedly local works, and more and more festivals thrive on the ideological purchase of being "global."[34] However, they do so as they engage in generic innovation and formalistic experiments, both of which aspects tend to be overlooked by critics.

We have now arrived at the cusp of the second phase of global Shakespeare performance; theatre and film artists are challenging fixed notions of tradition and a narrow definition of cultural authenticity. Shakespeare performances have entered a postnational space, where identities are blurred by the presence of international performers, tourist audiences, transnational corporate sponsors, and the logic of international festivals. The postnational space shares characteristics of liminal spaces that are discursively formed. As Ian Watson writes in his observation of culture (which is defined by inclusion, exclusion, and a sense of belonging), the liminal spaces are sites of "conflict, eruption, compromise, debate, and above all, negotiation."[35] Cultural ownership is a fiction, and familiarity with traditional cultural practices does not align with ethnicity. In fact, certain Asian theatrical practices such as *jingju* and Noh are unfamiliar genres on their home turfs today, and Shakespeare's language has more immediate impact in modern translations, even as it grows more distant from the universe of English speakers. Outside the region, Asian cinematic and theatrical idioms such as *kung fu* and *jingju* are becoming more common in English– and European-language performances.

The transnational cultural flows go beyond the scope of geopolitical divisions of nation-states and cultural profiling. In other words, performances have deterritorializing and reterritorializing effects that unmark the cultural origins of intercultural interpretations because they work against assumptions about politically defined geographies. These performances tend to regard such geographies as artificial constraints that no longer speak to the realities of globalized art. Gilles Deleuze and Félix Guattari developed the concept of deterritorialization to analyze cultural relations that are in flux. *Deterritorialization* is a process that separates cultural practices from their "native" habitats or points of origin. Performance styles such as Kabuki are available for appropriation by all artists, and, conversely, Japanese directors' use of Kabuki is not by default more authentic than a French practitioner's deployment of Kabuki elements. Touring productions can also *reterritorialize* the plays upon arriving in a new location, taking root in a new venue and taking on local colors.[36] As a result, intercultural works are best understood through theatrically defined cultural locations influenced by transnational networks of collaboration and funding (e.g., a French–Japanese *Richard II* by Ariane Mnouchkine in Paris and on tour, or a "culturally neutral" *Richard III* made in Beijing by Lin Zhaohua, set in a no place, and presented in Berlin).

Therefore, my approach is marked by a fundamental departure from the national lens; it emphasizes the connections between distinctive and often conflicting interpretations of "Shakespeare" and "Asia" in different cultural and visual contexts. Numerous performances recast Shakespeare and Asia as condensed collective signifiers of cultural values through their marketability for audiences in different locations. Outside their country of origin, intercultural works attract audiences who are enthralled by the performance of the exotic, whether it's Shakespearean or Asian motifs. Within their local market, the name brand of an editorialized Shakespeare with Anglophone lineage helps to boost their production value.

Focusing on aesthetic and social functions of performances, this book situates adaptations of Shakespeare and Asian narratives in a postnational space of exchange. Chapters do not create or celebrate new centers for the postcolonial cachet of these adaptations, such as the sentiments expressed by the Calibanization of *The Tempest* or the quip of Malian singer Ali Ibrahim "Farka" Touré that Timbuktu is "right at the heart of the world" despite its obscurity on the world map.[37] In addition to giving us a critical category to examine how knowledge about performance is organized, the complexity of the transhistorical and translingual migrations of Shakespeare and Asian performance idioms compels us to maintain a productive critical distance from assumptions of familiarity and knowability.

My approach, which mines rhizomatic and horizontal connections among adaptations, reevaluates the perceived lack of connections between a known Western body of dramatic works and lesser-known East Asian traditions. Deleuze and Guattari use the botanical metaphor of "rhizome" to describe multiplicities, as opposed to an "arborescent" model of knowledge, which is hierarchic like a tree's trunk and branches.[38] A rhizome is characterized by its horizontal stem with lateral shoots. Since a rhizome provides nonlinear, trans-species connections in plants, a rhizomatic network of knowledge captures multiplicity more effectively through nonhierarchical entry and exit points in data sets and the interpretations of culture. My interpretive model for embodied performances connects what may otherwise seem to be isolated instances of artistic expression. The field has come a long way in the four decades since J. L. Styan demonstrated the value of "stage-centered criticism" in Shakespeare studies in 1977.[39] The primary focus of Shakespeare criticism in the late 1990s was on the author-function in performances, though James Bulman cautioned against replacing "the old textuality with a new form of performance textuality which may be 'read.'" The move was driven by recognition of the "multiple material existences" of any single play.[40] As variously articulated notions of performativity penetrate ever deeper into cultural studies, the Shakespearean oeuvre is no longer a repository of "textual obligation[s]" detached from "performative option[s]."[41] Concepts such as the politics of visibility and repetition with a difference have transformed our understanding of the perpetual struggles for primacy between text and representation, and my approach acknowledges these theoretical developments.[42]

Cinematic Stage and Theatrical Film

There are deep connections among adaptations that extend through different media and genres. Few monographs in the field bring film and theatre studies together, but the nature of the material at hand demands that these two major genres be placed in a comparative context. To account for structural and narratological connections that are articulated through fusions of genres, this book looks at films and theatre works to explore the following questions: What cultural values associated with Shakespeare do Asian and Western artists appropriate? Why do characters' gender identities take a personal turn in appropriations? How do these artists use Shakespeare's plays to reframe modernity and reinvent local and global genres of performance in the international circuit of festivals?

There are compelling reasons to bring the genres of theatre and film to bear on each other rather than placing them in isolated silos. Several works examined in this book are products of metacinematic and metatheatrical operations, contestations among genres for primacy, or experimentations with features of disparate genres. It is more productive to examine samples from both dominant genres (theatre and film) for comparative analysis. For instance, although scholarship on global Shakespeare tends to focus more on theatre, East Asian cinema holds an important place in world cultures: Japanese feature and animation films have become source material for adaptation around the world; South Korea is projecting soft power through its exported films, television dramas, and the Korean Wave (*hallyu*); and Hong Kong cinema is the world's third largest film industry in terms of global influence after Bollywood and Hollywood, according to the UNESCO Institute for Statistics' 2013 report on cinema infrastructure. Analyzing works of adaptation from a key film culture enhances our overall understanding of global Shakespeare.

Chapter 1 offers new methods for looking at and listening to Shakespearean films and stage productions by focusing on the works and aesthetic claims of Akira Kurosawa and Yukio Ninagawa. Kurosawa used traditional Japanese theatrical elements in his cinematic depictions of Macbeth and Lady Macbeth; his signature long shots, which remain emotionally detached, are echoed in Ninagawa's stage version of *Macbeth*, particularly in scenes played behind semitransparent screen doors. Ninagawa was well known for the cinematic quality of some of his stage productions, and Kurosawa derived inspiration from Noh and Kabuki styles of presentation and makeup.

Among the works discussed in Chapter 2, the theatre occupies a central place in the Hong Kong comedy film *One Husband Too Many* (dir. Anthony Chan, 1988). The rustic stage where the play within a film is mounted serves as both a dramatic device and a venue where cultural values are negotiated. Following a couple aspiring to introduce Western culture to backwater Hong Kong through their iffy performance of *Romeo and Juliet* (itself an imitation of Franco Zeffirelli's 1968 period screen version), the film pits the decidedly local vibe of the stage against the perceived universal values of cinema. When the onscreen audience's booing prompts an unplanned intermission, they do not leave while the couple collect themselves backstage; rather, the audience seems invested in seeing how the production will turn out, even if they do not endorse it. Through its protagonist's Quixotic insistence on staging Shakespeare for enlightening messages, the film grinningly contrasts the contrivance of Zeffirelli's film with any fantasy that the allegedly greatest (British) love story of all time can ameliorate social conditions in Hong Kong.

One of the films analyzed in Chapter 3, *The King and the Clown* (dir. Lee Joon-ik, 2005), from South Korea, brings the life of two fifteenth-century traveling players to bear on Hamletian narratives of the discoverability of truth. King Yeon-san of the Joseong era hires these vagabond players to help him catch the conscience of corrupt court officials. With a transgender figure, the clown, at the core of its narrative, the film creates ironic distances to both the craft of filmmaking itself and to traditional Korean puppet and cross-gender theatres.

The Singaporean film *Chicken Rice War* (dir. Chee Kong Cheah, 2000), featured in Chapter 4, draws its comedic energy from its rehearsals and performances of *Romeo and Juliet* and the offstage life of the actors in that college production. The film inserts an aspiring television news anchor to report on the conflicts between two families who own competing chicken rice stalls next to each other ("Two families, both alike in dignity and profession . . . "). Against moments where the stage asserts its putative Shakespearean or local authenticity (students performing in English; an elderly woman singing about the "feud" in Cantonese operatic tunes), cinematic elements of camerawork and editing (cutting between shots of the failed stage performance and reaction shots of parents interrupting the performance) strive to reclaim the superiority of film as a genre. As shown in Chapter 4, the film's opening and closing scenes, narrated by the news anchor, simultaneously parody Shakespeare's prologue, epilogue, and Baz Luhrmann's film, *William Shakespeare's Romeo + Juliet*. Like *The King and the Clown*, *Chicken Rice War* thrives on the tension between theatricalized presentation (such as the play within a play) and verisimilitude in cinematic representation.

These crossovers instantiate formalistic experiments and expressions of a range of ideological positions. Though theatre and film are distinct forms, we gain a fuller understanding of adaptation by taking stock of the cross-currents and common threads between them. Their intergeneric dynamics are best understood in a holistic context and through comparative analysis.

Form, Ideology, Reception, Diaspora

Shakespeare and East Asia identifies four themes that distinguish interpretations of Shakespeare in post-1950s East Asia from works in other parts of the world:

(1) formalistic innovations in sound and spectacle,
(2) ideological investments in art's remedial functions,
(3) conflicting and polity-driven production and reception, and
(4) multilingualism in diasporic adaptations.

More specifically, these four themes form a series of concentric circles of analysis that move from form to ideology, from local to global contexts, and from production to reception.

The book is structured around modes in which one might encounter Asian-themed performances of Shakespeare. Each chapter—unhindered by divisions of plays or performance genres—offers an approach to reading particular works. Although there is significant intra-Asian cross-fertilization, each chapter generally examines works from one cultural sphere. There are a multitude of approaches to Shakespeare and East Asia, and this book offers but one possible path through the historical material. Readers are encouraged to explore the connections across these works and languages. Many of the works selected contain teachable moments and are readily available in replayable media, such as digital video. Among the criteria for selection have been availability and accessibility, positionality within Asian and Anglo-European cultures, and curricular applicability.

Since Japan has historically been a gateway for the filtration of Western ideas into East Asia, Chapter 1 focuses on the achievements of Kurosawa's postwar film version of *Macbeth* and Ninagawa's contemporary stage version. The two directors have been influential in both the West and Asia: both pioneers—perhaps unwittingly—in the internationalization of Asian Shakespeares, they were discovered by English-speaking critics early on and became part of the canonical critical framework. As the "default" Asian directors for discussion, they have emerged, over time, as more palatable and "less foreign" to Western minds. Mindful of Ninagawa's and Kurosawa's representative function in canonical criticism, this chapter delineates methodologies to listen to and view performances by analyzing the aural, musical, and visual compositions of Kurosawa's and Ninagawa's works. Both directors combine a visual language borrowed from Japanese painting and Shakespearean motifs to defamiliarize and unpack stock images of *Macbeth* and Japan. A prime example would be Ninagawa's *Macbeth*, which takes place under a large cherry tree within an enlarged, stage-size

Buddhist altar for home worship. As Macbeth wades through blood, spring turns to autumn and the petals fall. Another example is the final scene of Kurosawa's film. The Macbeth figure dies from arrows made of the forest, symbolizing that the forest encroaches upon his castle to consume him. Complex and multidimensional, the works of both directors compel us to reexamine our assumptions about Japanese and Shakespearean performance cultures.

Chapter 2 continues the line of inquiry into the intersections of form and ideology in the Sinophone world. One prominent strand of adaptation is an imagined remedial effect that Shakespearean motifs and East Asian aesthetics can have on each other, on the artists, and on the audiences. Works analyzed in this chapter either amplify Shakespeare's purported remedial merit and instrumentality, using it to promote social justice, or ironize it in parodies of the political efficacy of a "reparative" Shakespeare. With case studies from Hong Kong, Taiwan, and China, this chapter examines the politics of reform, the myths of Shakespeare's remedial merit, and the operating principles of these myths. Such metacriticism allows us to move beyond national profiling by bringing formalistic features to bear on the ideological purchase of adaptations. Feng Xiaogang's *kung fu* feature *The Banquet* (*Ye yan*, 2006), for example—made in the same genre as *Crouching Tiger, Hidden Dragon* (dir. Ang Lee, 2000)—adapts *Hamlet* in a way that remedially recasts gender roles. The film gives Gertrude and Ophelia, women characters who are traditionally silenced, a strong presence. One might even say that *The Banquet* "rescues" Ophelia from a fate of being silenced by the patriarchy. Parody, on the other hand, provides quite a different take on the idea of remediation. Though the emergence of parodic rewritings can indicate a society's familiarity with the Western canon and confidence in its own performance genres, there are subtle distinctions between actual familiarity and using parody to construct a familiarity that does not yet exist. Taiwan, a society more Westernized than many of its East Asian neighbors,[43] with an American system of secondary and higher education, has produced more irreverent approaches to Shakespeare—a prominent example being *Shamlet*, Lee Kuo-hsiu's long-running (since 1994) stage parody. Chapter 2 also situates select works in the international contexts of such *Hamlet*-inflected works as Tom Stoppard's *Rosencrantz and Guildenstern Are Dead*.

Building upon the foundation of formalistic and ideological criticism, Chapter 3 examines the metacritical question of the production and reception of adaptations. It first tunes in to the diverse, both parallel and conflicting, voices behind the production of select works from South Korea in a polyphonic framework. Each of the voices—artistic and political, drawn from shamanistic traditions and Shakespearean narratives—has its own trajectory, authority, and weight in the arc of development of an adaptation from inception to reception. Among the different sites for the engagement of Asia and Shakespeare, two of the richest, yet understudied, cities are London and Edinburgh; there, the commercialization of festivals is complicated by the expectations of compulsory realpolitik of Asianized spectacles and, sometimes, Asian exceptionalism. Shakespeare makes Asian theatre legible in the British context, and Asian performance styles played an important role in the rise of Shakespearean theatre as a global genre, as evidenced by the British reception of Oh Tae-suk's *Romeo and Juliet* (London, 2006) and *The Tempest* (Edinburgh, 2011). This chapter argues that performing Shakespeare in Asian styles and manufacturing Asian identities through Shakespearean theatre are reciprocal processes that have contributed to the emergence of Asian productions.

Cultural identities are not always rooted in one place or one national language. Moving from monolingual to multilingual performances, Chapter 4 explores the dilemma of intercultural identity in the Asian diaspora, examining works that not only feature translation as a political metaphor but also dramatize the interstitial space among languages. One such case is the aforementioned Singaporean film *Chicken Rice War*, a work that addresses local language policy and global teen culture, critiquing Singapore's multiracial policies that seek to erase ethnic differences. The chapter also asks: What are the political implications when an English-speaking Singaporean director such as Ong Keng Sen appropriates *King Lear* and Noh theatre to create the multilingual stage work *Lear* (1997 and 1999), a piece both intracultural ("pan-Asian") and intercultural? Ong's diasporic background informed the structure of his pan-Asian, multilingual *Lear*. Symbolizing a revisionist history of the Japanese occupation of Singapore (1942–45), the Mandarin-speaking Older Daughter kills her Japanese-speaking father, only to discover that she now inhabits the patriarchal role she has critiqued. Like Goethe's Wilhelm Meister, who searches for a national identity through his performance of the prince in *Hamlet,* Ong puts his actors in search of a new Asian identity through his multilingual productions. In what ways do Ong's works differ, formalistically and ideologically, from Ninagawa's Kabuki-style *Macbeth* or the British-born but France-based director Peter Brook's *Mahābhārata* (1985)? How "Asian" is a touring production when it is specifically designed for the context and taste of audiences at an international festival? Ong, who was invited in 2009 to speak at the Shakespeare Association of America's conference and to screen his *Lear* in Washington, DC, is not only a leading director in world theatre but also an influential playwright and curator. His highly self-conscious works are well known for their high-gloss postmodernism.

The four chapters of *Shakespeare and East Asia* thus move through concentric circles of analysis, from formalistic and sociological criticism to reception studies and the politics of multilingualism. The adaptations examined break new ground in sound and spectacle; they serve as a vehicle for artistic and political remediation or, in some cases, the critique of the myth of recuperation; they provide a forum where diasporic artists and audiences can grapple with contemporary issues; and, through international circulation, they are reshaping debates about the relationship between East Asia and Europe.

Caveat Lector

It should be noted that most of the directors and adapters examined in this book are male, which has long been a function of the setup of Asian theatre and film industries, particularly when it comes to adaptations of Shakespeare. The inequality is stark in the theatre circle, though there are a few prominent female artists, such as Chinese American director Tisa Chang, Taiwanese choreographer Lin Hsiu-wei, and Japanese playwright Kishida Rio. Born in Chongqing, China, and now a key figure in Asian American theatre, Chang founded the Pan Asian Repertory Theatre in New York in 1977. Her company's Asian American adaptation *Shogun Macbeth* is discussed in Chapter 1. Lin cofounded with her husband, Wu Hsing-kuo, the Contemporary Legend Theatre in Taipei in 1986. The company's solo *Lear Is Here* is discussed in Chapter 2. Lin also played a triply masked dancing doll in the company's *Kingdom of Desire* (Beijing opera based on *Macbeth*, dir. Wu Hsing-kuo, 1987). Kishida is a key collaborator with Singaporean director Ong Keng Sen on *Lear* and *Desdemona* (Chapter 4). As one of the few feminist playwrights in Japan with her own company and a member of the first generation of female directors, Kishida had several intra-Asian collaborative productions. She is best known outside Japan for her collaboration with Ong, notably on *Lear* (1997), a multilingual production with performers from Japan, China, Indonesia, Thailand, Singapore, and Malaysia. Unfortunately, these works have come to be known primarily as Ong's productions.[44]

There are, of course, also figures such as Miyata Keiko, a rare, award-winning woman director in a men's world. She was artistic director of the New National Theatre in Japan from 2010 to 2018. The dismissal of Hitoshi Uyama and subsequent appointment of Miyata was protested by Yukio Ninagawa, Hisashi Inouue, and other leading directors. She has directed productions of plays by Bertolt Brecht, George Bernard Shaw, Arthur Miller, Ibsen, and others. However, Miyata is not known for adaptations of Shakespeare.

Wherever possible, I have also made an effort to draw attention to works by women and gender minorities, such as Komaki Kurihara's landmark performance of Lady Macbeth (Lady Asaji) in Kurosawa's film *Throne of Blood* (Chapter 1), or Lee Joon-gi's embodiment of Gong-gil, a transgender court entertainer, in the film *The King and the Clown* (Chapter 3).

Conclusion

The history of East Asian Shakespeares as a body of works—as opposed to random stories about cross-cultural encounter—allows us to understand better the processes of localizing artistic ideas through transnational collaboration, processes that can unsettle assumptions about the stability of Shakespeare as a textual and verbal presence and about Asia as a privileged, unified visual sign. Going beyond what has been theorized by Walter Benjamin as the translational mode of survival (*Überleben*) and continuous, extended life (*Fortleben*) of art-works,[45] adaptations register the negotiations between fiction and history, between genres and modes of representation, between text and performance, between what happens in the narrative in the past and the social discourse in the present. Adaptations activate the historicity of a play and mobilize differences to achieve an impact onstage and onscreen. They lead us away from an overdetermined concept of the canon.

"To unpath'd waters, undream'd shores"

Sound and Spectacle

Following the sounds of gongs on a dimly lit proscenium stage, the "Sanctus" from Gabriel Fauré's *Requiem* (1887–1900) swells softly as two meanly dressed elderly women walk down the aisles, carrying with them bento boxes, sewing kits, and grocery bags. Although they wear ragged clothes, they are well provisioned. When they finally reach and climb up to the stage, they pray at a gigantic set resembling a blown-up version of a *butsudan*, or Buddhist household altar, which dwarfs the performers and audiences, and remain onstage for the entirety of the production. The two women push the massive, multipanel folding shutters outwards to the sides of the stage and take their places there, facing in towards the stage and the audience. When the lights come up, long-haired witch figures played by male Kabuki actors specializing in female roles (*onnagata*) dance to falling cherry petals behind the semitranslucent screens in a cinematically inspired slow-motion scene (Fig. 1.1). These screen doors are opened to reveal a 2018 New York revival of Ninagawa Yukio's (1935–2016) landmark 1985 touring production of *Macbeth* (Amsterdam and Edinburgh) in Japanese (which show premiered in Tokyo in 1980). The two women start knitting and eating nonchalantly. Occasionally they pay attention to stage action and weep, but most of the time they seem indifferent to the unfolding of prophecy, scheming, and bloodbath onstage, as if outside both the play's world and audience's world. Two years after the director passed away, New York's Lincoln Center revived this production with the original cast as part of their Mostly Mozart Festival in 2018. A portrait of Ninagawa appeared onstage during

Shakespeare and East Asia. Alexa Alice Joubin, Oxford University Press (2021). © Alexa Alice Joubin.
DOI: 10.1093/oso/9780198703563.003.0001

Fig. 1.1 Ninagawa's *Macbeth* (Lincoln Center New York, 2018). Falling cherry petals behind semitranslucent screens. Reproduced by permission of Stephanie Berger.

curtain call to pay tribute to one of the most revered directors of modern times, which speaks to the influence of Ninagawa beyond East Asia.

This well-traveled production seamlessly blends theatrical and cinematic modes of expression. The performance is in conversation with multiple early modern and modern Japanese stage genres (including Noh), classical music, samurai film, and Akira Kurosawa's (1910–98) influential film adaptation of the same play entitled *Throne of Blood* (*Kumonosu-jō* [lit.: Spider's Web Castle], Toho Company, 1957). Along with other versions of Shakespeare's plays on the global stage, East Asian performances create a space for imagination that is neither here nor there, taking audiences, as *The Winter's Tale*'s Camillo puts it, "to unpath'd waters, undream'd shores" (4.4.566–67).

We begin our journey through Shakespeare and East Asia in Japan, because Japan is historically the first port of entry for western ideas and canons into the region, including Shakespearean motifs and plays. For example, a group of Korean intellectuals studying in Japan (Geugyesul yeonguhoe, Theatre Arts Research Association, also known as Performing Arts Research Association) in 1933 staged the trial scene from *The Merchant of Venice*.[1] Chinese students studying in Japan in the early twentieth century also played a key role in appropriating western classics. Japan's influence in East Asia is part of its colonial history, for Japan colonized Taiwan from 1895 to 1945 and annexed Korea from 1910 to 1945.

In Japan, two directors stand out in the history of reception of Shakespeare: Ninagawa and Kurosawa. Ninagawa, modern Japan's theatre guru, and Kurosawa, a virtuoso master in cinema, are both known for their reinventions of Shakespearean and Japanese aesthetics. Situated at the crossroads of East Asian and Anglophone visual cultures, both of them are what François Truffaut defined as *auteurs*, directors who leave a palpable personal signature on their works even as they themselves are undeniably also products of their culture and historical era.[2] They contributed to East Asian Shakespeare traditions by offering viable models of adaptation and by inspiring new cinematic and theatrical approaches to Shakespeare in subsequent generations.

Ninagawa is one of the few directors in the world to have directed all thirty-seven of Shakespeare's plays including *Pericles*, a task he began in 1997 as the artistic director of the prestigious Sai-no-kuni Shakespeare series. He even directed the same plays multiple times over the years, for example, doing *Hamlet* six times on different occasions in Japan and the United Kingdom. (*Hamlet*, by the way, has a special place in the history of Japanese reception of Shakespeare: there are more than a hundred different translations in Japanese.) Meanwhile, Kurosawa holds the distinction of having directed striking film adaptations of *Hamlet*, *Macbeth*, and *King Lear* that are as canonical in the Anglophone world as they are in the Japanese cinematic tradition. His *Throne of Blood* envisions the tragedy of *Macbeth* in a Buddhist landscape in medieval, feudal Japan. The film has been hailed as "the greatest masterpiece among Shakespeare films" and "the most successful Shakespeare film ever made" by esteemed directors Peter Brook and Sir Peter Hall, respectively.[3] Beyond the Shakespeare circle, he has also been a source of inspiration in world cinema history through his acclaimed samurai films such as *Yojimbo* (1961) and *Seven Samurai* (1954), films with sword-fighting sequences that portray psychologically scarred warriors and feature stylized action and, often, exaggerated death scenes. Kurosawa's craft influenced westerns such as *The Magnificent Seven* (dir. John Sturges, 1960), modeled on *Seven Samurai*, and *A Fistful of Dollars* (dir. Sergio Leone, 1964), which pulls from the plot of *Yojimbo*. The theme of revenge in samurai epics is parallel to the theme of frontier-town shootouts in westerns, and Kurosawa consciously draws on both genres for kinetic energy in his adaptations of Shakespeare's tragedies.

Beyond the genres of samurai and western, the visual structure of Kurosawa's films—while itself in dialogue with postwar Japanese national identity—has provided templates for works by Steven Spielberg, Martin Scorsese, and George Lucas, including the latter's *Star Wars* films. Kurosawa tends to begin his films *in medias res* and offers vignettes of epic history. We infer the larger, animated historical context of feudal Japan from small details, such as armor left behind by displaced soldiers in endless battles. Audiences are plunged into action already unfolding before the start of the film. Similarly, George Lucas begins *Star Wars* with Princess Leia battling the troops of Darth Vader. Stephen Prince compares Lucas to Kurosawa in terms of their shared cinematic narrative strategies of "reaching for the general through the specific." He writes that "by going deeply into history to find myth, Kurosawa furnished Lucas with a singularly powerful narrative method and template." *Star Wars* "places the viewer in the midst of a huge narrative cycle with its elaborately detailed fantasy universe," which, like in Kurosawa's epic films, comes with "minimal explanation of the shape and stakes of the struggle."[4]

Both Ninagawa and Kurosawa are influential figures in their respective fields: intercultural theatre and film. Their works showcase the intraregional cultural flows within East Asia and the larger significance of East Asian–western cultural exchanges. Ninagawa is a household name in Japan, the United Kingdom, and festivals throughout Europe and Asia. Some of his most memorable Shakespearean productions in Britain include *A Midsummer Night's Dream*, set in a Zen rock garden in Kyoto (1996); *Hamlet* (1998, 2004, 2015); a major production of *King Lear* (RSC, 1999–2000) starring Sir Nigel Hawthorne; *Pericles* (at the National Theatre at the invitation of Trevor Nunn and RSC, 2003); a highly stylized *Titus Andronicus* (RSC's Complete Works Festival, 2006); and *Coriolanus* on a stage filled with mirrors (2007). His 2015 *Hamlet* at the Barbican in London, staged when Ninagawa was about to turn 80 and starring Fujiwara Tatsuya (who also played Hamlet for Ninagawa in 2004), uses the conceit of a nineteenth-century rehearsal in a slum and features Kabuki elements. Ninagawa's company has a long-term relationship with the British producer Thelma Holt. He was awarded an honorary Commander of the Most Excellent Order of the British Empire (CBE) by the British government in 2002. While Kurosawa's *Throne of Blood* and *Ran* are not the earliest Asian Shakespeare films, they are two of the most internationally influential works. Likewise, Ninagawa's widely toured productions have been a staple at international venues and festivals. He was a shrewd producer of palatable intercultural elements in Britain, among other countries, and his international stature allowed him a relatively high degree of control over artistic intent and his image in the media. Ninagawa and Kurosawa represent pinnacles of artistic achievement in theatre and cinema in their respective eras and styles.

A Winding Path

Shakespeare's dramatic works first appeared in Japan in the form of performances and rewrites of select scenes. The first public performance was a staged reading that took place in Yokohama in February 1866, two years before the Meiji Restoration (1868) initiated large-scale translation projects. Hosted by the Silk Salon, the reading of "Hamlet's Instructions to the Players" in English aimed to entertain British expatriates. The earliest exposure to Shakespeare by the locals was through translations of Charles and Mary Lamb's 1807 prose rendition of *Tales from Shakespeare*. The Lambs' Victorian, didactic appropriations of select tragedies (by Charles) and comedies (by Mary) were initially intended for women and children who would not otherwise have access to Shakespeare's plays, but the collection was one of the most popular English-language rewritings, with 97 Japanese versions and reprints between 1877 and 1928 and a dozen Chinese editions between 1903 and 1915. The Lambs' *Tales*, rather than complete translations of the plays themselves, formed the foundation for such adaptations as Inoue Tsutomu's 1883 best-seller, *A Strange Story from the West: The Trial of Pawned Human Flesh* [*Seiyō chinbun jinniku shichiire saiban*], which is based on *The Merchant of Venice*.[5]

The outlandish story was adapted into Kabuki by Katsu Genzō in a production entitled *A Time of Cherry Blossoms and a World of Money* [*Sakuradoki zeni no yononaka*] (May–June 1885; revived in 1886 and 1894).[6] Japanese translations of western classics were retranslated into Chinese and other languages in the late nineteenth and early twentieth centuries as part of related but ultimately distinct pursuits of modernization in several East Asian countries. Later on, East Asian intellectuals such as Lu Xun (1881–1936), who studied in Japan, would bring some of the plays' ideas, such as portrayals of class conflicts and gender identities, to their home countries through translation and rewriting.

Some of the most influential early touring productions for local and foreign residents were those of the Miln Company, led by British-American actor George C. Miln, who had served as a Unitarian preacher in New York and worked as an actor-manager in Chicago before turning to London to train in theatre.[7] The Miln Company's 1891 productions of *Hamlet, The Merchant of Venice, Macbeth, Othello, Richard II*, and several other plays in English in Yokohama inspired such important translators as Tsubouchi Shōyō (*nom de plume* of Tsubouchi Yuzo, 1859–1935) who translated all of Shakespeare's plays.[8] Like many of his contemporaries, Tsubouchi appropriated Shakespearean aesthetics to reinvent Japanese theatre.[9] What is notable in the era of modernization is the general zeal to analyze and appropriate Anglo-European literature and political philosophy.

While Ninagawa is internationally renowned for his repeated uses of cherry blossom, the motif of schadenfreude appeared early on in Japanese theatre history, first in Kabuki, and later in modernist productions. In 1885, journalist Udagawa Bunkai popularized cherry blossom as a symbol of ephemerality in his serialized novel in an Osaka newspaper, an adaptation of part of the Lambs' *Tales*. Katsu Genzō drew upon Ugadawa's imagery of cherry blossom in his 1885 Kabuki production of *The Merchant*.[10] The reference to cherry blossom in central Osaka in Ugadawa's novel, which was retained in Katsu's dramatization, would literally blossom in Ninagawa's *Macbeth* a century later in Tokyo, London, and Edinburgh, where it signified not the beauty of Osaka (which stands in for Venice) but transience and death in the tragedy. Cherry blossom appeared again in another Ninagawa production, the Kabuki-style *Ninagawa Twelfth Night* (performed by the Shochiku Grand Kabuki Company). When it toured to the Barbican in London in 2009, it opened with a lovesick Orsino against the backdrop of a sea of cherry blossom, followed by a ship gliding across the stage into a storm of billowing cloth.

In the early twentieth century, it was common for directors to apply a modernized, realistic framework to staging western plays in Japanese. Shakespeare is sometimes treated as a modern playwright in Japan, even though Japanese directors know full well Shakespeare's roots in early modern English culture. There are exceptions, of course. Fukuda Tsuneari (1912–94) did not regard Shakespeare as a "modern" author like Gorky or Ibsen. In fact, Fukuda did not approve of the *shingeki* ("new drama," a form of Japanese theatre drawn on modern western realism), believing that *shingeki*'s approach to psychological motivation and inside-out characterization is anachronistic for performances of Shakespeare and Greek tragedies.[11] Fukuda's own play *Akechi Mitsuhide* (1957) fuses narratives of Mitsuhide's life as a sixteenth-century feudal lord with the life story of Macbeth, similar to how Kurosawa approaches *Macbeth* in his 1957 samurai film.[12] Whether employing modern settings and theatrical realism or taking a more historical approach, Japanese directors regard Shakespeare as a usefully foreign author who comes from outside the immediate circle of Chinese, Korean, Confucian, and Buddhist influence.[13] By contrast, twentieth Anglophone directors either embrace or repudiate Shakespeare as the epitome of classic high culture.

Historically the Japanese mentality towards foreign ideas is both closed and open. Japan holds the unenviable position of being both a closed society insisting on native exclusivity and one of the first East Asian countries to appropriate a large number of Anglo-European cultural texts. In 1801 Shizuku Tadao used the term "closed country" (*sakoku*) to describe Japan when translating from Dutch into Japanese the three-volume *History of Japan* by Engelbert Kaempfer, a German physician to the Dutch Embassy in Japan during 1690–92.[14] While it may be difficult for foreign ideas to assimilate fully in Japan, the country is a gateway to new ideas in the history of East Asia's westernization and modernization. The contentious process of modernization created new traditions as it reinvented classical traditions.[15]

While western audiences may expect, say, a Japanese adaptation of Shakespeare to offer something uniquely Japanese or be representative of Japanese performance traditions today, intraregional borrowing and fusion of Asian and western motifs are part of an increasingly common approach, as exemplified by Ninagawa's stage productions and Kurosawa's film adaptations. (The deep connections among Asian and western adaptations were theorized in the Prologue. Theories and politics of reception of Asian performances are examined in Chapter 3, which delves deeper into varying audience expectations of a work as it tours to different locations.)

Three Approaches

Since the late nineteenth century there have been three approaches to Shakespeare, which are not mutually exclusive. Ninagawa and Kurosawa employed all of these approaches in their works at different points while making unique contributions to theatre and film histories. The first approach involves *localization and assimilation.* Shakespeare's narratives are dressed up in localized *mise en scène*, as had been the case with Tsubouchi Shōyō's strategy of using his "naturalized" translation of *Julius Caesar* in 1884 to promote a progressive political agenda.[16] In *Throne of Blood*, Kurosawa brings the relationship between humans and nature in *Macbeth* to bear on a highly localized *samurai* narrative set in feudal Japan. Ninagawa tends to closely follow Shakespeare's scripts in translation, and so his stage works do not use this approach as often. However, Ninagawa's uses of direct translations rather than localized adaptations introduced unfamiliar but innovative narrative patterns into the Japanese audiences' horizon of expectation. Otojirō Kawakami's 1903 *shinpa* ("new school drama") adaptation of *Othello* localizes the characters and narratives in the playwright's contemporary period. The adaptation chronicles General Muro Washirō's military campaigns during the Japanese colonial expansion in Asia. Sent from Tokyo to quell an anti-colonial insurrection on Taiwan's Penghu Islands, the general ends up killing his wife, Tamone, daughter of the Minister of Finance.[17] Kawakami's play exhibited a double colonial gaze: Japan looked to some nations as colonizable subjects while Japan itself was in a subaltern position in relation to certain European cultures.[18] The country's rapid postwar development, cultural export, and economic prowess in the 1980s changed the dynamics.

The second approach uses Shakespeare as a *cultural catalyst* to revitalize certain genres.[19] The new roles of the director and dramaturge transformed genres traditionally led by actors, such as the male-dominated Kabuki. *Shingeki* emerged as a director-centered genre. Actresses joined actors onstage in Kabuki and Noh, sometimes alongside male actors specializing in female roles, in experimental productions. The theme of militarism in *Macbeth* serves as a cultural catalyst in Kurosawa's *Throne of Blood*, which draws on Noh-inspired facial makeup and mannerism. Ninagawa is well know for applying techniques from one tradition to another. Noh stage structure contrasted with Heian-era costumes in his 1998 production of *Twelfth Night* at Saitama Arts Theatre outside Tokyo. His other version of the play, the *Ninagawa Twelfth Night* (2005, 2007, 2009), employed the Kabuki technique of rapid role changes (*hayagawari*). Onoe Kikunosuke V played Viola, her disguise Cesario, and her twin brother Sebastian, sometimes in rapid succession, and brought a new perspective to the masculine, feminine, and androgynous identities of Cesario who is a fusion of part of Viola's self-identity and her impersonation of Sebastian. Specializing in female roles on the Kabuki stage, the actor disappeared as one character and immediately reappeared as another, sometimes with a different costume. *Hayagawari* was also used to highlight gender dynamics in *Japanese Woodblock Prints of Hamlet* [*Hamuretto Yamato Nishikie*] directed by Koji Oda, a Kabuki-style coproduction between Shochiku and the Panasonic Globe in Tokyo (Tokyo Globe, 1991; Sunshine Theatre, 1997). Ichikawa Somegorō played Hamlet, Ophelia, and Fortinbras. He effectively showcased the duality of the psyche of Hamlet and Ophelia as well as Fortinbras as Hamlet's foil. Novelty does come at a price, however: according to Izumi Kadono's study, cuts to Hamlet and Ophelia's dialogues and the fact that the pair never appear together in the same scene diminished Ophelia's inner struggles.[20] Innovations can also be seen in Kyōgen theatre, which is traditionally performed as an intermission between Noh acts. Takahashi Yasunari's well-known Kyōgen comedy *The Braggart Samurai* (starring Nomura Mansai, Tokyo Globe, 1991) used *The Merry Wives of Windsor* (the plotline of Mistress Ford and Mistress Page's deception of Falstaff) as a vehicle to bring Kyōgen to international audiences at the World Shakespeare Congress. Similarly, Katsu Genzō's 1885 *Merchant of Venice* and Ueda Kuniyoshi's *Hamlet* (1982) introduced new strategies of characterization to the stately stylization of all-male Kabuki and to the mask theatre of Noh, respectively. A pioneer in English-language performances of Noh, Ueda believes it was necessary to expand Noh practices.[21]

Ueda went on to create the *Noh Othello* in English in 1986 and in Japanese in 1992, featuring the renowned Kyōgen actor Nomura Mansai as Emilia; this represents a third approach, one of *fusion*, that blends two or more Japanese and European genres to support the director's artistic vision (as is the case for Kurosawa) or to communicate with audiences at international festivals (as is the case for Ninagawa). Tadashi Suzuki combined Kabuki and Noh techniques (gracefully walking without lifting feet from the ground) and conventions (blurring of present and past, of dream and reality) in his all-male metatheatrical adaptation of *The Tale of Lear* (1984). To view a video of the Suzuki Method, please visit globalshakespeares.mit.edu/the-tale-of-lear/?video=the-suzuki-method-stomping

Suzuki's signature training and performance method of the actors stomping or beating the ground with their feet is born from this fusion of physical theatre and traditional Japanese theatres.[22] Combining dialogues from Shakespeare with those from other writers, Suzuki's works often focus on a central character who is "insane":

> The structure of my theatre is that a person with excessive illusions sits alone in a room in real time, . . . and the texts of . . . Shakespeare possess him or her. It's not a drama in which the action follows chronological time. The real drama is what transpires in the consciousness of someone who may just be sitting quietly in one moment of time. . . . Shakespeare writes speeches that the characters themselves may not understand, but others do. [For example,] there is a gap between the character Macbeth and what he says. I am very sensitive to what lies in that gap.[23]

Whereas Suzuki incorporates Noh and Kabuki techniques to deconstruct them and to create an ironic distance between form and content,[24] Ninagawa, trained as a *shingeki* actor, tends to create a strong thread of visual imagery (such as cherry blossom) and a framing device (such as the family altar writ large). In his 2009 *Twelfth Night*, Ninagawa put cherry blossom in a Kabuki acoustic landscape and the music of harp and harpsichord. The fusion landscape signaled dialogues between Japan and the UK.

The Panasonic Globe in Tokyo, a premier indoor venue designed by Arata Isozaki, was an important venue where fusion works were staged. The 700-seat arena theatre opened in 1988, a decade before the London Globe was built, and internationalized Japanese Shakespeare while bringing global Shakespeares to Japan. Nearly all of the Japanese performance genres were represented there. The Tokyo Globe hosted important performances from an eclectic range of countries, including Ingmar Bergman's *Hamlet* (Sweden), Lin Zhaohua's *Hamlet* (China), and Robert Lepage's *The Tempest* (Canada). Tadashi Suzuki's famous adaptation of *King Lear* was staged there in 1989. It is striking that Tokyo had more productions of Shakespeare (33) than London in 1994.[25] Over a period of fourteen years until it closed in 2002, the Tokyo Globe "allowed Japanese Shakespeare an unbridled license that resulted in almost limitless experimentation."[26]

Ears of the Other

What is the significance of the mixture of Japanese and European musical and acoustic landscapes in Ninagawa's *Macbeth* before any word is spoken onstage? What might the intercultural sounds suggest in Ninagawa's scenography? What are we to make of the unconventionally sparse music in Kurosawa's *Throne of Blood*, whose use of music is largely limited to a piercing Noh bamboo flute and drum beats? How do sound and music demarcate cultural and interstitial spaces? Should certain sounds, including incidental music, be culturally prescriptive in their symbolic representation of a cultural location? What about silence?

There is an important distinction between incidental music called for by a scene (music designated by the playwright) and contemporary theatrical and cinematic uses of music (at the discretion of the director or composer). When Shakespeare's plays call for songs or music to play alongside dialogues or in particular scenes, such as Feste's songs in *Twelfth Night* or mad Ophelia's singing in *Hamlet*, the actors (their characters) hear, register, and respond to such music, which is constitutive of dramatic action. That is, the audiences are not the only ones hearing the music. In contemporary theatre and film, however, incidental music underscores dramatic actions but is not "heard" by actors in the scene. Rather, such music has an emoting function in dictating the affect of the audience. In Ninagawa's and Kurosawa's works, the characters often do not respond to the nondiegetic incidental music;

or, if they *are* affected by such music, their affective labor is primarily constituted and carried by physical performance. As David Lindley and Bill Barclay theorize, "music that existed entirely outside the world of the drama . . . dictated both the presentation of that world and the audience's response to it."[27] Understanding theatre and film calls for reverse engineering various performative components. It is a useful exercise to keep an ear out for soundtracks that are superimposed on dramatic action and the gap between music and narrative.

Listening to the voice of the other is an integral part of intercultural communication. French philosopher Jacques Derrida believes that communication in a broad sense involves processes of handing over and signing off on messages. He speaks metaphorically of how a recipient of a message "signs" off (upon receipt) with their ear, "an organ for perceiving difference." It is *l'oreille de l'autre* (the ear of the other) that signs. Listening to others is an act of registering differences. As he writes, "A keen ear is an ear with keen hearing, an ear that perceives differences."[28] Intercultural performances, just like other texts, are "signed only much later by the other" within a "structure of textuality."[29] There is a degree of reflexivity in listening to the cultural other, as Derrida writes of a "borrowed ear" to listen to and tune in to cultural difference: "Do we hear, do we understand each other already with another ear? The ear does not answer. Who is listening to whom right here?"[30] Thus an intercultural performance cannot be constituted solely by the artist's subjectivity, because as a form of communication it is contractual in nature. A contract must be seen and heard by an audience who acknowledges and honors it, as in signing off on the communication. Ninagawa notably appropriates Japanese and western sounds and music motifs in his productions to disassociate particular sounds from one single cultural origin. Kurosawa, too, listens to film soundtracks with borrowed ears in order to construct a language for his own work.

Although visual motifs play an important role in intercultural theatre and cinema, listening to these performances is as productive as taking stock of their visual cues, such as cherry blossom. As Marcus Tan shows in *Acoustic Interculturalism*, "music and song . . . form the vertebrae of Asian performance traditions" because they move the plot forward, "delineate character and manoeuvre the dramatic action by dictating the rhythms of the performance." Since culture is to be seen as well as heard, music and sound are important elements that, in Tan's words, "assist in the construction of the culturally kaleidoscopic *mise en scène*."[31] Ninagawa and Kurosawa employ music and soundtrack in manners that contrast not only to each other but also to contemporary uses of sound and music in Hollywood films and main-stage productions by the Royal Shakespeare Company. Typically RSC productions feature live music at the beginning or end of a scene. The volume of this live or prerecorded programmatic music is usually kept to a minimum so as not to interfere with the dialogue onstage. It is in line with what we might call *ambient* music, although when the dramatic situation calls for it, music—whether live or prerecorded—can also be amplified to provide thematic guidance of a play or scene's emotional landscape. Rarely, though, does it dominate the dialogue.

Since there are many variables in East Asian adaptations of Shakespeare, I focus in the following comparative analysis on Kurosawa's and Ninagawa's adaptations of the same play, *Macbeth*, with occasional reference to their other works and, whenever appropriate, to the larger contexts that informed their works and East Asian Shakespeares. *Macbeth* and *King Lear*, works adapted by both directors, have diagnostic significance in modern East Asia: *Lear* offers material for an exploration of the emerging political order after World War II, and *Macbeth* has been used to help audiences overcome the trauma of wars.

Kurosawa, as we've seen, uses music sparingly, whereas Ninagawa has often allowed programmatic music to drown out dialogue, and his actors resort to shouting or machine-gun-style rapid delivery as they compete against music to make themselves heard. Daniel Gallimore suggests sympathetically the subordination of language (or speech) may be "typical of [Ninagawa's] era . . . in which directors have succeeded translators in importance."[32] Ninagawa's dominating musical motifs are a strong contrast to Kurosawa's spare soundtracks. The 2018 New York revival of Ninagawa's *Macbeth* notably featured, in nearly every scene, Fauré's *Requiem* and a small number of other pieces of classical music by Samuel Barber and Franz Schubert, which helped establish emotion and mood. In some instances such reliance on scores that drown out the actors' words might be perceived as too heavy-handed.

While Ninagawa mixes Japanese and western musical themes, Kurosawa employs atonal soundtracks that seem to work against what is being depicted in a scene, creating a sense of detachment. There is a jarring or jolting effect that is not present in post-1990s Hollywood film adaptations of Shakespeare, such as those of Kenneth Branagh. In Branagh's films, the function of music is to cue and direct emotive responses. In *Henry V*, Patrick Doyle's heroic musical theme—already threatening to engulf Derek Jacobi's passionate delivery as Chorus—swells to float Branagh's speech "once more unto the breach" (1.3.1), setting the tone and stage for the speech to motivate soldiers to launch another attack of Harfleur. Scholars tend to agree that Doyle's scores are "characteristically sweeping and grandiloquent."[33]

By contrast, the soundscape in Kurosawa's *Throne of Blood* creates a chilling effect. The music mimics the position and function of the multiperson Chorus in Noh theatre—typically onstage, offering a detached perspective on the dramatic actions—and provides an aesthetic framework for the film. Satō Masaru's *Throne of Blood* soundtrack is presented in an understated manner, yet its piercing bamboo flute at times resembles shrieks. Similarly, the melancholic score by Tōru Takemitsu is used sparingly for only 32 of the 160-minute-long *Ran* [Chaos], Kurosawa's well-received adaptation of *King Lear*. Music in *Throne of Blood* plays a number of roles in the grim cinematic narrative. A more conventional use is found in the scene where Kunimaru Tsuzuki (Duncan) and his retinue arrive at Washizu's (Macbeth's) castle. Shots of farmers in the field are supported by light music and beats. As the new lord of the North Castle, Washizu seems content in his position and new community. The blissful, if brief, scene of farmers working under pleasant sunlight and young characters rejoicing in some kind of paradise stands in stark relief to the rest of the film, which advertises a grim outlook based on Shinto-Buddhism's idea of retribution. We hear laughter in the background, which, as we will realize later, is the calm before the storm, as Lady Asaji (Lady Macbeth), behind closed doors, is pressuring Washizu to make up his mind about their joint, bloody enterprise. Most of the other scenes in the film use atonal music either to convey messages that seem at odds with the visual themes or to create a sense of alienation. Nature is depicted as a fearsome force that is indifferent to human suffering and striving. While Kurosawa's films are known to symbolize Buddhist enlightenment, critics have considered them to be not overtly religious in nature. Melissa Croteau, for example, suggests that *Ran* carries a "*secular* ethical message of selflessness and sacrifice . . . [through] grim pessimism punctuated with glimmers of hope," and J. M. Shields categorizes Kurosawa's films as a "unique brand of skeptical humanism."[34] Indeed the Buddhist motifs are drawn from Shinto-Buddhism specific to the feudal period and a syncretic *shinbutsu shūgō*—a hybrid of *kami* (forces of nature) worship and Buddhism—that is still practiced today.

"Full of sound and fury"

One sonic strategy Kurosawa employs is using sounds to contrast with visual or verbal signs. When Lady Asaji denies she is possessed by supernatural powers, drum beats and the high-pitched Noh flute suggest otherwise. Sometimes the film reframes otherwise familiar sounds to create a sense of horror and perversion. For example, early in *Throne of Blood*, when Washizu and Miki (Banquo) encounter the mysterious mountain spirit (a composite of Shakespeare's three witches), composer Satō uses Noh musical motifs to create a sense of estrangement in the dense forest. We encounter the lost soldiers through Kurosawa's signature long shots and panning shots as they gallop disoriented back and forth through the woods. Diegetic sounds of rain, galloping, and whinnying are interwoven with the Noh flute that exists outside the world of Washizu, creating a sense of other-worldliness. The single long pitch of the flute is unsettling. As Evelyn Tribble observes, the key to understanding Kurosawa and Satō's soundscape is the human response to fear "in an environment rendered unfamiliar and strange because of an originary act of violence." Atonal music and unpleasant sounds signal potential sources of violence and, therefore, fear. Familiar sounds become terrifying "because of their capacity to evoke the unknown."[35] We hear the laughter of the mountain spirit, for example, in the fog. In film, a disembodied voice is often more authoritative, mesmerizing, sinister, or all of the above. Everyday sounds such as horse galloping become eerie and unnatural in the soundscape. As the narrative progresses, the flute seems to become an aural signifier of supernatural power or spirit. The occasional note of the flute piercing the silence further heightens the sense of isolation.

In addition to the flute, drum beats and atonal strings accentuate the disorientation the soldiers experience. Part of the alienating effect comes from the Noh music motif superimposed on western orchestra music, as Mark Thornton Burnett has observed.[36] Even after the fog recedes, there is no relief, as we hear the soft chanting of the mountain spirit, who is spinning cotton on a spinning wheel, her lips barely moving. An otherwise innocuous form of domestic labor is now placed in nature. As the soundtrack disappears and the mountain spirit's androgynous voice takes over, the audience finds itself trapped between the reaction shots of Washizu and Miki and the otherworldly spectacle of the spinning wheel sans soundtrack. Burnett notes another form of oppositional binary, namely the Spider's Web Castle looming in the distance between Washizu and Miki. A static shot implies that the castle, now possessed, is the object over which the two battlefield buddies will fight in the future. Silence here enhances the difficulty of the choices to be made. This sonic strategy harks back to the opening of the film, and presages its closing. After the deep, shimmering opening chorus ("Look upon the ruins | Of the castle of delusion"), the film cuts to a long sequence of visual and aural whiteout. Without any nondiegetic sound and without a musical soundtrack, the film audience's attention is directed toward silence and howling wind, accompanied by fog over barren land. The camera eventually pans over to a castle, but strikingly there is no human in sight other than a single samurai on horseback rushing toward the castle gates. The film's closing scene shows the image of a stele shrouded in fog, with isolated mountain ranges in the background, accompanied by the piercing Noh flute and percussion. The stele marks the spot where the once glorious Spider's Web Castle stood, and the beginning and end of Washizu's career and ambition, and it symbolizes as well the solitude of Washizu in his quest for power. We learn from the chanting of an unseen male chorus that nature is the sole witness to human folly and the pains people inflict on one another: "Within this place | Stood once a mighty fortress | Lived a proud warrior | Murdered by ambition." Clearly the narrative alludes to the vanity and transience of human ambition, as the castle has now given way to nature, dust returning to dust.

Music also plays a role in highlighting the parallel themes of the mountain spirit's supernatural power and the madness of Lady Asaji, suggesting she is possessed by the spirit (despite her denial when confronted by Washizu), either herself a witch figure or contaminated by the spirit's power. Lady Asaji is linked to the prophetic spirit through similar musical patterns, and like the spirit she is dressed in pale clothes. Her presence is accompanied by a soundtrack that musically mirrors the appearance and disappearance of the spirit. Projecting her ontological anguish and hatred toward Washizu, Lady Asaji does not so much speak to him as to herself. Asaji remains eerily calm even as she gives advice on murder. She maintains emotional and physical distance from Washizu and, by extension, the murderous act.

Lady Asaji is herself isolated from any community, including the small community of women. There are few women characters in *Throne of Blood*. The most striking scenes of Asaji's lady-in-waiting show her huddling with her lady—once to mourn the death of the Great Lord and, on another occasion, to express sympathy after Asaji's stillbirth. They are shot from behind; the camera does not show their faces. We hear the women's crying rather than see them. This arrangement alludes to the men's world in which they find themselves. Yet Lady Asaji is isolated even from the already marginalized community of women. As is discussed in the next section, visual signs conspire to connect her to the supernatural.

Interestingly, the soundtrack contradicts, in a productive manner, Lady Asaji's denial of being possessed. This is an instance where music offers a narrative counter to the dramatic action. In musicologist Kendra Leonard's astute analysis, the music indicates that Asaji's power over Washizu does not diminish but rather increases despite Washizu's mistrust, as the thematic soundtrack assigned to her and sounds associated with her persist in "echoing . . . the music first assigned to the [mountain spirit]." As the instigation scene progresses, and as she convinces Washizu to murder the Great Lord, her own body becomes "a musical instrument through which the [spirit's] motifs are broadcast."[37] Washizu begins to suspect Asaji's advice is influenced by some supernatural power, and the nondiegetic Noh flute, accentuated by a diegetic bird cry in the same pitch pattern, seems to confirm that Asaji is no longer herself. Leonard notes how even Asaji's white tabi (socks worn with thonged sandals) make noises that echo the flute motif. The screech of the owl when Asaji succeeds in persuading Washizu to move forward with their scheme is in the "same pitch range and rhythmic pattern as the flute motif" earlier.[38] Later, all the sounds of screeching crows, Noh drums, and high-pitched flute recede. The audiences become keenly aware of the deathly silence. The only sound penetrating the dead of the night is the ruffling of Asaji's tabi across the tatami floor panels. The swishing of her kimono as she shuffles—or rather, floats—around the tatami floor stands out against the silence. The rustling sound as she glides across the room to wash the bloodstained dagger becomes associated with her person and action. In these ways *Throne of Blood* connects a demonized, femme fatale Lady Asaji, both visually and sonically, to the androgynous mountain spirit.

Silence plays an important role elsewhere in the film too, as in the famous sleepwalking scene. Significantly, it is Washizu, rather than a court physician, who witnesses his co-conspirator Lady Asaji's strange behavior, and her isolation is foregrounded when even Washizu turns his back on her. As she repeatedly tries to wash the imaginary blood off her hands, in maddening fashion and in eerie, dead silence, Asaji appears to lack the confidence and self-restraint of the earlier instigation scene. Scholars have offered contrasting interpretations of her psychological transformation. For instance, Kendra Leonard believes that at this point the mad Lady Asaji is "no longer an instrument of possession" as "she is no longer linked with the prophetic witch but suffers alone." The contrast between this Asaji–Washizu encounter and the instigation scene lies in their differing use of music. Whereas an unsettling Noh flute punctuates the ideological tug-of-war of the instigation scene, the sleepwalking scene is defined by its startling silence. In Leonard's interpretation, this is because Lady Asaji is deflated: her body no longer channels supernatural powers and therefore no longer echoes the pitch range and rhythmic pattern of the mountain spirit.[39] Anthony Dawson offers a different reading, emphasizing the merit of depicting Lady Asaji's human weakness in this scene under her "steely exterior." A character "so single-minded, so passionate, [and] so self-contained," Asaji sports a blank white face devoid of emotions as she goads Washizu and mocks his innocence in the instigation scene. While sleepwalking, though, Asaji has lost her "hidden energies" of "wary intelligence." Dawson suggests this turn is driven partly by the cinematic narrative and partly by Kurosawa's ambivalence in portraying powerful women.[40] Whether Asaji's hand-washing is symptomatic of her resistance to demonization (her perceived kinship with the mountain spirit) or symbolic of her residual humanity (and conscience), and whether Asaji's power of persuasion comes from being possessed by supernatural forces (per Leonard) or her ability to reinterpret messages (per Dawson),[41] it is clear that the deafening silence is a trope as important as Lady Asaji's compulsory rite of cleansing. This silence, which marks either the emergence of her conscience or her departure from supernatural influence, also marks her return to her more innocent self. It is the lack of Noh soundtrack that signals this shift in her psyche. The same kind of silence envelopes the final scene of Washizu's death from the arrows of his own soldiers.

Gendered Pronouns

In addition to music, spoken language is also an important aspect of *Throne of Blood*, as salutations and word choices are intimately related to moral and political agency or the lack thereof. What stands out in the film—but is obscured by the English subtitles—is how and when some characters choose informal language. Subtitles are simultaneously a heuristic and filtering device, revealing as much as they repackage for consumption by a target audience not proficient in the verbal language. Jessica Chiba made a similar observation about the exigencies of screen translation in her study of Kurosawa.[42] When conversing with each other, Washizu and Miki refer to each other with first names, deepen their voice, and use informal language and the informal, masculine "I" (*ore*). They often laugh things off, as in the scene when they are lost in the forest, as part of their bravura. Singular first-person pronouns in Japanese serve important discursive functions, according to discourse and cognitive linguistics.[43] In a world strictly governed by rigid hierarchy and titles, the men's move to undermine formality has profound implications. It could be interpreted as a gesture towards building a masculine bond and camaraderie, but also as a move to reassert their masculine identity in a world full of uncertainties. The bravura around the pronoun *ore* buttresses their denial that they are lost. Yet even if they are, they remain brothers, lost together in the woods.

Washizu attempts to create a similarly intimate bond with Lady Asaji in private, but she rejects his attempt and maintains verbal and physical distance. It is notable that when Washizu addresses Asaji, he does not use any honorific; he does not address her as *tsuma* (wife) or *okusan* (lady of the house). Meanwhile, Asaji uses the most formal, singular first-person pronoun *watakushi*, rather than the informal, feminine *atashi* (or *atakushi*), which would be what a private conversation between a husband and a wife normally entails. Moreover, she addresses Washizu with the general second-person pronoun *anata*. This word, though often used in television commercials to refer to a general audience—that is, in the absence of information about the addressee's age, gender, or class—is also used by women to address their husbands. Asaji's combination of the formal *watakushi* and usually more casual *anata*—the latter here spoken in a register that conveys condescension and rejects intimacy—creates another layer of the uncanny beyond the atonal music. The use of these pronouns creates tension and conflicts between desired intimacy and rejected informality; it confuses Washizu, who is unsure how to respond. (The significance and weight of singular first-person pronouns is given a spin in the animated 2016 box-office hit *Your Name* [*Kimi no na wa*, dir. Makoto Shinkai, CoMix Wave Films].[44])

Ninagawa's Use of Music

Let us now consider how our other Japanese director used sound and music in his adaptation of this same play. Like Kurosawa, Ninagawa also deployed silence for dramaturgical purposes. Lady Macbeth (Komaki Kurihara) sleepwalks in silence, rubbing her hands in an imaginary stream. Her high-pitched, hysterical laughter fades into sobbing. As in Shakespeare, Ninagawa's Lady Macbeth is silenced after the scene where King Duncan is murdered. A profound silence underscores Macbeth's cold-hearted lament: "She should have died hereafter. | There would have been a time for such a word" (5.5.17–18). Ninagawa was as much a painterly director as a sound engineer. In fact, one went to the theatre to hear, as well as to see, his plays. Audiences heard the sound of aerial bombardment before seeing the first scene of Ninagawa's 2003 *Pericles* at the National Theatre in London. The sonic and musical landscape was a nod to Gower's prologue about "man's infirmities" (1.Prol.3) and the atrocity of war. It is "a dream dreamt by modern people in the period of distress immediately after [an unnamed] war." Ninagawa detached the narrative from identifiable geographical locations. The costumes cannot be traced to any specific culture or period except for "the traditional Shinto costume worn by maidens at Diana's temple."[45] It is the sounds that set the tone for the production.

Music also creates varying pathways to language and, in some instances, plays a pragmatic role. There is an interesting relation between Ninagawa's sound design and his actors' performance. Elton John's music drowns out the actors' awkward and sometimes failed delivery of their lines in *Romeo and Juliet*, the first Shakespearean play Ninagawa directed (1974). Music helps to augment the shortcomings of some of his actors who are not versed in classical drama. This strategy is most visible in his 1999 *Richard III*, where loud rock music drowned out Richmond's concluding remarks on "unit[ing] the white rose and the red" in a "fair conjunction" (5.5.19–20). The music echoes the chaos onstage as animal carcasses are dropped from above, reminding us of a scene in *Monty Python and the Holy Grail* (dir. Terry Gilliam and Terry Jones, Python Pictures, 1975). In fact, the production opens with a similar setup, which the concluding scene echoes visually and aurally, indicating that chaos continues to reign despite the union of the Houses of Lancaster and York. Drowning Richmond's speech in loud music ironizes his words and denies any sense of closure.

Both visual and sonic elements made important contributions to Ninagawa's signature metatheatrical framing devices, and his stage works often featured intra-Asian thematic and transhistorical allusions to styles borrowed from traditional Japan, as well as from other Asian and western cultures. This is especially evident in the music in his productions. He regarded himself as a "listener" of foreign cultures, emphasizing the significance of music in his *Tempest* (1987) and other works.[46] At once visceral and intellectual, many of his productions used classical music and strong visual motifs to blend elements of familiarity and strangeness. (Our focus here is on Ninagawa's theatre works, though he directed a number of films, including *Hebi ni piasu*

[*Snakes and Earrings*, Amuse Soft Entertainment, 2008], which is based on Hitomi Kanehara's novel of the same name.)

Sounds can shape or contradict sets onstage, and scores can contradict each other as well. Three children sing the Christmas carol "Emmanuel" in Japanese in the opening of Ninagawa's 2005 *Twelfth Night* to greet the arrival of a white-faced Orsino. In his production of the Scottish Play, Macbeth's order to the assassins to go after Banquo is accentuated by a lone flute. When Macbeth dies in the final scene, Samuel Barber's "Adagio for Strings" (1936) carries the emotional arc of the demise of the tragic hero and Macduff's bittersweet victory. Marcus Tan suggests that Barber's music "interjected with a foreignness that has now become 'localised' through music's emotive and atmospheric qualities."[47] Japanese and western music share the stage to create a hybrid sonic environment. Ninagawa often reuses the same music in new contexts. The same piece by Barber accompanies the presence of war victims in the aforementioned *Pericles* to highlight the themes of death and rebirth after the war. Appropriately enough, the medieval narrator Gower is represented by a pair of musicians playing a Japanese lute.

As was mentioned at the beginning of this chapter, sounds of temple gongs open the production of *Macbeth*. These gongs initially give an impression of coherence between visual and aural motifs around the Buddhist altar, but they soon appear contradicted by classical music when a Catholic hymn, the aforementioned three-minute "Sanctus" of Fauré's *Requiem*, joins the scene. This music accompanies the appearance of the two elderly women in ragged clothes hobbling slowly toward and praying at the butsudan altar. Buddhist chants (*shōmyō*) accompany the praying women, and the chants fade as the altar doors open. These scores seem to be in conflict, drawing attention to their cultural significance and histories. The hybrid musical landscape of this *Macbeth* has elicited a range of responses from the British critics: some found it "intensely religious"[48] while others were drawn to the "specifically Christian music" that contrasts "heart-breaking pathos against the dark and glittering splendour on stage."[49] Ninagawa mixed scores from different cultures and eras to dramatize tension and characters at odds with each other.

The "Sanctus" recurs at the play's end, aurally bookending the production much as the butsudan visually frames it. After a few moments of silence following the death of Macbeth, the two elderly women slowly close the multipanel shutters as the "Sanctus" swells softly, the Catholic score once again contrasting strongly with the visual of the Buddhist altar. Appropriating the words of prayer in the Roman Catholic Mass for the Dead, the choir sings in Latin:

Sanctus, Sanctus,	[Holy, holy]
(repeats)	
Dominus Deus,	[Lord God]
(repeats)	
Deus Sabaoth.	[God of Hosts]
(repeats)	
Sanctus Dominus Deus,	[Lord God of Hosts]
Deus, Deus Sabaoth.	[God, God of Hosts]
Pleni sunt coeli et terra,	[Full are the heavens and earth]
Gloria, gloria tua.	[Glory, glory of you]
Hosanna in excelsis	[Hosanna in the highest]
(repeats)	

The soft harp figure and violin in the opening of the "Sanctus" allow for its gentle introduction into the scene. The rising and falling initial melody of the soprano comprises only three notes, which are repeated by other singers. After singing the initial phrase twice, a D-flat is added for a fourth note. The duet between the soprano and tenor builds toward the *forte* on "excelsis" and eventually the triumphant "hosanna." Although the Catholic score seems to contradict the Buddhist set, Fauré's musical minimalism matches and supports the simple set. In contrast to Mozart's and Verdi's *Requiem*s, similarly accompanied by vocal and instrumental expression, Fauré's "Sanctus" is more intimate in form. The piece climaxes with powerful major chords and a horn fanfare, and it concludes with the sopranos in diminuendo as the orchestral parts soften into dreamy harp arpeggios. The juxtaposition of the decontextualized "Sanctus" with the spiritual symbolism of the butsudan both comments on the postwar emulation of western high culture in Japan and ironizes the trope of "lost" westerners finding solace in enlightening Japanese spirituality. It also highlights the conspicuous flaw of post-World War II imagination of global cultures in stressing either homogenizing cultural sameness or irreconcilable difference.

The "Sanctus" exemplifies the type of music Ninagawa favored: slow-paced, atmospheric music, especially pieces involving choir and pipe organ. He also used soundtracks from Hollywood films, bringing cinema and theatre together. *Richard III* (1999), with its rock music, is an exception. Harp and harpsichord appear in other productions, such as *The Ninagawa Macbeth* (Kabuki-za Theatre, Tokyo, 2005).

Much as Branagh enjoys a strong relationship with composer Patrick Doyle, Ninagawa collaborated with his in-house composers to customize incidental music and original scores for his productions. The music serves both programmatic and aesthetic functions. In some cases, key characters are identified by their own musical themes, such as *jingju* (Beijing opera) percussions and western music for the doppelgänger Puck in his 1996 and 2000 *A Midsummer Night's Dream*. Here, Puck is voiced by a black-veiled Japanese actor yet embodied by the simultaneous acrobatic performances of a *jingju* actor wearing an identical costume but no veil. The musical contrasts underscore Puck's role as a liaison between the fairy and human worlds. Drums and woodblocks typically found in *jingju* contrast with synthesized organ music in act 2, scene 1.

While both Ninagawa and Kurosaw often used music to contrast the spectacle, there are notable exceptions. Before turning to visual motifs in the next section, it is worth mentioning an instance in Kurosawa's *Ran* where visual signs merge seamlessly with the soundscape. A great diegetic silence encases the scene where Jirō's (Regan) samurai wipe out Tarō's (Goneril) and Hidetora's (Lear) forces in the castle. The carnage unfolds in silence, only to be punctuated by a dirge, a mournful death march. Kurosawa's screenplay identifies this as a scroll painting of hell writ large. In the absence of verbal language and diegetic sound, the elegy takes over to guide our ears to see the horrific violence. Kurosawa explains the significance of a soundtrack of cyclical music here:

Hidetora . . . slips and tumbles down the stairs like a dead man falling into Hell. A terrible scroll of Hell is shown depicting the fall of the castle. There are no real sounds as the scroll unfolds like a daytime nightmare. . . . The music superimposed on these pictures is, like the Buddha's heart, measured in beats of profound anguish, the chanting of a melody full of sorrow that begins like sobbing and rises gradually as it is repeated, like karmic cycles, then finally sounds like the wailing of countless Buddhas.[50]

Music here thus helps to complete the visual sign of an unfolding scroll of hell. In this famous mad Lear scene, Hidetora loses his wits and staggers through the castle. Jirō's samurai are stunned and watch silently the formerly authoritative leader drift into the wilderness. Since Hidetora is already mad, Jirō spares his life. As Stephen Prince writes, with evil becoming the category through which to understand humanity, "what was once a materialist . . . program of reform has become instead a transcendental lament."[51] Tōru Takemitsu's score consists of a main theme of strings and heavy percussion led by booming bass drum beats.

Eyes of the Other

. . . for the eye sees not itself,
But by reflection, by some other things.

—Brutus to Cassius in *Julius Caesar* (1.2.51–3)

Nowadays we see before we hear.

—Richard Eyre, director of *King Lear* (2018), *The Hollow Crown* (2012),
Stage Beauty (2004)[52]

tWhat is the relationship between seeing and being seen, between the spectator and the performer? Brutus in *Julius Caesar* reminds us that we can see ourselves only through others' eyes or a mirror. In Ninagawa's 2005 *Twelfth Night*, at Tokyo's Kabuki-za Theatre, floor-to-ceiling mirrors lined the entire stage, inviting—or rather forcing—the actors, characters, and audiences to see themselves through the eyes of the other. As a powerful framing device, the mirrors highlighted the themes of doubling and mirroring in the comedy.

Looking at any intercultural performance is to view one's own presuppositions and worldview through the eyes of the other. This chapter, focused on the sensory aspects of experiencing Shakespeare, began with sound and music; it now turns to the spectacle onscreen and onstage, to the visual framing devices, visual motifs, and me-tatheatricality in Kurosawa and Ninagawa. Both directors had a painterly eye when they envisioned their adaptations. Steven Spielberg described Kurosawa as "the pictorial Shakespeare of our time."[53] With scroll painter Kōhei Ezaki as art consultant for the *Throne of*

Blood, Kurosawa explicitly envisioned the film as an ink painting that is characterized by minimalist interiors of the castle and foggy outdoor scenes. Ninagawa, too, had a keen eye for scenography, for he trained as a tailor before becoming a *shingeki* actor in the Seihai Company in Tokyo in 1955. Kurosawa and Ninagawa, two of the most spectacular and internationally known East Asian directors, have served as eyes through which Asian audiences see Shakespeare—and as eyes of the other that gaze at western audiences.

Like a performance's soundscape, its scenography usually invites audience reactions within the designer's context. Alluding to the literary and textual bias in performance studies—which leads to a preoccupation of how Shakespeare's text is cut or rearranged (textual significance) and ignores other performative elements (dramaturgical significance)—Dennis Kennedy writes, "The theatre leaves wide scope for visual interpretation of a script, a much wider scope than that granted to verbal interpretation," and there is a relationship between scenography and "what its spectators accept as its statement and value."[54] In the field of global Shakespeare, what a performance looks like (for example, the motif of cherry blossom in Ninagawa's *Macbeth* or the Spider's Web Forest in Kurosawa's *Throne of Blood*) may not always correspond to what an audience might perceive as the significance of the visual. Once the production tours or a film is screened internationally, the constituency of the audience changes. For audiences—whether Japanese or western—who are not familiar with the samurai code, the world of *Throne of Blood* can appear stylized and rigid for no obvious reason. Conversely, for audiences familiar only with samurai film as a genre, the layered psychological development of Lady Asaji—inspired by Shakespearean dramaturgy—may seem ungrounded. For audiences of Ninagawa's *Macbeth*, the sheer grace of a cherry tree onstage with falling petals can create shocking contrasts with the dark tragedy and bloodshed. In contrast, playgoers who are familiar with the connotations of cherry blossoms might see the set as an expression of beauty and mortality.

Macbeth thus becomes a twice-told and doubly removed story in *Throne of Blood* and Ninagawa's production. This is not unusual in East Asian adaptations of Shakespearean tragedies that try to balance Asian and western elements. It speaks to the importance of learning what to look for and how to see, in addition to how to listen to the intercultural vibe. Stephen Prince observes that "the signifiers of word and image" are not interchangeable in *Throne of Blood*, as the "verbal texture of [*Macbeth*] is transformed into a dense, elaborate patterning of image and sound."[55]

Kurosawa's film is animated by his visual framing of both the natural and human worlds as inhospitable spaces, taking a cue from what Banquo calls "instruments of darkness" (1.3.122). These spaces have Foucauldian disciplinary functions on the characters, whose behaviors are affected deeply, dictated and molded, by the spaces they are in. The framing devices dramatize the themes of the tragedy of human isolation and the cross-pollination of nature and artifice. The characters' psychological and social isolation lead to tragic conse-quences. In terms of the symbiotic relationship between the natural and human worlds, the film repeatedly signals how a visual metaphor of entanglement structures the emotional landscape of both the forest and the castle. The visual structures of forest and castle mirror each other, as the castle apparently can be reached only through the wood, which serves as a "'natural labyrinth' that confuses enemies of the prevailing order," in the words of one of Great Lord Tsuzuki's (Malcolm) generals. Maurice Hindle suggests that, in fact, the forest is "not so much a natural as a *supernatural* labyrinth."[56] In a more recent study of presentations of the supernatural onscreen, Neil Forsyth argues that illusion gives way to delusion in *Throne of Blood*. The distinction between supernatural illusion and human delusion is an important one to maintain.[57] Infused with the vocabulary of Shinto-Buddhism, which believes that every being and object has a spirit, the film draws on samurai codes of honor, the *Sengoku jidai* (Warring States period, 1467–1600), and Japan's post-World War II identity crisis and disillusionment with militarism. Imagery of the supernatural is simultaneously buttressed and undermined by psychological isola-tion. By contrast, Orson Welles's 1948 and Roman Polanski's 1971 *Macbeth* films are firmly located within the genre of horror.

How does the film's grammar of visual signs dramatize the tragedy of human isolation? When a character is isolated from society and becomes an unaccommodated creature, whether caught in the storm or in an inhospitable castle, the experience of horror and solitude is intensified. It is no coincidence that the film opens and closes with images of isolated mountain ranges in fog, shot on the iconic Mount

Fuji. The exterior scenes of the castle were shot around a custom-built set on Mount Fuji, while the courtyard scenes were shot at Toho's Tamagawa Studio. This nature, like Kurosawa's camerawork, conveying apathy through its signature long shots, maintains a distance from the events as an indifferent observer.

The opening and closing shots of a landscape devoid of humans bear cinematic significance as a framing device. They set the moral and the tone of the film. Paralleling Laurence Olivier's *Hamlet* (Two Cities Films, 1948), which opens with visual extratextual material and an announcer stating that "this is the tragedy of a man who could not make up his mind," *Throne of Blood* is bookended by disembodied baritone choric narrators, connecting the past, present, and future, for "what [the spirit of ambition] once was so, now still is true." This echoes Banquo's command to the witches: "If you can look into the seeds of time, | And say which grain will grow and which will not, | Speak then to me" (1.3.61–4). *Macbeth* is a tragedy concerned with multiple futures: an impending future when the witches shall meet again, a prophetic future imparted by the weird sisters, and the dynastic futures of Macbeth and Banquo's line. The child as a symbol is the materialist embodiment of these futures, but also a nostalgic representation of an adult's past. The opening and closing shots of the stele suggest that Macbeth's past is our future, and what was his future could well have been the audience's past: the audience, too, is connected to a history of human atrocity, which is particularly pertinent given the post-World War II context in which Kurosawa worked.

Our first introduction to the iconic Spider's Web Forest is the thickets through which Washizu and Miki gallop. Characterized by webs of tangled branches, strong verticals of tree trunks, and heavy rain, the scene draws us in with its perfectly lateral, fast tracking shots. These shots begin to resemble one another as Washizu and Miki double back on previously trodden trails. Each sequence is composed of several long takes, giving the illusion that they are simply racing back and forth on the same spot. According to Brian Parker, they "cross the same location no fewer than twelve times."[58] Eventually Washizu shoots an arrow into a tall treetop, which triggers an unearthly laughter.

Following the uncanny laughter, Washizu and Miki stumble upon a modest bamboo hut deep in the Spider's Web Forest. The hut consists solely of thin vertical sticks, and the image evokes a prison cage while echoing the vertical lines in the galloping scene. Sitting inside the hut is an androgynous being with long, uncombed hair, who is spinning yarn—like a spider spawning threads to weave and entrap—and seems oblivious to the presence of Washizu and Miki. The spirit appears to be turning a double-spooled spinning wheel, but the otherwise mundane domestic chore takes on an eerie overtone when the film audience realizes that the spirit does not in fact touch the fiber: it is simply spun from the smaller wheel onto the larger one. What is uncanny is that the spirit does not seem to twist together the thread of fiber. This scene empties out the otherwise productive domestic labor of spinning the yarn, suggesting that Macbeth's pursuits are but insubstantial vanity projects. Washizu's arrow and the subsequent laughter might be interpreted as an instance of a warrior's arrogance provoking and bringing into being the spirit of the dead to presage his demise. It might also be interpreted as Washizu's belated awareness that "an evil spirit is blocking our way," as he tells us later. In either case, intertwining branches frame the image of Washizu and Miki on horseback, now confined by a nature that—as is revealed later—has reached its limit in taking over the corpses generated by human atrocity. The visual narrative device for entrapment would attract Japanese-speaking audiences' attention, because *ito* (糸), the word for "thread," is homophonous with "intention" (意図), "design," and rhymes with "treasonable intent" (異図).

When the mountain spirit vanishes into the fog and Washizu snaps out of his trance—induced by listening to the spirit's Buddhist chant on the vanity of human ambition—he and Miki rush into the hut to look for any traces of the mountain spirit. They tear down the hut's cloth wall and walk through; when they turn around, the hut has vanished. They occupy the same space as previously occupied by the mountain spirit, a space of perverse nature—and now, as they come upon a pile of skulls, skeletons, and weapons, a symbol of human mortality and transience. The samurai warriors have stepped into the realm of death and curses, where they are stuck metaphorically and, as the narrative reveals later, are "forever . . . doomed."[59] The transition suggests that the mountain spirit embodies the grudging souls of the dead, likely the casualties of wars.

Much as Ninagawa's framing device is metatheatrical, Kurosawa's is metacinematic. The act of spinning yarn on double-spooled wheels in the woods is a metacinematic device that brings an otherwise domestic activity into nature, rendering the chore perverse and presaging the tension between nature and artifice. Like a filmmaker who edits scenes to form a narrative, the mountain spirit edits the life story of Washizu. This allegory parallels Clotho who spins the thread of human life in Greek mythology.[60] Several critics have pointed out the parallel between the wheels that are spun and reels of film.[61] Buchanan theorizes that Washizu and Miki are both "*verbally* confronted" with their futures and "*visually* [confronted] by the medium in which it is told."[62] Further, the act of spinning calls to mind Washizu and Miki's running in circles in the previous scene. Jack Jorgens points out that the spinning wheels "inscribe the circles followed by Washizu and Miki as they ride in circles in the forest" as they are caught up in cycles of violence. The spinning wheels "give the illusion of movement in [the warriors'] futile form of feudalism."[63]

This is but one of many examples of how Kurosawa pioneered the techniques of defamiliarizing the quotidian by featuring ordinary daily objects writ large and presenting human tableaux in stark contrast against nature. Ninagawa would appropriate this practice for his stage productions, which frequently featured framing devices inspired by an ordinary object writ large, such as a family altar.

The forest and its attendant thematic concerns permeate and eventually invade the castle. We witness an army cutting down branches in the Spider's Web Forest to serve as their camouflage, disrupting the habitat of birds. These displaced birds fly to nest in the castle, even disrupting a meeting, where they are seen as a bad omen. The mountain spirit's prophecy of the forest's uprising is realized when soldiers march towards the castle, disguising themselves with these branches. The illusion of movement first witnessed in *Throne of Blood*'s opening scene has come full circle, becoming the illusion of the forest's moving to encroach upon the castle, grown inhospitable to its human occupants. In the final scene, Washizu, with his soldiers turning against him, dies a brutal death, his body like a pincushion or porcupine, pierced by thickets of arrows. It is noteworthy that Washizu, a samurai warrior, is deprived of the opportunity to die an honorable death by *seppuku* (suicide by disembowelment), or a Shakespearean death in one-on-one combat. Significantly, he dies at the hands of his soldiers and from arrows made of the forest. Judith Buchanan makes a cogent argument for the material connection between arrows and elements already highlighted in earlier scenes: wood (the shaft), feathers (the fletching), and bones (arrowheads).[64] The arrow, here a metonym for the forest, comes for and devours Washizu in a final act of poetic justice.

Another notable example of how the forest and the castle are interlinked is the spirit's hut and the room in the castle where Washizu and Lady Asaji plan and wrap up their murderous act. Kurosawa dramatize the cross-pollination of nature and artifice through a hybrid cinematic–Noh grammar. The spatial structure of the spirit's flimsy hut foreshadows that of Washizu's castle. Imagery echoing the hut's vertical sticks is visible and evoked explicitly on multiple occasions in the room's partition, behind Asaji. While resembling the Noh stage for Asaji's Noh-inspired makeup, performing methods, and mannerisms, the room is an unsettling space due to its uncanny echoes of the forest and the hut. The painted pine tree on the wall evokes both the thickets in the forest and patterns of bloodstains.[65] The partition, resembling the hut and a cage, encroaches on Washizu and Asaji as they increasingly murder their way into a corner.

Another key connection between the forest and the castle is Lady Asaji who is visually and sonically linked to the mountain spirit. In Shakespeare, Macbeth echoes the witches' rhetoric patterns ("Fair is foul, and foul is fair," 1.1.10–11) when he observes that "so foul and fair a day I have not seen" (1.3.36). In Kurosawa, it is Asaji who becomes a sonic and visual channel through which the mountain spirit in the Spider's Web Forest inhabits the castle. Asaji's mannerisms call to mind those of the spirit. The androgynous mountain spirit remains still; only her hand moves, spinning the wheel. Even as she chants, her mouth appears to not move at all. Asaji's bearing and manner— wearing her hair down, scraggly, and staying still most of the time— echo those of the spirit, who seems indifferent to the strife and conquest of Washizu. Even when Asaji speaks, her mouth, like the spirit's, seems not to move, as if she is ventriloquizing, channeling voices from another realm. Other visual signs also suggest a pathway between the forest, which bewilders and traps the uninitiated, and the castle, constructed of wood from the forest.

The performances of both the mountain spirit and Asaji are highly stylized, and Asaji wears heavy Noh-style, masklike makeup, obscuring most of her facial expressions. Similar to the mountain spirit's act of prophesying without making eye contact with Washizu, Asaji avoids eye contact with her husband as she prophesies Miki's (Banquo) eventual, perceived betrayal. As Buchanan points out, the implied and ideological connections between Asaji and the mountain spirit dissolve "the boundaries between the two competing domains in Washizu's world, the forest and castle." The vertical lines defining the forest and the horizontal beams of the castle initially seem oppositional to each other. As the film progresses, the superficial difference between them begins to dissolve, as "both are agents of torment . . . and collaborate in closing in on Washizu."[66] Asaji's sonic connections to the mountain spirit (analyzed in the preceding section) and the visual parallels between them (stillness, whiteness, lack of affect) suggest a further resonance between the castle and the forest where the unenlightened may become trapped.

In contrast, Washizu is far more expressive than his wife, pacing up and down while Lady Asaji remains seated. Even when she moves in other scenes she seems to float, head to toe remaining still. Washizu confers with his aids in warfare, but in the matters of prophecy and dynastic futures, he speaks to Asaji. (He does discuss the prophecies with Miki before arriving at the castle, but he defers to Asaji in actions to take regarding them.) Washizu's and Asaji's competing worldviews are the thrust of this scene. While Washizu stresses the value of loyalty to his lord, Asaji takes a cynical view of the feudal world order, stating that the Great Lord comes into power by killing *his* lord—thereby urging Washizu to follow his model. Asaji's reasoning echoes Claudius' advice to Hamlet who is mourning Old Hamlet: "But, you must know, your father lost a father | That father lost, lost his" (1.2.89–90). In this moment of sober reasoning, Asaji offers her reading of feudal history, though Washizu resorts to demonizing her reasoning and her person. Although Shakespeare's Macbeth commits a terrible transgression by murdering Duncan, Washizu could be considered to be conforming rather than rebelling. He is following in the footsteps of his lord—who rose to power by killing his predecessor—and submitting to the fate foretold by the mountain spirit. Further, Washizu (Mifune Toshirō) conforms to the Noh archetype of Heida, the warrior, whereas Yamada Isuzu's Asaji draws directly on the role type of a madwoman.

Throne of Blood shows that Kurosawa does not romanticize Japanese history, departing from the trend of popular period films (*jidai-geki*) in the 1950s. Despite Noh-style makeup and stylized movements, the castles in the film look lived in, and the costumes are meaningfully embodied by the actors. The framing and narrative devices work in tandem to connect nature and artifice, and the palatial space with the natural world.

Like Kurosawa, who combined Noh, American westerns, and Japanese scroll painting in his *Throne of Blood*, and Peter Brook, who regarded theatre as iconographic art,[67] Ninagawa often worked from a set of compelling images for each production as if he were a designer. He did this to spark the audience's interest while introducing them to the play world in the first few minutes of the performance.

Ninagawa's visual strategy was an integral part of his sound design. The gentle and shimmering "Sanctus" echoed his visual motif of cherry blossom. The cherry tree on stage was inspired by Motojirō Kajii's (1901–32) widely circulated phrase, "dead bodies are buried under the cherry trees." In the play, death is associated with a cherry tree in full blossom, a symbol of transcendental beauty and the repose of the soul. Ninagawa's rehearsal notes for act 5, scene 6, where Malcolm, Siward, and Macduff's army covers itself with branches from Birnam Wood outside Dunsinane, usefully sum up the significance of cherry blossom as the dominant visual and sonic frameworks: "memories of cherry blossom at night [morph into] a sensuous invitation to death."[68]

The goal of Ninagawa's framing device was to set the mood and immerse the audience in the world of the play. Many of his productions featured surprising ways to use cultural elements. Ninagawa found inspiration for the striking set described at the beginning of this chapter from daily life:

[W]hen I went back home and opened up our family Butsudan to light a candle and pray for my father, at that moment, I thought, "this is the right image [for *Macbeth*]." I had two overlapping complex ideas: ordinary people watching *Macbeth*, and a Japanese audience looking at the stage and seeing through it to our ancestors.

He elaborated on his synesthetic experience of a dialogue across different spaces:

When I was in front of the Butsudan, my thoughts were racing. It was like I was having a conversation with my ancestors. When I thought of *Macbeth* in this way, I thought of him appearing in the Butusdan where we consecrate dead ancestors.[69]

Like Wu Hsing-kuo's solo Beijing opera *Lear Is Here* (2001), discussed in Chapter 2, the *Ninagawa Macbeth* is a personal dialogue with his father, as the director confided:

While I was praying [at our family altar] I recalled my dead father and elder brother and I felt as if I was conversing with them. At that time it occurred to me that if the drama of *Macbeth* were a fantasy which developed from a conversation with my dead ancestors, then this could really be my own story.[70]

In a typical Japanese household, a butsudan family altar contains ancestral tablets (*ihai*) that enshrine ancestral spirits. Thus the larger-than-life set of the butsudan was born, with giant sculptural warrior-god figures serving as the backdrop to Malcolm and Macduff's meeting. As already noted, throughout the performance, the two old women sit on either side of the altar to pray to their ancestors, to watch the play with the audience, to serve as stagehands, and to carry on with their day—detached from the action. They eat, drink, sew, and even nod off. From time to time, they do respond to the dramatic action. They weep when Macbeth says, "my way of life | Is fallen into the sear, the yellow leaf" (5.3.22–3) and at his "Tomorrow and tomorrow and tomorrow" (5.5.22) speech. The *fabulae* of *Macbeth* could be stories told to the two women by their ancestors, or their hallucination—old wives' tale, in other words. The two-woman silent chorus plays a role similar to that of the *waki* in Noh, witnessing the heinous acts and mediating between the spectator's world and the play world.

This theory holds up, since the dramatic actions take place within the altar. Their aloofness outside contrasts with the earnestness of the characters inside. As Malcolm delivers the tragedy's last lines, screen doors slide shut. Later, the two women slowly close the multipanel shutters outside the screen doors to further separate the playing space from the audience. They exist outside the play's narrative time, which calls to mind Macbeth's attack on the order of time.

The screen doors serve another important dramaturgical function: they divide the stage into two areas for physical and allegorical actions. The upstage area behind the screens is reserved for action that is farther removed from the quotidian, while the downstage area in front of the screen doors, closer to the audience, is used as a space that is alternative to what passes as normative in the upstage area. Intimate scenes and casual discussions take place downstage, in front of the screen doors. The witches initially appear behind the semitransparent screen doors, visible thanks only to lightning. Banquo is murdered there, and that is also where the apparitions are seen when Macbeth consults the witches. The banquet scene takes place behind the screens where Banquo's ghost replaces the warrior-god statue on a pedestal upstage. Jolted by Banquo's ghost out of the semblance of guilt-free peace he works so hard to maintain, Macbeth opens the screen doors to step "outside" for fresh air and therefore downstage. He is not only dethroned by the ghost who has taken his seat at the table but also jolted out of the family altar. Lady Macbeth follows Macbeth there and urges him to keep his dignity in front of his guests: "You do not give the cheer: the feast is sold" (3.4.32). This is also the space where Fleance escapes to when pursued by the assassins. As such, the downstage space is disconnected from the violent world behind the screens.

Just as silence is part of Ninagawa's sonic strategy, the empty space plays an important role in his use of the stage. Act 5, scene 1, Lady Macbeth's sleepwalking scene, opens with a single flickering candle without stage lighting. There is a clear parallel between the candle—which could extinguish at any moment—and the weakened mind of Lady Macbeth. As Macbeth later mourns the passing of Lady Macbeth and the passing of time, he lights more candles on the stage floor. It should be noted that act 5 scene 5 is not always performed as a mourning scene. Ian McKellen's Macbeth was dismissive in his 1977 production in Stratford-upon-Avon. In Ninagawa's version, Macbeth lights the candles around him methodically in a circle in order to "conquer his fears,"[71] only to engage in futile attempts to extinguish the ever-burning candles later on. Macbeth's feverish collection of the candles resembles a childish obsession: "His behaviour appears just like that of a child who cannot feel at peace until he gathers all his toys around him," writes Ninagawa.[72] Whereas the single candle symbolizes Lady Macbeth's mental state, the group of candles embodies Macbeth's guilt; he cannot put out the candles, because he cannot undo the atrocious crimes he has committed. This circle of inextinguishable candles creates an ironic distance between redemption and Macbeth's speech: "Tomorrow, and tomorrow, and tomorrow." Encircled by the candles, Macbeth says, appropriately, "Out, out, brief candle! | Life's but a walking shadow" (5.5.23–24), as his shadow is cast by the candles' light. Like the altar writ large, the ingenious use of candles exemplifies Ninagawa's signature approach to creating a sense of estrangement through quotidian objects. The candles commemorate lost souls, including the Macbeths, soldiers who will die in the next scene, and those whom Macbeth had already killed.

The candles also reference the stone statues of Buddha at Adashino Nenbutsuji Temple on a hill overlooking Kyoto. This ninth-century Buddhist temple served as a charity site of last resting place, where those who could not afford proper burial rites could leave the deceased, from the Heian (794–1185) to Edo (1603–1868) periods. Thousands of stone Buddhas tend to the dead without graves and pray for their souls. As such, the arrangement of candles evokes death, proper rites, and Macbeth's anxiety about not having any offspring—which, in the Japanese context, would mean no descendants would pay tribute to his departed soul. As is foreshadowed by the banquet scene, Macbeth is pushed out of the family altar by Banquo's ghost. Macbeth will not have a place in any family altar where respect is paid to ancestors. He is deprived of the privilege to be anyone's ancestor. That is his ultimate tragedy.

Unexpected transformations of quotidian objects surprise and delight Ninagawa's audiences. A dominant, rising sun in the back-drop, along with techniques from Noh and Kabuki styles, are the most memorable features of his 1999 *King Lear*, an English-language coproduction with the RSC in England. The cast included Nigel Hawthorne in the title role and Hiroyuki Sanada as an androgynous Fool. The scenes of the blinded Gloucester being led by his disguised son Edgar evoked a Japanese watercolor (4.1, 6). Cherry blossoms, a rain shower of flower petals, and snowstorms were Ninagawa's visual trademarks. An enlarged Capitoline wolf statue dominated the stage of his 2012 *Cymbeline* in London, an adaptation that presented Japanese courtiers against Roman sceneries. A gigantic, tiered *hina*-dolls display in *Hamlet* (Barbican, London, May 2015) turned actors into human-sized dolls in the play-within-a-play scene. According to the handout, Ninagawa drew inspiration from the Japanese Girls' Day (Hinamatsuri, or Dolls' Day), a festival celebrating girls' development. As part of the festival, dolls are displayed for well wishes for the girls' future. Since the dolls represent hope, Ophelia's giving away dolls rather than flowers in her mad scene carried with it a grave tone, playing as a disruption to established rituals. This production evoked the metaphorical connection between drowning—dolls adrift—and despair evident in the eleventh-century *Genji-Monogatari*. The floating-doll ritual is still performed by Kamigamo and Shimogamo Shrines in Kyoto. In some instances, the previous year's dolls are brought to the shrines to be burned. Ophelia's life-sized dolls drew attention to the artificiality of rituals and the performance. The audience's attention was thus redirected from the representational aspect of theatrical realism to the presentational aspect of metatheatrical narratives.

Coda

Kurosawa's cinematography inspired Ninagawa's stage directing, and Ninagawa expressed his ardent admiration of Kurosawa.[73] Ninagawa's signature metatheatrical framing and use of stylized Kabuki, Noh, and Bunraku techniques may seem radical for Japanese theatre practitioners, but his works shed light on the often-overlooked aspect of English Shakespeares: the naturalized filtration through realism and naturalism. Both stylized Asian theatres and western realist techniques are governed by their respective stage conventions, but from a western perspective the conventions of realist theatre can sometimes seem so transparent due to their familiarity that one is no longer able to see them.

Kurosawa transformed, rather than translated, Shakespeare's language into imagery, whereas Ninagawa worked with direct translations of Shakespeare's plays (in many instances keeping proper names intact, in Japanese transliteration). Ninagawa did, however, impose a new framework on the play. The distinction between verbal and nonverbal signs in theatre works is an important one; it has empowered modern directors, and particularly Ninagawa, to engage in meaningful conversations with classical drama.

Once we think we have heard or seen something, it is difficult to unhear or unsee it. Listening to and looking at the voices and spectacles of the other is not in itself an endorsement of the journalistic tendency to ignore verbal language in touring or foreign-language productions or films, be it Kurosawa in New York or Ninagawa in London, Tokyo, or Shanghai.[74] Local reviewers tend to put more emphasis on a foreign spectacle, due to the linguistic barrier, thereby dismissing or underappreciating the value of verbal representation. This was exemplified by Lyn Gardner's assessment of Ninagawa's 2012 *Cymbeline* at the Barbican during the World Shakespeare Festival in London: "It's all about display. . . . [The production] captures *Cymbeline*'s fairytale qualities, but seldom gets its psychological detail."[75] Michiko Suematsu's candid response to such viewpoints rejects such stereotypical characterization of Japanese Shakespeares: "[to say that] 'a Japanese-language production [abroad] must stand or fall on spectacle [alone]' . . . sounds utterly nonsensical."[76] Achieving a contextual understanding of a work is far more important than singling out any one element, which is why this chapter situates Kurosawa and Ninagawa within larger cultural contexts. Journalists are not the only ones fetishizing the spectacle of Asian performances. Scholars have suggested various levels of cultural exclusivity, buying into such myths as Asian Shakespeare performances standing out by their unique visual and aural signs—as if Shakespearean drama excels in the verbal, Asian performances "the corporeal,"[77] a tendency that I critique in Chapter 3.

An iconic director, Kurosawa has become source material for other artists. *Ran* and *Throne of Blood* (Fig. 1.2) in particular have influenced subsequent Japanese films. For example, the animated film *Millennium Actress* (*Sennen joyū*, dir. Satoshi Kon, Bendai Visual Company, 2001; Fig. 1.3), which follows former actress Chiyoko Fujiwara down memory lane as she is being filmed in a television documentary, pays homage to *Ran* in a sequence on the siege of a castle. For all her life and acting career, Chiyoko has been chasing after an anonymous painter whom she idealizes as both her prince and a means to escape socially prescribed gender roles. The photography of the scene is

Fig. 1.2 *Throne of Blood*. Soldiers shoot arrows at Macbeth-Washizu.

Fig. 1.3 *Millennium Actress*. Cameraman Ida Kyōji (Masaya Onosaka) being shot by arrows.

reminiscent of Kurosawa's cinematography, and the character of the cameraman, Ida Kyōji, inserts himself into visual sequences of Chiyoko's narration. Chiyoko dresses up like Lady Kaede in *Ran* (the equivalent to Edmund in *Lear*), a woman bent on revenge and seeking to escape the patriarchal structure. Like Kurosawa's films, *Millennium Actress* features painterly scenes that draw on Ukiyo-e–themed woodblock prints. Its bloodstained wooden walls, for instance, recall the scene where Washizu and Lady Asaji murder the Great Lord in *Throne of Blood*. In this scene, Chiyoko is wearing a twelve-layer kimono and the same Heian-period eyebrows that Lady Asaji wears. In several other scenes, the television interviewer Genya Tachibana's mannerism calls to mind Mifune Toshirō, who acted in many of Kurosawa's films, including the *Seven Samurai*, *Throne of Blood*, *Yojimbo*, and *Rashomon*. The witch who haunts Chiyoko throughout *Millennium Actress* curses or imparts prophecy while operating a set of spinning wheels, a visual motif that echoes the mountain spirit in *Throne of Blood*. The witch's chanting and tone resemble those of the mountain spirit as well. As what W. J. T. Mitchell calls a "metapicture," the film draws attention to itself as a motion picture.[78] Felicia Chan suggests that the film's self-reflexivity is not only "constituted by its performed awareness of filmic devices [and Kurosawa . . .] but also by the insertion of itself into" Japanese film history. It "re-memorialis[es]" cultural screen memories.[79] Kurosawa stands at the center of the collective memory.

Throne of Blood has also inspired other works outside Japan in a rhizomatic network of cross-citations. In 1985, John R. Briggs combined cross-media and cross-cultural citations when he brought the Scottish Play, Kurosawa, and Asian America together in his *Shogun Macbeth*, performed by Pan Asian Repertory Theater in New York (founded by Tisa Chang), as mentioned in the Epilogue. Regarded as a Kurosawa-lite adaptation, in both the positive and negative senses of the phrase, the adaptation (in English) is interspersed with a great number of Shakespearean lines and set on the island of Honshu in twelfth-century Kamakura Japan (1192–1333). All of the action took place on a minimalist stage set in front of an eight-foot statue of Buddha behind a Torii gate ("bird abode," a traditional gate commonly found at the entry to a Shinto shrine), a statue that seemed to look down at the dramatic events with a sense of aloofness, a transcendental indifference. The set calls to mind the two indifferent, elderly women in Ninagawa's *Macbeth*. The itinerant blind narrator Biwa Hoshi (Tom Matsusaka) opened the production with lines from the *Sutra* that echoed the chanting of the mountain spirit in Kurosawa's film and anticipated some of Macbeth's later lines ("Life's but a walking shadow," 5.5.23):

Life is a lying dream, he only wakes who casts the world aside. The bell of the Gion Temple tolls into every man's heart to warn him that all is vanity and evanescence.[80]

Just two years later, in 1987, Wu Hsing-kuo's *The Kingdom of Desire* redefined Beijing opera by paying tribute to and fine-tuning Kurosawa's visual language. Wu's Macbeth faces a similar fate of being killed by his soldiers' arrows. In 2010, the Oregon Shakespeare Festival staged an English-language stage version of *Throne of Blood* directed by Ping Chong. Kurosawa's approach of turning familiar artifacts into venues of estrangement has proven influential. To view video clips of *The Kingdom of Desire*, visit the page curated by Alexa Alice Joubin on *MIT Global Shakespeares*: globalshakespeares.mit.edu/kingdom-of-desire-wu-hsingkuo-1986/

Kurosawa and Ninagawa, members of the postwar generation, came of age during the politically conscious era. As a result, they often used metacinema and metatheatricality in their works to draw attention not only to the ideological payload of the narrative but also to the craft of filmmaking and playmaking. Building on the analysis of forms (sound and spectacle) in this chapter, Chapter 2 considers ways in which stage and screen conventions intersect to carry ideological weight when "time is out of joint" and actors' "toil shall strive to mend" social circumstances (*Romeo and Juliet*, Prol. 14).

"Our toil shall strive to mend"

Politics of Remediation

Performing Shakespeare is an act of remediation. It involves, as the Chorus proclaims in the Prologue to *Romeo and Juliet*, making amends to suit the dramatic action to the cultural location and zeitgeist of the era. Modern actors "strive to mend" (Prol. 14) both the play and the social circumstances through their performance, deploying new narratives for social justice. The hypercanonicity of Shakespeare has inspired remedial uses of his plays that beseech the audiences' attendance "with patient ears" (Prol. 13) and discerning eyes. Many screen and stage adaptations are informed by a preconceived notion that performing the Shakespearean canon can improve not only local art forms (such as attracting a larger audience or securing invitations for international festivals or tours) but also personal and social circumstances (such as addressing issues like trauma or voicing political opinions that are otherwise difficult to discuss publicly). Michael Dobson has used the term "sentimental myths" to characterize the tendency on the part of enthusiasts to imagine socially remedial, politically effective Shakespeares. Examples include the idea that "all productions . . . in the former Eastern Bloc were urgently political." Additionally, there is the myth that Shakespeare is interculturally transparent because his oeuvre has been translated into multiple languages (which in turn is used as evidence that his work "must somehow transcend all of them").[1] These myths fuel the growth of remedial adaptations—works that engage with reparative interpretations of Shakespeare.

Central to these ideas about a politically remedial Shakespeare is the dramaturgically constructed locality—setting, performance venue,

Shakespeare and East Asia. Alexa Alice Joubin, Oxford University Press (2021). © Alexa Alice Joubin. DOI: 10.1093/oso/9780198703563.003.0002

and cultural origins of the performers. Place figures prominently in adaptations that subscribe to the belief in arts' remedial function. Directors and performers need to find a new space between fiction and reality in which actors, characters, and audiences interact. Once a new locality is constructed, Shakespearean motifs and East Asian aesthetics are deployed as agents to cure each other's perceived deficiencies, sometimes with a straight face, sometimes with parody.

Building upon the formalistic analysis in Chapter 1, this chapter locates actors, their characters, and their embodied, gendered identities in new dramatic and political spaces and proposes artistic remediation as a thematic lens to read selected adaptations. My goal here is not to adjudicate, but rather to analyze the myths of Shakespeare's remedial merit and reveal the operating principles of such myths, whether in earnest proposals to employ Shakespeare to usher in social justice or in parodic gestures that problematize the political efficacy of reparative Shakespeare. Similar to racial and gender stereotypes, myths derive their staying power from half-truths. Equally important here is that this metacritical lens enables us to move beyond national profiling to account for the discrete qualities of individual artists and performances. Many films and productions do not have one single point of cultural origin and cannot be flattened against a cultural profile. As has been discussed in the Prologue, one of the most influential but thoroughly critiqued modes of criticism is Fredric Jameson's idea that non-western cultural productions operate as national allegories—that is, allegories of the national histories.[2] Shakespeare in non-western cultures is not necessarily allegorical but it is often part of the remedial cultural work. Jameson has since offered a corrective in his book, *Allegory and Ideology*, in which he states that works do not in and by themselves contain meanings; rather, as they move through the world, they soak up and accrue meanings.[3] Theorization of recuperative art in this chapter is followed by analyses of how place shapes this cultural work; case studies from Hong Kong, Taiwan, and China; and finally an overview of Sinophone performances.

Remedial Functions of Art

There are two types of reparative adaptations: (1) an earnest, moralistic reading that hinges on the reparative efficacy of the arts; and (2) an open-ended approach that is skeptical of the efficacy of reparative performances. Some film directors consciously offer a corrective to Shakespearean narratives and to local genres of performance. In the Mandarin-language film *The Banquet* (*Ye yan*, dir. Feng Xiaogang, Huayi Brothers and Media Asia, 2006; alternative release title: *The Legend of the Black Scorpion*) the Ophelia figure, Qing Nü, has more moral agency than her counterpart does in *Hamlet* and is able to express her thoughts without going mad or resorting to singing as her only form of communication. Gertrude, recast as a love interest and stepmother of the Hamlet figure, actively participates in court politics for personal gain. East Asian feminism and ideals of femininity are deployed to counterbalance traditional Anglophone interpretations of Gertrude and Ophelia. At the same time, Hamlet's insistence on interiority—inner life—brings a new element of characterization to the genre of *wuxia*, which would otherwise focus more on the physical prowess of the knights-errant and the elegance of their choreographed fights. Prince Wu Luan rejects the idea that identity is defined by exterior factors (cf. "I know not seems," 1.2.77) and nourishes his interior self by remembering his idealized father (and his ghost). Echoing both *Hamlet* and Sir John Everett Millais's Pre-Raphaelite painting *Ophelia* (1851/1852), *Prince of the Himalayas* (dir. Sherwood Hu, Hus Entertainment, 2006)—set and filmed in Tibet, with a Tibetan cast, and in the Tibetan language—makes a bold move to bring Sino–Tibetan relations to bear on the discourse of a corrupt court in *Hamlet* and gives Ophelia a more active role in the dramatic action. Both films, discussed below, are set in fictional premodern periods and draw heavily on Shakespeare's global canonicity to avoid censorship and bolster their marketing efforts.

In other cases, Shakespeare is imagined to have a reparative effect on the artist's or a society's outlook on life when the time is "out of joint" (*Hamlet*, 1.5.190) or during identity crises. These works cast performing Shakespeare as a strategy to set things right. Appropriations by politicians and artists have tapped into Shakespeare's putative remedial functions. *Cymbeline*, for example, became a channel through which Taiwanese college students voiced their concerns about Taiwanese identity in the face of threatened militarism from and economic dominance by the People's Republic of China. I-Chun Wang reported that her students found strong parallels between

Roman-British relations in *Cymbeline* and Sino-Taiwanese relations during the Sunflower Student Movement of 2014, when students protested the Taiwan legislature's passage of the Cross–Strait Service Trade Agreement without adequate review.[4] As a foreign platform, Shakespeare creates a safe space for the discussion of contentious topics. In a classroom with divided opinions about the kind of relationship Taiwan should maintain with China, Shakespeare became a common denominator and a vehicle through which students of different political persuasions could discuss Taiwan's political future.

Inspired by Karl Marx's frequent uses of literary classics, leaders of the People's Republic of China have repeatedly repurposed quotes from Shakespeare for politically expedient reasons, especially with regard to Sino–British relations. On June 26, 2011, during a three-day visit to Britain, Chinese premier Wen Jiaobao visited the birthplace of Shakespeare. He alluded to his boyhood love of Shakespeare in his speech to British Prime Minister David Cameron. In a moment when international economic relations and political capital were at stake, British culture secretary Jeremy Hunt was blunt: "I am hoping that a billion Chinese might see some pictures on their TV of their premier coming and visiting the birthplace of Shakespeare" and flock to Britain in droves.[5] During Chinese president Xi Jinping's 2015 state visit to Britain, he quoted *The Tempest* ("what's past is prologue"; 2.1.253) during his eleven-minute speech to the House of Parliament and urged the two countries to "join hands and move forward." In a reciprocal gesture, Queen Elizabeth II gifted Xi with a special collection of Shakespeare's sonnets.[6] Both the British and Chinese leaders appropriated Shakespeare's cultural capital for their own purposes. Politically reparative merits and economic returns, in this case, become the primary function of art. With the sonnets, Elizabeth II reminded Xi of Britain's superior and often dominant cultural position. Xi used references to Shakespeare to project an image of a cosmopolitan China. Both sides saw Shakespeare as providing some common ground. The outbreak of the global pandemic of COVID-19 caused by SARS-CoV-2 (severe acute respiratory syndrome coronavirus) in early 2020 disrupted live theatre events, cinemas, and travel worldwide. It also gave rise to new forms of anti-Chinese racism and deepened distrust of the Chinese government in international and trade relations.

Interestingly, Xi's quotation of Antonio's phrase "what's past is prologue" from act 2, scene 1, could perform double and conflicting duties. It could, on the one hand, imply that the two nations will overlook their ideological differences and work together despite the antagonistic history between them—a history that includes the Opium Wars and, more recently, the Chinese government's treatment of the activist-artist Ai Weiwei's human-rights-themed art. On the other hand, it could also betray Xi's thirst for power domestically and internationally, as indicated in China's One Belt, One Road Initiative. As the tone changes, the phrase could carry more sinister meanings of a threat, hinting at escalating the conflict. The phrase has frequently been misquoted in the first sense. It is engraved on the National Archives building in Washington, DC, where it is often assumed to suggest the ways history shapes the present or that history can help shed light on the present.

Theatre directors have drawn on the remedial effects of art on performance traditions and personal identities. Psychological realism, a feature that actor-director Wu Hsing-kuo attributes to Shakespearean tragedy, expands the repertoire of *jingju* (Beijing opera) performance routines. Wu's solo *jingju* performance of *King Lear* (*Lear Is Here*, which premiered in 2001 and had been on tour worldwide) uses an aging father figure and recalcitrant younger generations to reimagine the story of his personal life and theatre career. Ideas for the adaptation began in a workshop in Paris hosted by Ariane Mnouchkine, founder of Théâtre du Soleil, that was designed to address limitations in the acting methods of both the European avant-garde and *jingju* practices. Wu believed that Shakespeare would provide material for an effective remedial experiment. On an allegorical level, Wu uses the idea of Lear's two bodies, as both a monarch and a father and as a character and an actor, to address his own divided identities as a Taiwanese practitioner of *jingju*, a decidedly Chinese art form, in Taiwan, an island nation constantly under threat of invasion from the People's Republic of China. This Buddhist-inflected reading of *King Lear* and Wu's autobiography, in which he plays multiple characters, including himself, brings Lear's character arc to bear on the events in Wu's personal and professional life. As the Lear in the production awakens to a renewed sense of self-recognition, Wu the actor also arrives at a new stage of self-knowledge.

The Special Place of *King Lear* in Remedial Arts

Wu's choice of play is not coincidental. *King Lear* has held a special place in the genre of reparative Shakespeare in Asia since some scenes were performed in English in the Chowringhee Theatre in Calcutta in 1832. Passages from it have been used to play a healing role in narratives about aging and dying with dignity. In Rituparno Ghosh's 2007 film *The Last Lear*, which is inspired by Utpal Dutt's play *Aajker Shahjahan*, an eccentric, aging stage actor in Kolkata, Harish "Harry" Mishra (Amitabh Bachchan), reenacts scenes of plays he used to perform. In the final scene, the actress Shabnam (Preity Zinta), who comes to visit Harry, wakes him from a coma by reading lines from act 4, scene 7, the scene where Lear and Cordelia reunite and reconcile with each other. Shabnam slips into the role of Cordelia, while Harry dies reciting the lines he knows by heart: "You are a spirit, I know. . . . Where have I been? . . . I know not what to say. . . . I am a very foolish, fond old man." It is a scene of reconciliation and self-recognition because in his career, Harry is ill-suited for the transition from stage to screen. In an earlier scene, while shooting a film, Harry is injured from a fall, which parallels the blinded Gloucester's imaginary fall at the Dover Cliff in *Lear*.

The theme of domestic tragedy in *Lear* has inspired appropriations that examine the wounds of diasporic communities and tensions between different generations. Sangeeta Datta's 2009 film *Life Goes On* depicts the conflicts in an immigrant family of Hindus that moves from Bengal to London. Drawing on Bollywood conventions, the film alludes to *King Lear* through the family's redemptive arc. After his wife passes away, the father—who is more attached to Bengali traditions—struggles to reconnect with his three daughters. The youngest daughter is cast as Cordelia in a college production. Hong Kong-British director David Tse Ka-Shing staged a Mandarin-English version of *King Lear* in 2006 with his London-based Yellow Earth Theatre, in collaboration with Shanghai Dramatic Arts Centre, in Shanghai and Stratford-upon-Avon (part of the RSC Complete Works Festival). Focusing on the questions of heritage and filial piety and set in 2020, this adaptation framed the different worldviews of Lear and Cordelia in terms of linguistic difference, as is examined in Chapter 4. Lear, a business tycoon, solicits declarations of love from his three daughters. Regan and Goneril, who live in Shanghai, are fluent in Chinese, but Cordelia, who lives in London, is unable to communicate in Chinese with her father. Her silence is both a result of her inability to speak Mandarin and a gesture of resistance of the patriarchy. Cordelia, a member of the Chinese diaspora in London, participates in this important family and business meeting via video link. Ironically but perhaps fittingly, the only Chinese word at her disposal is *meiyou* ("nothing").

Similarly, Singaporean director Ong Keng Sen uses language as an identity marker in his multilingual adaptation of *Lear* in collaboration with Japanese playwright Kishida Rio (1997 and 1999). The Lear figure speaks Japanese and walks in the solemn style of Noh theatre, while the Older Daughter, a composite figure of Goneril and Regan played by a *jingju* actor, speaks Mandarin. Their philosophical conversation, which is carried out in two languages and two distinct performance styles, is followed by a ritualistic division-of-the-kingdom scene. The younger sister (Cordelia) speaks Thai, although she remains silent most of the time. Ong's *Lear* is set up as a corrective to the prevalent preconception about Asian languages and cultures as interchangeable.

King Lear also features prominently in reparative discourses beyond Asia. Similar to *The Last Lear*, John Kani's play *Kunene and the King*, performed by Kani and Anthony Sher (Stratford-upon-Avon and Cape Town, 2019; a coproduction of RSC and Fugard Theatre), depicts how characters come to terms with aging, cultural biases, and their mortality through situations that parallel those in *Lear* and their reenactment of scenes from the play. *Kunene and the King* features Lunga, a South African black male nurse, and Jack, an ill-tempered white actor coping with terminal liver cancer in South Africa. Throughout the play they recite passages from *King Lear* to expose each other's cultural biases and eventually reconcile their differences. In a similar vein, in the independent film *Lear's Shadow* (dir. Brian Elerding, 2019, based on a 2017 play at Lineage Performing Arts Center, Pasadena), two friends engage in an argument use *Lear* to prove their points. Stephen (David Blue) and Jack (Fred Cross) act out scenes of *Lear* while attempting to rebuild their friendship and deal with grief, with Stephen playing all three daughters to Jack's Lear.

Parodies of Remedial Arts

As much as the first approach celebrates individual struggles and triumphs, it risks compartmentalizing social inequality by aestheticizing suffering. The second approach challenges the therapeutic ethos. In contrast to more earnest pursuits of remedial Shakespeare, some films and productions mock the conviction that Shakespeare—as a repository of western values that are often deemed progressive—has any recuperative or ameliorative function in hybrid cultural spaces, particularly in Taiwan and Hong Kong. Whereas Chapter 1 examines adaptations of tragedies by Kurosawa and Ninagawa, some works examined in this chapter turn tragedies into parodies and comedies. A number of Hong Kong films as well as several Taiwanese stage works engage productively in this parodic mode. The late Taiwanese playwright and director Lee Kuo-hsiu's (Li Guoxiu) *Shamlet* (*Shamuleite*, 1992), drawing on the Mel Gibson film *Hamlet* (dir. Franco Zeffirelli, Icon Productions, 1990), mocks western realist performances and turns high tragedy into comic parody. A struggling theatre company rehearses and stages *Hamlet* during their tour around Taiwan, seeing Shakespeare as part of their strategy to reboot their company. However, instead of following the typical arc of redemption, *Shamlet*, rife with scripted onstage mishaps presented as improvisation, concludes with the company's eventual defeat.

Indeed reparative adaptations often feature underprivileged actors as unlikely heroes who eventually succeed in playing Shakespeare. The precarious state of experimental theatre is reflected in the actors' futile attempt to revive their company through Shakespeare, as depicted by the Hong Kong comedy film *One Husband Too Many* (*Yi qi liang fu*, dir. Anthony Chan, Bo Ho Film, 1988). The protagonist, Hsin (Ah-Hsin, or Hsia Chih-Hsin, in the film; this chapter follows the English subtitles in terms of characters' names), pins all his hopes on bringing western culture to a backwater village by staging his version of *Romeo and Juliet*. He takes on the role of Romeo; his wife plays Juliet. In the end, Shakespeare fails to resuscitate not only his theatre career but also his personal love life. Another Hong Kong film, *Trouble Couples* (*Kai xin wu yu*, dir. Eric Tsang, Cinema City, 1987), draws on the trope of the reluctantly paired and unlikely couple, Petruccio and Katherine, in

Taming of the Shrew to deconstruct ideas of cultural subjugation and assimilation. Mui Tai-heung (Anita Mui), a motherly figure, forbids her three younger sisters from dating before she is married. The three sisters conspire to find Mui a husband, and they recruit an unlikely hero, the loser and loner Tsang Jo-choy (Eric Tsang). In the film's Shakespeare-esque denouement, Tsang's friends set up a wager. The man whose spouse is the most docile would win monetary rewards. Tsang wins the wager thanks to Mui's contrived public display of obedience and her speech on wives' duty to their husbands and female humility. The couple leaves the party triumphantly, but as soon as they are out of the sight of the guests, Tsang bows to thank Mui for her enactment of submission according to their prior agreement and reaffirms his servitude to her. While the film's marketing material draws on the tropes of discipline and feminine subjugation in *Taming of the Shrew*, Shakespeare ultimately fails to "save the day," for it is Tsang who is being conditioned to serve. To view this scene, visit www.youtube.com/watch?v=QVjlkbbPdWE

In contrast, Lim Won-kook's *Frivolous Wife* (*Nallari jongbujeon*, Lotte Entertainment, South Korea, 2008) turns *The Taming of the Shrew* into a romantic comedy by drawing on the South Korean trope of rich, bold, rude, self-reliant women, which was popularized by *My Sassy Girl* (*Yeopgijeogin geunyeo*, dir. Kwak Jae-young, ShiCine, 2001; American remake dir. Yann Samuell, 2008). The "shrew" figure in *Frivolous Wife* goes through parodic, *My Fair Lady*-style self-reform to be accepted by her boyfriend's family, only to realize that her future in-laws are ruthless gangsters. Similar to *Trouble Couple*, *Frivolous Wife* hints at redemptive arcs only to quickly burst the illusion of reparative interpretations of the canon and the promised reward.

Shot nine or ten years before the July 1997 handover of Hong Kong from Britain to China, *Trouble Couples* and *One Husband Too Many* have been interpreted, in the few available studies so far, as allegories of Hong Kong's positionality between two empires.[7] An important but overlooked feature of these films—along with *Shamlet*—is their fundamental distrust of Shakespeare's moral authority. These parodies of remedial functions of art leverage their ambiguous location between cultures to dismantle monolithic constructions of cultural authenticity—the assumed stability of the canonical texts and their moral universe—by repurposing Shakespeare for political criticism.

A Theory of Reparative Adaptation

These works point to a larger phenomenon that I call remedial performances of Shakespeare. Remedial interpretations as a mode have spread from academics to practitioners since the 1980s. Informed by an urge to excavate ideologically appealing messages from narratives, remedial criticism is rooted in what Rita Felski calls a critical predilection for "expos[ing] hidden truths and draw[ing] out . . . counterintuitive meanings that others fail to see."[8] Under this model, the professional interpreter of a text sees through the superficial appearance to show less well-informed readers its hidden meanings. In a different context, Douglas Lanier has raised questions about "reparative Shakespeare," performances of socially conscious, inspirational narratives that use Shakespeare as their centerpiece.[9] Fictional and documentary films in this genre often feature a foolhardy troupe or director working with unlikely Shakespearean actors for a high-stakes performance. Kenneth Branagh's film *A Winter's Tale* follows a group of aspiring thespians who attempt to stage *Hamlet* during Christmas in a church, a time and place of reconciliation. Inmates in a rehabilitation program spare no effort in their performance of *Julius Caesar* in Paolo Taviani and Vittorio Taviani's Italian film *Caesar Must Die*. They find peace with themselves even if their production is far from perfect. Real-life actors, too, follow a recuperative trajectory in documentaries. Mike Jonathan's *The Road to the Globe* reveals creative ways in which a New Zealand company rose to the challenges and brought their *Troilus and Cressida* in Te Reo Māori to the Globe-to-Globe Festival in London in 2012 during the Olympics. Tom Weidlinger's *A Dream in Hanoi* offers a rosy picture of post-war reconciliation through an American-Vietnamese coproduction of *A Midsummer Night's Dream*. Mel Stuart's *The Hobart Shakespeare* chronicles the journey of an inner-city teacher and his underprivileged fifth-graders. They are an unlikely cast for *Hamlet*, but renowned actor Ian McKellen agrees to attend their performance.[10] While divergent in their agenda, these works share several features in common. They depict fictional characters or real-life actors seeking rehabilitation through theatre-making, and Shakespeare empowers them morally and politically.

Despite seemingly insurmountable obstacles and setbacks, the narratives invariably end with a triumphant performance. Lanier theorizes that such works "invest Shakespeare with magical reformational power," and that they can empower the socially marginalized, such as refugees, women of color, and inmates. Lanier is primarily concerned with the ethics of criticism, asking whether "a bad misreading of Shakespeare" can "nevertheless create a positive effect in a performer" and asking what constitutes "bad reparative Shakespeare."[11] He connects reparative Shakespeare as a mode of performance to politically oriented criticism of Shakespeare. Case studies in the present chapter cover a broader spectrum of reparative interpretations of Shakespeare, ranging from transformations of performative genres to autobiographical narratives and parodies of the reparative impulse.

Reparative performances carry substantial affective rewards, which is why the impulse to use the classics for socially enlightened goals remains strong, and there is a long history of using Shakespeare as a catalyst for social change and appropriating the canon as source material for feel-good narratives. Contrary to popular belief, affective and cognitive approaches to the arts—emotions and reasoning—are not mutually exclusive. As Sarah Cavanagh's research in psychology and cognitive science demonstrates, "the brain systems involved in emotion and those involved in cognition are not . . . separate systems pulling us in opposite directions."[12] A reparative approach to the arts, coupled with political reasoning that makes an adaptation relevant and compelling, fosters stronger affective connections to a play, because the neural mechanisms underlying emotion and motivation are intertwined.

The cases in this chapter exemplify both strands of recuperative adaptations. The first comprises more conservative approaches to Shakespeare based on an assumption that the dramatic situations exemplify moral universality. Earnest performances of artistic reparative efficacy propose that Shakespeare can improve one's character and social circumstances. That said, not all reparative adaptations are ideologically conservative. The second consists of adaptations, particularly those in a parodic vein, that problematize heteronormativity and psychological universals in liberal humanist visions of Shakespeare. This approach is self-conscious of deeply contextual meanings of the canon. As a result, it lends itself to the genres of parody, metatheatre, and metacinema. Both strands emerge out of the tradition of using literature as a coping strategy in times of crisis. Audiences maintain, simultaneously, a distant and personal relationship to actors' words and embodiment. Both strands respond to, as Todd Landon Barnes has theorized, the "concomitant rise of neoliberalism and emotional capitalism which employ therapeutic discourses to individualize social inequality."[13] The moralist approach is informed by the therapeutic self-help ethos, while the parodic approach questions the canon's capacity for emotional transformation.

A Place-Based Myth

Remedial art is a place-based myth because of the important role played by place in metatheatre and metacinema, practices that render the tension between presentation and representation visible. In some adaptations, place is more important than period, as evidenced by Peter Brook's *King Lear*, because place provides an anchor for actions that are perceived to have an impact across multiple time periods.[14] Recent scholarship by Andrew Bozio has highlighted the importance of characters' and audiences' perception of place in *King Lear*.[15] Brook's own film version of *Lear* (1971), set and shot in snow-capped Northern Jutland (Denmark), is informed by Jan Kott's and Samuel Beckett's nihilistic view of humanity. Its bleak landscape without music—which is both nowhere and everywhere—signals despair in the tragic narrative.

Further cementing the importance of place, multiple historical monuments and reconstructed sites, such as the "Juliet's balcony" in Casa di Giulietta in Verona, Elsinore Castle in Helsingør, Shakespeare's Birthplace in Stratford-upon-Avon, and the Globe Theatre in London, are given near-sacred status due to their (mostly) fictional connections to Shakespeare's life, scenes, or characters. Over time, they have created a mythologized sense of site-specific authenticity. Expanding the notion of playing space, these sites serve as palpable and tangible shrines where visitors imagine they can touch the past, or even Shakespeare's fictional events, when they lay their hands on, say, the balustrade of Juliet's balcony. "Site-specific epistemologies" have been shown to carry weight ideologically to the extent that art continues to be produced in postnational spaces where cross-cultural borrowings occur. As a result, Shakespeare has been "repositioned beyond national boundaries and traditionally understood colonial authority" in places such as Hong Kong and Singapore.[16] The cultural setting of a dramatic narrative, the geopolitical site of performance, and the trajectories of the artists (where they are from, where they are going) are the primary factors in the cultural and political significance of reparative performance. Festivals and performances dedicated to commemorating cultural figures emphasize the place, such as the birthplace of Shakespeare, the home country of Henrik Ibsen, or the hometown of Shakespeare's contemporary, the Ming Dynasty Chinese playwright Tang Xianzu.

In some instances, places of origin are not only alluded to in a metaphorical sense but are also being actively reconstructed. In 2018, in the spirit of overcoming past cultural misunderstanding, the Shakespeare Birthplace Trust and Fuzhou Culture and Tourism Investment Company Ltd entered into an agreement to recreate Shakespeare's birthplace and his home in adulthood in Tang's home-town, Fuzhou, located in Jiangxi Province, China. The recreation will be situated in a 220-acre replica of parts of Stratford-upon-Avon, complete with Tudor architecture. Interestingly, the architecture of New Place, where Shakespeare lived until his death in 1616, was demolished in 1702. Only a commemorative site and garden remain today in Stratford-upon-Avon. Its recreation in China brings a new meaning of mobility to the notion of place, which is usually rooted in a geographic site. The Chinese replicas are part of San Weng (Three Masters), a new tourist attraction celebrating Shakespeare, Cervantes, and Tang Xianzu, three writers who died in 1616. This is the first time the Shakespeare Birthplace Trust, an independent charity, has author-ized a recreation of its iconic buildings. Reversing the cultural exchange, a replica of "Peony Pavilion" as depicted in Tang's play of that name was built in Stratford-upon-Avon in April 2019. Con-structed in China, shipped to the UK, and assembled on-site, the six-meter-high wooden pavilion occupies ten square meters. The sign below its roof reads "Mudan ting" (牡丹亭, Peony Pavilion) and is accompanied by a couplet extolling the impact of Tang's plays across cultures and historical periods.

In reparative performances, the idea of place remains an important denominator that has become more fluid and hybrid. In 2016, the

Oregon Shakespeare Festival produced Desdemona Chiang's *Winter's Tale* with an Asian American cast. The adaptation set the romance in premodern China and America's Old West, combining both Asian and Asian American senses of place. In this instance, Shakespeare, a familiar but exoticized other, served as a platform for minority performers who themselves are sometimes perceived to be outsiders even at home. Similarly, on the early modern English stage, characters think through and with their surroundings. They orient themselves in unfamiliar places, and the environment in turn offers scaffolding for their memory. Playgoers, as Andrew Bozio demonstrates, go through a parallel process to imagine the stage as the place and setting of the dramatic action.[17]

Another example is the dance-mime production *Dreamer* (dir. Rich Rusk and Chris Evans). Coproduced by the English company Gecko and the Shanghai Dramatic Arts Centre, it moves its characters between the real world and a dreamscape. Inspired by *A Midsummer Night's Dream* (1595/1596) and Tang Xianzu's *Peony Pavilion* (1598), the piece was commissioned by the British Council for the 2016 Shakespeare Lives program to commemorate the 400th anniversary of Shakespeare's and Tang's deaths. One of the memorable features of *Dreamer* is how it constructs place and space. The timid Helena (Yang Ziyi) is a hybrid character drawn from one of the four young lovers in Shakespeare's comedy and the derogatory notion of "leftover women" in China. The term *shengnü* 剩女 is used to refer to women who remain unmarried in their late twenties and beyond; the Chinese word is homophonous with *shengnü* 聖女, saintly women. Helena moves between her mundane world of a dead-end job and her dream where she encounters Du Liniang (Wu Jingwei), the heroine of Tang's tragedy. Like Du, Helena pines for a lover who can be found only in dreams. Helena pines for Demetrius (Lan Haimeng). While Helena originates in a Greece imagined by Shakespeare, her Chinese doppelganger is a character rooted in contemporary Shanghai's fast-paced life. The production brings Shakespeare and Tang together in a hybrid cultural space to dramatize and repair social ills that have affected the millennials.

The sense of place is also constructed and articulated through the set. The modular, flexible set and industrial scaffolding help create a sense of a floating, interstitial place. Fluid movements between places correlate to the two companies' identities. The Essex-based Gecko provided choreography, theatrical conception, and music; actors from the Shanghai Dramatic Arts Centre performed the nearly wordless sequences. In one scene, Helena's bed dissolves seamlessly, having been taken apart swiftly by Oberon, Titania, and unnamed stagehands who remind us of Shakespeare's fairies. In the blink of an eye, Helena emerges in a new place. An invisible trickster transports Helena back and forth between the two worlds, and in the process she gradually breaks free of her overbearing parents and, by extension, the constraints her cultural position imposes on her. The props are fluid as well. For example, a telephone cord morphs into an umbilical cord that connects different places, disparate dreams, and ultimately different cultures. This piece, designed to commemorate two national poets, seems to suggest that Shakespeare and Tang help characters and by extension actors and audiences articulate moral universals. Case studies in the following pages cover both strands of recuperative performances, beginning with more conservative remedial Shakespeares and concluding with more open-ended adaptations that critique moral universals.

Ophelia Empowered: *The Banquet* and *Prince of the Himalayas*

Two 2006 films based on *Hamlet* exemplify the first approach to reparative adaptation. *The Banquet* addresses issues of female empowerment, and *Prince of the Himalayas* dramatizes the agency of Ophelia. In Feng Xiaogang's Mandarin-language *wuxia* (martial knight-errant) film *The Banquet* (aka *The Legend of the Black Scorpion*, 2006) the Ophelia figure expresses her thoughts assertively and forcefully in private and public scenes. Set in fifteenth-century China with an all-star cast, this film depicts a Hamlet seeking justice amidst other characters versed in swordsmanship. This genre is distinct from *kung fu* films that emphasize the hero's fist-fighting skills.[18] Director Feng is a household name in China, known for his invention of a new genre, the comic and often farcical New Year celebration film that is screened during the Chinese New Year. Highly profitable and entertaining, the genre subverts the didacticism that is standard fare in films produced by state studios. *The Banquet*'s Ophelia (Qing Nü, played by Zhou Xun) dominates many scenes with her songs and dance and is not shy

Fig. 2.1 *The Banquet*. Ophelia-Qing Nü (Zhou Xun) hugging Hamlet-Wu Luan (Daniel Wu) in a rainy courtyard.

about expressing her affection for Hamlet (Prince Wu Luan, played by Daniel Wu), even when she is threatened by the Gertrude figure (Empress Wan, played by Zhang Ziyi), who is both the prince's stepmother and his lover. Significantly, Ophelia does not go mad. Although she is still associated closely with water, her songs allude to rivers and boating, and her intimate scenes with Hamlet often involve rain, Ophelia is not drowned in the end. An example of the water symbolism is a scene in a rainy courtyard where Qing Nü washes the prince's hair as the prince looks up at the falling raindrops (Fig. 2.1). To view a trailer of the film, please visit globalshakespeares.mit. edu/the-banquet-feng-xiaogang-2006/

This bold cinematic reimagination of *Hamlet* shifts the focus from the question of interiority and self-knowledge—traditionally embodied by Hamlet—to the ambition of a very articulate Empress Wan and the assertiveness of Qing Nü. Both characters do not hesitate to express their love for the prince. Empress Wan has kept her romantic relationship with Prince Wu Luan secret. Qing Nü's naïveté and purity make her a desirable and unattainable figure of hope, in contrast to the calculating empress. Her innocence and passion present an idealized contrast to China's postsocialist society, which is driven by a market economy that turns everything, including romance and love, into a commodity.[19]

In its remedial move, *The Banquet* turns Ophelia into a symbol of innocence in a corrupt court. She occupies the moral high ground. Significantly for a martial arts film, Qing Nü is the only character who is not versed in swordsmanship. Her sole "weapons" are her perseverance in the face of obstacles and her faithful love for the prince. Her name, Qing Nü, derives from the goddess of snow in Chinese mythology, and her robes are always white regardless of context. Her white robes—a color of mourning in the culture—contradict the mood of festive occasions. This highlights the sexist idea of female chastity, as snow is used as a trope for chaste women in traditional poetry.[20] Remaining aloof throughout the film, Qing Nü is uninterested in politics and refuses to succumb to her father's advice to "learn from the empress" and use marriage as a political stepping-stone. Empress Wan, by contrast, marries her brother-in-law in exchange for power and security after her husband is killed by a scorpion's sting. However, there is a clear distinction between Qing Nü's childlikeness and what is typically regarded as emotionally immature childishness. In response to her brother's reminder that the prince is too dedicated to studying art to care for her—"you are not in his heart. Do not fool yourself"— Qing Nü indicates that she is fully aware of the situation but has "promised to always wait for him." She chooses to stay by his side and sing to him so that he will not be lonely. The figure of Ophelia is modeled after the trope of chaste widows. The consequences are painful. Jealous of Qing Nü's intimacy with the prince and her ability to offer unconditional love, Empress Wan orders her to be whipped. Ever defiant and refusing to be manipulated by anyone, Qing Nü almost gets her face branded, and the empress exiles her to the south. It should be noted that she is both empowered by her dedication to love and disempowered by Confucian expectations of young women.

Qing Nü publicly expresses her love for the prince. When Emperor Li (the Claudius figure) sends Wu Luan to the Khitans as a hostage, Qing Nü petitions the court to be allowed to go with him, echoing Desdemona's insistence on accompanying Othello to Cyprus.[21] Her passions are uncensored and her reason is simple: she wants to accompany the prince so he will not be lonely. Unlike Shakespeare's Ophelia, Qing Nü does not have to go mad or speak allusively about her desire, although she sings on multiple occasions, as Ophelia does in *Hamlet*.

Toward the end of the film, at a banquet to celebrate the coronation of the empress, she sings a song of solitude that the prince has taught her and leads a group dance. She seems to be content simply to love the prince without seeking anything in return. Qing Nü's entrance takes Emperor Li and Empress Wan by surprise. Her performance at the court commemorates her lover, whom everyone, including Qing Nü, believes has died en route to the Khitans. (Unbeknownst to Qing Nü and everyone in the court, the prince has returned and is disguising himself as one of the masked dancers.) Falling into the trappings of idealized femininity, this Ophelia defies another woman, the empress, only to gain access to a male love interest. Eventually the character follows a romantically motivated arc. The prince becomes her "redemption."

The remedial cultural work represented by the film deploys pop feminism to counterbalance the image of Ophelia as a victim and her marginalized role in *Hamlet*. This trope of "empowerment" has been critiqued by practitioners as well. *The Ophelia Project* (2010) directed by Rhiannon Brace for the Ophelia Collective in London, for example, critiques "romantic images of women such as Millais's *Ophelia* and other Pre-Raphaelite paintings [and their glorification of Nature]."[22] Sometimes pathologized, Ophelia has been used to name numerous other projects that support abuse victims, such as American writer Lisa Klein's 2006 novel *Ophelia*. Feng's *The Banquet* also participates in the trend to align innocence, femininity, and moral superiority. An example is the musical *With Love, William Shakespeare*, staged by Theatre Noir and Hong Kong Repertory Theatre in 2011. Increasing the prominence of women does not always translate into empowerment. *The Banquet*'s romanticization of Ophelia risks objectifying the character even as the film empowers her through her moral stance. The film does not pass the so-called Bechdel-Wallace test (named after Alison Bechdel and Liz Wallace), which stipulates a film should have two named female characters converse about topics other than a man; rather, Empress Wan and Qing Nü talk about the prince and are pitted against each other as they vie for Prince Wu Luan's attention. The film locates the dramatic action in a fictional historical setting to provide insulation from potential ideological criticism. The film's genre offers another layer of protection against what might be called pop feminism, in that the world of *wuxia* provides equal footing for male and female characters through access to swordsmanship. The fantastical, "fifth-century" world, much like the Forest of Arden serving as a space of liberation from gender roles in *As You Like It*, allows for the existence of characters such as Qing Nü. However, as critics have pointed out, some *wuxia* films such as *Crouching Tiger, Hidden Dragon* (dir. Ang Lee, Asia Union, 2000) disguise their adherence to the Confucian and patriarchal order in the *wuxia* world of disorder.[23]

Sherwood Hu's *Prince of the Himalayas* (2006), shot in Tibet with an all-Tibetan cast, offers a visual response to John Everett Millais's representation of the drowning Ophelia and provides—as does *The Banquet*—a redemptive arc through the Ophelia character. Tibetan actress Sonamdolgar as Odsaluyang presents a feisty and assertive Ophelia who links the secular with the sacred and death with life. Ophelia is associated with water throughout the film. Early on, we are shown a rather explicit, intimate scene between the Hamlet character (Prince Lhamoklodan) and Odsaluyang in her hut by a stream. Odsaluyang becomes pregnant as a result; the two are not married. In labor, Odsaluyang approaches the Namtso Lake, a sacred site to Tibetan pilgrims, in search of the prince, whom she loves but also hates because he has killed her father. She is shown picking wildflowers to make a wreath. She walks into the lake presumably to ease her pain, but the scene presents a haunting image of a watery death that amounts to a visual citation of Millais's painting (Fig. 2.2). Wearing a white garment and a floral wreath on her head, she lies down in the water and gives birth while she floats, then, sleeping deeply, she "sink[s] down to the river bed," where she "meets her father and mother."[24] The camera pans over the water to give us a glimpse of the baby floating away from the mother. Presumably Odsaluyang dies after giving birth in the lake, but her death is not depicted onscreen. To view a clip of this scene, please visit the page curated by Alexa Alice Joubin on the *MIT Global Shakespeares*: globalshakespeares.mit.edu/prince-of-himalayas-hu-sherwood-2006/

This scene takes Ophelia's association with the cyclic quality of nature in Millais to a different level, hinting at the necessary, if cruel, cycle of fading and emerging generations. This scene is depicted in a painterly mode in Hu's film to focus attention on her suffering. As Odsaluyang walks into the lake singing a song, the water runs red with her blood. The baby is carried by water to safety and is rescued by the

Fig. 2.2 *Prince of the Himalayas.* Ophelia-Odsaluyang (Sonamdolgar) dies in Namtso Lake in Tibet after giving birth to her and Hamlet's baby.

Wolf Woman, a prophetess. As one of the most interesting departures from *Hamlet*, this scene hints at the possibility of a saintly Ophelia figure who, in death, brings forth a new life and hope for the next generation. *Prince of the Himalayas* offers a courageous, independent Ophelia.

Millais's famous *Ophelia* (1851/1852) was exhibited in Tokyo, Kobe, and elsewhere and is well known to East Asian audiences. One of the themes of the painting is the cycle of growth and decay. Ophelia is portrayed as being in the transitional moment between life and death. Buoyed temporarily by the stream, the dying Ophelia is half-sunk, but her head is still above the water. Extending upwards, her open arms at first glance may resemble a prayer posture or the traditional pose of a martyr at the moment of her death. The blocking and camera in this scene in *Prince of the Himalayas* clearly pays homage to Millais.

Whereas Shakespeare's Gertrude's account of Ophelia casts her as a fairy-tale creature ("mermaid-like," 4.7.176), Odsaluyang in *Prince of the Himalayas* is a kind of goddess of nature, an immortal bride who returns to nature. The strong association between water and suffering women in Chinese art and film history contributed to Hu's decision to shoot Ophelia's death scene by the mirrorlike Namtso Lake near

Lhasa. Water can be a mirror of beauty or a gateway to darker realities lying beneath its surface.[25] Female water deities are celebrated in Chinese poetry and paintings as beings who ruled the waves. Hu's film associates Ophelia with a water goddess not unlike the Luo River Goddess or the goddesses of the Xiang River. Such goddesses, according to legends, start out as "unhappy spirits of drowned victims involved in female sacrifice, young girls given in local rituals as brides to pacify male river gods. Others may have been romantic love suicides (nobly following their deceased husbands) . . . or victims of no-love situations . . . while still others represented punishment for female sexual transgression."[26] As ecofeminist studies have shown, the association of women and nature have detrimental consequences.

Prince of the Himalayas gives birth to a more sexualized and spiritual vision of Ophelia in the water, transforming Ophelia from "a document of madness" (4.5.178) to an embodiment of resistance of the patriarchy. By eradicating the ambiguity surrounding Ophelia's death, the film grants the character more agency. Both *The Banquet* and *Prince of the Himalayas* are preoccupied with Ophelia's placement and displacement in relation to sources of authority. While her songs still occupy the center of attention, Ophelia does not stand in for lost girlhood or female madness. At the same time, the strands of empowerment and fragile womanhood coexist as the Chinese and Tibetan Ophelias lay claim to their moral agency by acting on their own behalf. However, they are simultaneously limited by the new cultural locations, by the cultural logics of the new locations they seek to sustain. The double bind of Confucian ethical codes and pop feminism make Ophelia both a symbol of the abject and a mediator. The internal contradictions do not indicate the failure of the remedial work carried out by these two films, for, as Elaine Showalter has argued, there may be no "'true' Ophelia for whom feminist criticism must unambiguously speak."[27] Nor do the examples analyzed here seek to posit a nationalist category of "Asian" women.[28]

The King's Two Bodies and Lear's Two Faces

Beyond gender, spirituality is an area that has been explored by directors in the remedial work they carry out. East Asian directors have engaged with various notions of spirituality in the twenty-first century. The self-problematizing nature of *King Lear* allowed space for Buddhist interpretations of the meanings of spiritual life. Akira Kurosawa's Japanese film *Ran* (1985), a retelling of *Lear*, blends secular ethical messages with ideas of Buddhist enlightenment, as discussed in Chapter 1. Discourses of the making and unmaking of the self that echo religious formulations have played a key role in contemporary Shakespeare performance. Examples include French New Wave director Jean-Luc Godard's metacinematic film *King Lear* (Cannon Group, 1987) and Wu Hsing-kuo's Buddhist-inflected solo stage production *Li'er zaici* (*Lear Is Here*, 2001 and 2007). In Godard's film, Peter Sellars' William Shakespeare Jr. the Fifth meets a Lear figure (Burgess Meredith) and Cordelia (Molly Ringwald) as he attempts to restore his ancestor's play after the Chernobyl nuclear disaster. Deployment of spirituality to ameliorate life narratives can be found in the work of other directors. In Michael Almereyda's film *Hamlet* (double A Films, 2000), a scene that features Vietnamese monk Thich Nhat Hanh draws on the director's interest in Asian spirituality. In Taiwanese playwright Stan Lai's three-man production in Hong Kong in 2000, *Lear and the Thirty-seven-fold Practice of a Bodhisattva*, a prerecorded Jigme Khyentse Rinpoche recites a fourteenth-century Tibetan Buddhist scripture. A Rinpoche, an honorific title, is reserved for an incarnate lama in Tibetan Buddhism. In Ong Keng Sen's multimedia stage work *Desdemona* (2000), the Singaporean director addresses social oppression and Desdemona's endurance (see Chapter 4). In the Ryutopia Noh Theatre's Japanese *Hamlet* (dir. Kurita Yoshihiro, 2007), the titular character's costumes and mannerism call to mind a Buddhist monk. In several South Korean productions, Ophelia is recast as a shaman who comforts the dead and guides the living (see Chapter 3).

An example of the remedial, autobiographical approach to Shakespeare and self-knowledge is Wu's solo Beijing opera *Lear Is Here*, in which Wu plays ten characters. They play was presented by the Lincoln Center Festival (July 2007) and was produced by Taiwan's Contemporary Legend Theatre.[29] The 2007 staging at the Rose Theater, Lincoln Center, New York, contained revisions from its previous versions. To view the full video along with annotations, visit the online learning module edited by Alexa Alice Joubin and Peter S. Donaldson: globalshakespeares.mit.edu/modules/

One of the most compelling scenes involves a metatheatrical inquiry of the self. A dispirited King Lear stands in the center of the stage after the storm scene on the heath (3.2). The mad Lear proceeds to take off his *jingju* headdress and armor costume in full view of a packed audience. The onstage costume change breaks the fourth wall and *jingju* conventions, revealing an actor who is dressed as if he were backstage. The actor interrogates himself and the eyeless headdress in a somber moment while touching his own eyes. He removes and methodically joins the stage beard to the hairpiece on the headdress, making it a faceless puppet. Wu's work with this prop makes clear that the empty eyes raise questions about his own identity and that of the character whose costume he no longer inhabits. Raising it above him and pondering it intently, he asks "Who am I?" before shifting his gaze to the audience and asking the same question, slightly revised, in the third person: "Doth any here know him?" Then he answers his own question: "He is not Lear." The prop thus functions as both an emblem of the emptiness of stage representation and of the actor's emptied self when he is not inhabited by the character. The prop also represents the character King Lear, who now—like a puppet—has no life without an actor performing him. Wu's manipulation of the faceless puppet parallels the ghost in Kim Kwang-bo's production of Jo Kwang-hwa's *Ophelia: Sister, Come to My Bed* (dir. Kim Kwang-bo, Cheong-u Ensemble, 1995), in which Old Hamlet appears as a large puppet operated by three Buddhist monks, to signal a tug-of-war between different forms of human and spiritual agency and identities. The monks, serving as the Chorus, sing an elegy.

As the actor gestures toward the eyeless prop and his own eyes, he evokes the blinding of Gloucester in the narrative about sight and truth. "Who am I?" Lear asks rhetorically of Oswald (1.4.76). Wu's lines here are based on a word-for-word translation of the Folio text. The aging father rants on, rhetorically: "Doth any here know me? Why, this is not Lear. / Doth Lear walk thus? speak thus? Where are his eyes?" (1.4.208–12). He walks in circles on a stage with just one rock and no other sceneries as he says these lines. The actor's eyes become Lear's eyes only when the character's eyes are emptied out.

The actor reflects on his and Lear's somatic and psychical discombobulating experience. The process bears significance here as a key trope in Jacques Lacan's psychoanalytical theory. In what he calls the mirror stage, the subject comes to own their self-image by creating an ideal ego.[30] Seeing oneself in a mirror is one of the first steps towards establishing one's subjectivity before mastering language and entering the society. Lacan maintains that the idealized ego—distinct from the material body—remains a coherent and stable image that the subject aspires towards. At later stages, as Lacan explains, the idealized image of oneself—role models—is filled in by others whom one emulates. Even then, the mirror image—whether of oneself or a stand-in—has a fundamentally anarchistic relationship to oneself. The actor's gaze of the eyeless prop and of Lear is Lacanian, because Wu's performance interprets Lear's relationship to himself as a narcissist one. Lear's rhetorical question in the third person, "Doth any here know me?" thus reflects unconscious internal conflicts that eventually lead to bodily afflictions.

Further, the two pairs of eyes of Wu and the opera prop represent the double consciousness many performers experience onstage. Actors are aware of their situatedness onstage and in the dramatic narrative. They are also aware of the emotional state of the characters they are embodying. There is a necessary split of identity. Actors erase their personal identity so that they become the character they are performing. Wu's creative performance carries double duty. He probes the psyche of the *jingju* actor and his character while simultaneously reinventing the *jingju* convention of stylization. The scene of onstage costume change and metatheatrical inquiry complicates the popular understanding of acting in traditional Chinese operatic theatre, which is often regarded as sophisticatedly coded for aesthetic appreciation by the connoisseurs but as lacking any sense of interiority and depth of interior character development in the Aristotelian sense. Here, perhaps for the first time in the history of Beijing opera, Wu lays bare the process of embodiment in a metatheatrical exposé.

Dialogues between the actor and his prop are at the core of Wu's transformation from "Lear" to "the actor" (as the program lists this character). Wu's dual performance as Lear and as the actor playing Lear resonates with several metatheatrical moments in other Shakespearean plays, including Macbeth's evocation of the "poor player" who struts and frets and is heard no more, Hamlet's instructions to the players, and Hamlet's comparison of the fates of Yorick and Alexander the Great. The face without eyes is, like Lear's shadow, a figure of death. When the headdress with beard is held aloft and Wu gazes at it, the hollow face, like Yorick's skull, symbolizes self-knowledge through a meditation on death and embodiment. Wu's previous works also examine the meanings of death and ritual; he has adapted *Hamlet* before and played the Prince in *The Prince's Revenge* (*Wangzi fuchouji*, 1989) as well as the Greek tragedy *Medea* (*Loulan nü*, 1993; starring Wu as Jason and Wu's long-time collaborator Wei Haimin as Medea).

Lear's and Wu's questioning of the construction of the self shares similarities with Buddhist meditative practices. As James Howe suggests in *A Buddhist's Shakespeare*, there is rich material on meditation in the Shakespearean canon that has not been explicitly defined as Christian.[31] The meditation therefore lends itself to Buddhist interpretations. When Lear asks "who is it that can tell me who I am?" and the Fool answers "Lear's shadow" (1.4.213), the exchange moves close to well-known memento mori discourses and practices, framed by the wisdom of the Fool's suggestion.

However, religious redemption is initially rejected by Wu's two characters. Both the actor and Lear shy away from Christian-inflected humanism that tends to interpret Shakespeare's tragedy as a narrative of redemption through "pity" (4.7.53).[32] Instead of redemptive sufferings, anguish self-recognition becomes the leitmotif. Wu's "decision" to return to the stage after a hiatus and the near-disbandment of his company "is tougher than entering some monastery," as he tells us onstage. Wu's view is closer to Jonathan Dollimore's cultural materialist reading of *King Lear*.[33] Presumably it is a tougher decision to keep the show going despite seemingly insurmountable challenges because the monastery is seen as a form of escapism. Interestingly, as soon as that decision is taken, religious tropes surface again, more explicitly in the scene in which Wu as the blinded Gloucester "looks" to Dover as a site for his redemption. In a deliberate slip of the tongue during his continuous chanting of "Duofo" (the Mandarin Chinese transliteration of Dover, which rhymes with the Mandarin for "many Buddhas"), Gloucester conflates Duofo with Amituofo (Amitabha, or Buddha of Light). Gloucester moves from contemplating suicide to seeking refuge in the Buddha of Light (Amituofo). The shift from Dover to the Buddha of Light is significant because it hints at Wu's and Gloucester's wish to seek Buddhist redemption, which explains why, a moment later, his chant includes a series of additional names of

Buddha. One might say there is triple redemption of Wu, his onstage persona, and Lear.

The theory of the king's two bodies is evoked in Wu's reparative discourse. He connects his self-identity as an actor and the roles he embodies onstage. The duality can be seen on several levels. The scene of Wu—an actor—in dialogue with the emptied-out role of Lear (represented by the opera beard and headdress) echoes the medieval political theology of the king's two bodies, a theme highlighted by Shakespeare's *Richard II*, *King Lear*, and other plays. Ernst Kantorowicz argues that the theory posits a distinction between the "body natural" (a monarch's corporeal being) and a transcendental "body politic."[34] In this context, Lear's natural body shares biological attributes with other human beings. Lear would experience hunger, suffer under the elements, and die, as do all humans. Lear's transcendental body symbolizes his divine-ordained right to rule. The succession of monarchs is captured in the formulation "The king is dead. Long live the king." One human body dies, but the institution of monarchy survives. Within the *fabula* of *King Lear*, this scene also points to Lear's conflicting roles as a father and a monarch. Wu's adaptation provides metatheatrical commentary on the succession of characters and roles onstage, as well as on actors throughout history who embody those roles.

On a personal level, Wu struggles to reconcile his dual identities as a *jingju* actor and a citizen of Taiwan. He finds himself negotiating between art and politics, as *jingju* is commonly associated with China. Historically, the island nation of Taiwan has articulated its cultural and political identity in opposition to its colonizers and neighboring countries, including the Dutch, the Japanese, and now the Chinese. In the mid-twentieth century, the Kuomintang (Nationalist Party)-led government renamed Beijing opera *guoju* (national theatre) and used it to promote appreciation of the culture of an imaginary Chinese fatherland among the Taiwanese who had been "liberated" from the Japanese colonial rule. After martial law was lifted in July 1987, Beijing opera's association with Chineseness became an unbearable weight for its development. In the following decades, Beijing opera evolved from a state-endorsed theatre genre to an art form rejected by the majority of Taiwanese audiences who had not emigrated from China. The theatre genre became politically suspect. Political and military tensions between China and Taiwan exacerbated the situation, and Taiwanese nativist campaigns further alienated Beijing opera which already faced competition from popular entertainment, such as glove puppetry and Taiwanese opera. The anti-Chinese sentiment was fueled by large-scale protests in Hong Kong against a proposed law allowing extraditions to China in 2019 and the enactment of the Hong Kong national security law in 2020. Wu uses *Lear*, among his other adaptations of western classics, to save Beijing opera from its demise and its public image as an art form from China, turning it into an intercultural, fusion theatre. In other words, Wu decouples Beijing opera from the People's Republic of China.

The idea of the king's two bodies is therefore relevant to Wu on both personal and political levels. A country with a distinct blend of Chinese heritage and (colonial) Japanese and western influence, Taiwan is a "contact zone."[35] The duality demonstrated in *Lear Is Here* manifests itself in Lear's two bodies (character versus actor), in the two faces of Beijing opera, and in Wu's own dual identities. *Lear Is Here* heals Wu's identity crisis and simultaneously resolves the tension between Taiwan's need to assert its own cultural identity and the political ramifications of *jingju*.

The production as a whole concludes with a meditative scene in which Wu, dressed in a Buddhist monastic robe, circles the stage as himself, as Lear's ghost, as a transcendent being, or perhaps as a personification of the *jingju* tradition in crisis. The scene evokes again the performer's conflicting Taiwanese identities on and off the stage. His performance echoes the Buddhist meditative practice of moving around a sacred pagoda or idol. Wu as monk asks: "Who am I? I am me." He continues: "And I am looking for me! I think of me; I look at me; I know me. . . . I kill me. I forget me! I dream about me again," thereby laying a strong claim to the centrality of the artist's self in spiritual traditions. The double consciousness Wu evokes speaks to the duality of racialized existence. W. E. B. Du Bois uses the term "double consciousness" to describe the black experience in the United States. His rhetorical question in 1903 about self-identity resonates with Wu's performance: "How does it feel to be a problem . . . of two souls, two thoughts, two unreconciled strivings?"[36] While Du Bois theorizes the black community's two irreconcilable strivings, Wu explores, through Lear's two bodies, the duality of his identity as a Taiwanese citizen and a Beijing opera actor.[37]

Wu's secularization of religion is similar to the role of religion in the works of Philip Roth and Salman Rushdie. Wu performs Buddhist tropes in his quest for self-identity. The flouting of orthodox religious practices is part of his pursuit of a cosmopolitan identity. Wu's secular humanism de-transcendentalizes both Buddhism (as religion) and *Lear* (as high art) into instrumental, heuristic cultural texts.[38] Instead of letting an adaptation be a derivative, ancillary footnote to Shakespeare, Wu repurposes these texts as footnotes to his reparative, autobiographical performance. Canonical literary texts and religious beliefs are presented in Wu's production as cultural practices and as his personal, lived experiences.

Buddhism in Michael Almereyda's *Hamlet*

Asian spirituality has also been appropriated outside East Asia. Wu's question "Who am I?" in *Lear* parallels Ethan Hawke's performance of Hamlet's "to be or not to be" soliloquy in Almereyda's Buddhist-inflected film *Hamlet* (2000). Although set in modern-day New York City, the film contains multiple references to Buddhism, including a clip from Ulrike Koch's documentary about a pilgrimage, *Die Salzmänner von Tibet* (*The Saltmen of Tibet*, Bayerischer Rundfunk, 1997), which appears on the back-seat video monitor of Claudius's limousine. In the moment when the tribesmen pass through the boundary between the secular world and the sacred territory of the salt fields in the documentary, Claudius, who has been praying, covers the screen with his hand and laments the failure of his words to reach Heaven ("what if this hand be blacker than it is with brother's blood" in the film; "What if this cursed hand / Were thicker than itself with brother's blood?" in the play) as he is jolted by a nasty and dangerous swerve. Hamlet is driving the limousine, as chauffeur, without Claudius's knowledge.

The most sustained infusion of Buddhism in the film is the appearance of Thich Nhat Hanh, the leader of the Engaged Buddhism movement, on a television set in Hamlet's apartment, presenting a rendering of the "to be or not to be" scene (Fig. 2.3; video clip at www.youtube.com/watch?v=BnzwbKbLuXk). His

Fig. 2.3 Almereyda's *Hamlet*. Footage of Vietnamese Buddhist monk Thich Nhat Hanh's lecture on "inter-be" on the television in Hamlet's apartment. He says "We have the word 'to be,' but I propose the word 'to interbe.'".

teachings on "interbeing" focus on the notion of interdependency ("We have the word 'to be,' but I propose the word 'to interbe.' Interbe. Because it is not possible to 'be' alone. We must 'interbe' with everyone and everyone else—mother, father . . . uncle. . . ."). His words echo repeated video loops of Hamlet reciting the half-line "to be or not to be" while making suicidal gestures. Engrossed in his own footage of an erotic encounter with Ophelia on the handheld monitor, Hamlet is not looking at the television or listening to Thich Nhat Hanh. The book Ophelia is reading, and with which she partly covers her face, is Krishnamurti's *On Living and Dying* with a big photo of the sage on its cover. Thich Nhat Hanh and Krishnamurti encode Asian spirituality as a source of wisdom that could redeem Hamlet. The Buddhist meditation highlights the contradictory nature of identities that can be constructed only in opposition to others.

Like Wu's *Lear*, Almereyda's *Hamlet* deploys Buddhism to signal the possibility of redemption and an alternative philosophy of life. The conversation that emerges among Shakespeare's *Hamlet*, Koch's *Saltmen of Tibet*, and Thich Nhat Hanh's *Peace Is Every Step* (dir. Gaetano Kazuo Maida, Festival Media, 1998) parallels Wu's Buddhist litany of contradictory states of the self at the end of his production. Both works juxtapose Buddhist teachings about the illusory and shifting nature of the self with Hamletian skepticism and with secular elements drawn from Shakespeare. Almereyda's *Hamlet* posits that the Buddhist ideal of "interbeing" can counteract Hamlet's cynicism, whereas Wu in *Here Is Lear* moves from rejecting the monastery as a site of redemption at the beginning of the production to embodying the role of a monk at the end, when he dons the Buddhist robe. In many ways, Wu's performance points to the future of East Asian Shakespeares. He gives primacy to his personal life stories and to the interaction between his personas and his audience rather than attempting "authentic" representations of the Shakespearean tragedy or of *jingju*. The fusion of *Lear* and Wu's autobiography is also deployed as a tool to innovate the style of *jingju*.

The next section turns to works that take a parodic approach to the theme of remedial Shakespeare and combine generic hybridization with intraregional and transhistorical allusions.

Star-Crossed Lovers in Hong Kong: *One Husband Too Many*

Anthony Chan's 1988 vaudevillian film *One Husband Too Many* (*Yi qi liang fu* [lit.: One wife, two husbands]) exemplifies the irreverent approach to not only the canonical status of Shakespeare but also to any remedial potential Shakespeare might have. A sequel to Chan's comedy film *A Happy Bigamist* (*Yi wu liang qi* [lit.: Two wives under one roof], 1987) in the same style, *One Husband Too Many* dramatizes its characters' near quixotic insistence on performing and rehearsing *Romeo and Juliet* to ameliorate their conditions. *One Husband Too Many* follows the couple playing Romeo (Hsin, played by the film director himself) and Juliet (Hsin's onscreen wife, Yuan-tung, also known as Park, played by Anita Mui Yim-Fong) through their melancholic separation and Hsin's attempt to reboot his theatre company and his love life by producing *Romeo and Juliet*.

This film's use of *Romeo and Juliet* is part of the larger phenomenon of Shakespeare's plays entering into contemporary culture via quotation rather than in full performances. Mark Thornton Burnett observes that *Romeo and Juliet*, in particular, emerges in world cinema through quotations of such lines as Juliet's "What's in a name?" (2.1.85).[39] Or, as Celia R. Daileader theorizes, Juliet's balcony becomes a "metonymy for a forbidden world."[40] *Romeo and Juliet* features prominently in the history of East Asian filmmaking. Examples include the Taiwanese film *Juliets* (*Zhuliye*, dir. Chen Yu-Hsun, Hou Chi-jan, and Shen Ko-shang, Zeus International Production, 2010), an episodic film which reimagines Juliet as a physically disabled worker in a print shop who secretly helps a college student activist, a dancer who feigns madness and waits for her Romeo in an asylum, and an extra for a commercial who is pining for true love; *Young Lovers* (*Seyu yu chunqing*, dir. Michihiko Obimori, Shaw Brothers, 1979), which chronicles the life of a poor boy (Derek Erh Tung-Sheng) and a rich girl (Yu An-An) in Hong Kong; and *Crocodile River* (*Eyu he*, dir. Lo Wei, Aswin Film and Shaw Brothers, 1965), a Hong Kong film shot in Bangkok, in which an unlikely couple find themselves separated by a river filled with crocodiles.

One Husband Too Many opens *in medias res* when a performance of *Romeo and Juliet* is taking place at night. Even the first scene shows the inadequacy of the Anglophone model of performing the canon. On a makeshift stage in a fishing village center in the New Territories, Hong Kong, an actor wearing black-rimmed glasses prances onstage in costumes reminiscent of Danilo Donati's doublet-and-tights designs for Franco Zeffirelli's *Romeo and Juliet* (BHE Films, 1968) to the tune of that film's "A Time for Us" by Nino Rota, with new Cantonese lyrics. Zeffirelli has inspired other East Asian adaptations as well.[41] Nearby, a woman lies unconscious on what appears to be a sarcophagus. Next to the stage is an easel announcing a production of *Romeo and Juliet* in English and Chinese. The bulletin board is lined with cheesy theatre dressing-room lights, suggesting this production's low budget. The actors in the play within a film are dedicated to their performance despite booing from an unreceptive audience. It is either a visual and aural feast or a cruel parody of hybrid cultures, depending on your perspective. Before its initial pan to a red banner proclaiming "Promote Western Culture" above their stage, the camera passes through a night market, where we see crowds cheering Chinese acrobatics and Cantonese opera. As we arrive at the western-style *huaju* (spoken drama) stage, however, we hear the crowd's disapproving and frankly disparaging comments. One elderly lady in the audience concludes, for example, that it is taboo to stage a suicide scene on such an auspicious day. To view this scene, visit www.youtube.com/watch?v=mcZMbtDC8so

Meanwhile, Cantonese-opera percussion from a nearby stage intrudes on the Zeffirellian *mise en scène* of the final scene in the Capulet tomb. The actor playing Romeo is no less disruptive, though unintentionally. As he says to the nonresponsive Juliet: "Death . . . hath had no power yet upon thy beauty" (5.3.), he accidentally slaps her face as he strikes a pose. This startles the actor playing Juliet, who opens her eyes even though she shouldn't, and later seems to forget her lines. After Romeo commits suicide and as Juliet wakes up, she improvises: "Oh my cold Romeo, would you like me to take off my ugly aristocratic clothes to warm up your bosom?" Upon hearing this, the mostly male crowd, which has grown impatient and stood up, sits down in an instant, telling each other to quiet down in anticipation of a striptease. Their catcalls then distract the actress (Fig. 2.4).

The film is a response to the meta-theatrical feature of Shakespeare's *Romeo and Juliet.* Although the blundering of the actor and actress in the film breaks their fourth wall, Juliet improvising her lines takes inspiration from Shakespeare's Juliet, who becomes aware of playing a role. Sending away her nurse and her mother,

Fig. 2.4 *One Husband Too Many.* Yuan-tung (Anita Mui Yim-Fong) plays Juliet who wakes up in the Capulet's tomb in the final scene as Romeo is dying. The audiences are disruptive.

before she swallows the sleeping potion, she says, "My dismal scene I needs must act alone" (4.3.14–19). Elsewhere in the play she speaks of herself explicitly as an actress, of their "love-performing night" (3.2.5) and the nature of their "true love acted" (3.2.16).

One Husband Too Many is far from the only film to parody canonical cinematic versions of *Romeo and Juliet*. The action comedy *Hot Fuzz* (dir. Edgar Wright, Universal Pictures, 2007) features the final scene in a village production staged by bumbling actors with the same soundtrack (Lovefool by the Cardigans) and the same costumes as *William Shakespeare's Romeo + Juliet* (dir. Baz Luhrmann, Twentieth Century Fox, 1996). Set in Sandford, Gloucestershire, a fictional "model" village, *Hot Fuzz* is part of Wright's acclaimed trilogy of parodies. Sitting on Juliet's "death bed" surrounded by copious candles and three neon-lit crosses, Romeo (Martin Blower, played by David Threlfall), still in his shining knight armor costume from the masked ball, states, with each vowel elongated, that: "A dateless bargain to engrossing death! / . . . Here's to my love!" as he downs the poison. His unconvincing acting makes it seem as if he was taking a shot of liquor in celebration. After Romeo dies, Juliet (Eve Draper, portrayed by Lucy Punch) wakes up in the same angelic costume with white wings as Claire Danes' in Luhrmann's film. The feathers of her wings are glowing in backlight. She finds a pistol by Romeo's body and points it at her temple. As she pulls the trigger she yells in a cartoonish fashion: "bang!" There is no sound effect in the scene. In contrast to the unruly audiences in *One Husband Too Many*, the audiences in *Hot Fuzz* consist mostly of elderly villagers who sleep through the sup- posedly emotional scene. The scene in the theatre alternates between frontal shots of the audiences and long and medium shots of the action on stage. The production in *Hot Fuzz* draws attention to the over-the- top dialogues, stylized visuals, and campy nature of Luhrmann's *Romeo and Juliet*. Similar to *One Husband Too Many*, the theatre scene in *Hot Fuzz* remains at the first degree for characters within the film's universe. Despite their incompetence, the actors take their performance seriously.

The audience's disruption of Romeo's and Juliet's suicidal acts in *One Husband Too Many* deprives the actors of closure. Unable to complete their performance, they scurry backstage. There, the actors demonstrate confidence in their craft, in their "noble mission" of bringing culture to a backwater, and in the reparative value of Shakespeare in helping a rural village in Hong Kong fuse English and Cantonese cultures. During their backstage debriefing, the mayor joins them in the changing room to encourage them to continue, promising to send his assistants to maintain order. After the mayor's intervention, Hsin and Yuan-tung return to the stage to attempt for a second time to complete the play. Meanwhile, the mayor's bodyguards line up downstage and tell the audience members to quiet down; but after a while, seeing that the audience is now too quiet for their liking, they threaten them: "Applaud, or we will beat you up." Despite the assistance of the mayor, the troupe's second attempt at bringing closure to *Romeo and Juliet* is also disrupted by the unappreciative crowd, which this time ends up starting its own sideshow of tribal violence.

At this point, the film's interest shifts from parodies of the canon to critiques of the legacy of colonialism. The mayor's henchmen's display of authority suggests how colonial regimes have attempted to coerce the Hong Kong population to adopt British culture, with Shakespeare at its core. The scene also parodies the remedial discourse of bettering the natives' life by introducing the colonizer's language and culture. The audience is clearly not passive and is far from reverential of Shakespeare or any figure of authority. When physical fighting breaks out, Hsin and his wife become literally persecuted lovers. The disruptive audience storms the stage and comes face to face with the henchmen. Using a low angle, the camera moves between two rows of men lined up like two American football teams ready to charge. The standoff is depicted in a comedic manner, with the men twitching their pectorals to make them bounce up and down. This is meant as an aggrandizing gesture before the fight begins. "*Now* it's [really] *Romeo and Juliet!*" exclaims a distressed Hsin, who finds himself sandwiched between the two gangs. Before he flees, Hsin metatheatrically asks whether the standoff is a scene from a then-popular Hong Kong commercial for breast enlargement pills. Perhaps the audience members have now appreciated too well the tragedy about teen exuberance and violence: they have ingested the spirit of feud. Pursued by a torch-bearing mob, the couple has no choice but to flee the scene, carrying with them their idealized form of English theatre.

Two recurrent themes in *One Husband Too Many* are the inadequacy of a local troupe that has ambitions beyond its competency and the disruption of performances and rehearsals. The theme of the incompetent troupe also appears in films beyond those mentioned earlier in this chapter, such as Branagh's *A Midwinter's Tale*.[42] While mimicking and ironizing the canonical doublet-and-tights-style performance that was prevalent on the stages of China and Hong Kong in the 1980s, the troupe is also competing with local forms of entertainment for the audience's divided attention.[43] This is a commentary on the reality of contemporary theatre and film industries in Hong Kong.

The scene of a disruptive audience simultaneously reifies and undermines the authority vested in both Shakespeare's tragedy and the mayor. It also dramatizes the tensions between play text and performance. In a later scene, the crushed Hsin rehearses the balcony scene of *Romeo and Juliet* with his regrouped theatre troupe. Despite the troupe's earlier failure, Hsin does not choose a different play. Instead, he fetishizes *Romeo and Juliet*, not least because the play captures his struggles in his own love life. He rehearses the play with Sogo playing Juliet (Cherie Chung Chor-hung, also known as the Marilyn Monroe of the Hong Kong entertainment industry) and is unable to kiss her because he is too timid. Betting everything on the remedial power of Shakespeare's reputation for both his career and his relationship with his wife, Hsin mortgages his house and pawns his possessions to raise funds to support his troupe, only to face the rural audiences' irreverent attitude toward his production and English high culture (filtered through Italian filmmaker Zeffirelli's lens) in general. His strategy of modernizing and vulgarizing Shakespeare fails to win over audiences. To view this scene, visit www.youtube.com/watch?v=vqbLcUB-JSU

One Husband Too Many mocks Hsin's naïve dream of bringing modern western culture to a "backwater village." Casting himself in the lead role, film director Chan spares no opportunity for self-mockery by drawing attention to the tension between film and theatre as competing modes of representation and by problematizing his character's insistence on what he imagines to be Shakespeare's reparative function in his career and personal life. The film thereby deconstructs the dominant ideologies regarding the reparative functions of high culture overall.

Botched Reparation: Revenge Comedy in Taiwan

The emergence of parody is often an indication that the genre of reparative interpretation has matured. It is a sign that Shakespeare's global afterlife has reached a stage in which his works have become so familiar to cross-border audiences that the plays can be used as a platform exploring new genres. Parody, a genre that depends on its audience's familiarity with a canon, could be a sign of a society's self-confidence, but it could also manufacture a familiarity that does not yet exist. Taiwan has a slightly longer history of sustainable theatrical experimentation than does China. It was spared the devastating Cultural Revolution and was aided by an economic and political alliance with the United States that dates to the 1960s.

Lee Kuo-hsiu's (Li Guoxiu) *huaju* (spoken drama) play *Shamlet* (*Shamuleite*, 1992) bears a certain resemblance to Ernst Lubitsch's *To Be or Not to Be* (Romaine Film Corp, 1942) and Kenneth Branagh's *A Midwinter's Tale* (Castle Rock Entertainment, 1995), both of which chronicle fictional theatre companies' comical efforts to stage *Hamlet*. Lee's seven selected scenes from *Hamlet* appear as plays within a play that document the activities of a theatre troupe named Fengping (riffing on the company founded by Lee in real life, Pingfeng). The play has been very popular in the Sinophone world: there have been continuous revivals staged even after Lee's death in 2013.

The production's playful title combines the first character of the Chinese transliteration of Shakespeare (*sha* from Shashibiya) and the last three characters for *Hamlet* (*muleite* from Hamuleite). *Shamlet* also plays with the sounds of "sham" and "shame." Lee, who had no direct access to an English version of Shakespeare's *Hamlet*, worked with the Franco Zeffirelli–Mel Gibson film version (Icon Productions, 1990) and two popular twentieth-century Chinese translations, by the Taiwan-based Liang Shiqiu (1902–1987) and and the China-based Zhu Shenghao (1912–1944). The genealogical link between *Shamlet* and the Hollywood film remains unclear, but Lee indicates in an interview that the film inspired him to stage *Hamlet* on his own terms. An opponent of staging straightforward literary translations of foreign plays, he claims that if one chooses to stage a "translated foreign play" and "follow it slavishly line by line," one will be "deprived of the opportunity to create and rewrite."[44]

Among *Shamlet*'s more interesting generic potentialities is its treatment of genres of performance. Actors move from their real identities as the persons putting on the play *Shamlet* to their identities as actors in the story of the play and their phantom identities of Hamlet, Ophelia, Gertrude, and other characters in the play within a play (i.e., the failed production of *Hamlet* in *Shamlet*). The framing device is a possible evocation of Tom Stoppard's *Rosencrantz and Guildenstern Are Dead* (Edinburgh Festival Fringe, 1966; Brandenberg and WNET Channel 13, New York, 1990). Moving among these three different sets of identities, the characters explore their local identities as actors from a typical Taiwanese theatre troupe. They are tormented by the difficulties that face all small and experimental theatre companies, and these problems echo the difficult situations Hamlet faces. Full videos are available on two sections curated by Alexa Alice Joubin on the *MIT Global Shakespeares*: the 1996 production at globalshakespeares.mit.edu/shamlet-lee-kuohsiu-1996/ and the 2000 production at globalshakespeares.mit.edu/shamlet-lee-kuohsiu-2000/

Shamlet is rife with ingeniously scripted errors. These range from malfunctions in the routine mechanical business of the theatre to forgotten lines and accidentally switched roles. An example of how the production embraces the contingency of theatrical performance, one that highlights the perils of translation, is the Fengping presentation of the ramparts scene from *Hamlet* where the prince meets his father's ghost (1.5), which we see enacted in Taichung, the second stop of their round-the-island tour of Taiwan. After informing Shamlet of his assassination and urging vengeance, the Ghost prepares to ascend on a steel rope as he delivers his last lines, "Adieu, adieu, adieu. Remember me" (1.5.91). A mechanical problem traps the ghost on the stage. The actor playing Shamlet is paralyzed, and Horatio enters, as directed by the script, to deliver lines of weighty irony:

> HORATIO   My lord! My lord! My lord! Anything wrong?
> SHAMLET   How strange! [*Looking at the stranded Ghost*]
> HORATIO   Speak to it, my lord!
> SHAMLET   Never ever reveal what you see tonight.
> HORATIO   I will not tell. [*Improvises*] And I hope no one
> sees it! [*Looking at the stranded Ghost and then
> the audience*]
> SHAMLET   Come! Swear by your conscience. Put your
> hand on my sword.
> [SHAMLET   *discovers that he lacks this most vital of props*]
> HORATIO   [*Filling in and improvising*] Use my sword, my
> lord! . . .

SHAMLET   [*Soliloquizing*] Rest, rest, perturbèd spirit.
I . . . [*Forgetting his lines*] I've forgotten what
I had to say!

HORATIO   [*Prompting*] Perturbèd spirit, please remember
that whatever historical period it is, you shall
keep your mouth shut [*Indicating the stranded
Ghost*]. The time is out of joint. O what a poor
soul am I that I have to set it right!

SHAMLET   Yes, indeed!
                    [*The lights dim as the stranded Ghost keeps
                              trying to see if he can ascend*][45]

The scene calls to mind Stoppard's transformation of the sometimes-
omitted minor characters in *Hamlet*, Rosencrantz and Guildenstern,
into the leads. From the perspective of these two characters without
memories, *The Murder of Gonzago* (the play within *Hamlet*), the turn
of events, and even their mission do not make much sense and are
farcical. Though in *Hamlet* accidents lead to tragedy, in *Shamlet* they
are turned into comedy, a form that is as challenging to native theatrical
forms as it was to their Renaissance antecedents. By act 3, when the
Ghost still cannot ascend offstage, Laertes demands that he leave.
Whereas Stoppard's play explores the theme of existentialism, theatrical
contingency informs Lee's play. The scripted mechanical failures highlight the inner workings of a stage performance genre and invert the
process of theatrical illusion. The production invites real-life audiences in
Stoppardian fashion to reflect on their claimed familiarity with an editorialized, modernized *Hamlet* in Chinese and Taiwanese translations.

Like other postmodern playwrights who parody *Hamlet*, Lee takes
particular delight in playing with iconic lines. As the mounting pressure of swapped roles paralyzes the theatre company's production of
Hamlet, the line "to be or not to be" is projected in English on a screen
above the stage. Instead of invoking the image of Hamlet the thinker,
it initiates a series of dialogues among the characters who are searching
for their assigned roles.

QIANZI   May I ask a question? Who is Horatio now?

CHENGGUO   Everyone knows. Horatio is . . .

XIUGUO   Yes, I am Horatio.

CHENGGUO   Then who am I?

XIUGUO   [*Trying to cover up*] Who am I? Ha! What a
great philosophical question. Who am I? Every person

> will experience this self-interrogation, often in the
> middle of the night, when standing in front of a mirror.
> He will ask himself: "Who am I?" . . . Now, let me
> tell you who you are.[46]

Shamlet speaks to Taiwan's search for a national identity. Having emerged from half a century of Japanese colonization in 1945 and been drawn immediately into political whirlwinds that led to the two-Chinas problem, Taiwan has struggled for a viable, coherent identity since 1949. Fortinbras's footsteps allegorize the militaristic and ideological threat that Taiwan faces from the People's Republic of China. Not unlike the eternally distracted Joseph Tura (Jack Benny) in Lubitsch's *To Be or Not to Be*, the actors in *Shamlet* find themselves becoming souls adrift without meaningful identities; they remain at once in and out of their characters.

Closely linked to the European avant-garde and American post-modernism, *Shamlet* thrives on improvisation and pastiche. *Shamlet* belongs to the genre of plays within plays that go awry. One approach is to insert performances of a Shakespearean play into a larger, usually comical, story, as is the case in Alan Johnson's 1983 remake of Lubitsch's *To Be or Not to Be* (Brooks Films, 1983; starring Mel Brooks). The action centers on a Warsaw theatre company in Nazi-occupied Poland and on the comic effect of the lead actor who is never able to finish the "to be or not to be" soliloquy without interruption. Another approach is to use iconic Shakespearean scenes to comment on situations outside the play's world, as is common in the afore-mentioned versions of *King Lear*. Kristian Levring's film *The King Is Alive* (Newmarket Capital Group, 2000), shot in the avant-garde style of Dogme 95, features performances of *King Lear* as a desperate diversion by a group of tourists stranded in the Namibian desert. In other instances, new motives or new information are provided to expand the world of Shakespeare's play. The award-winning Spanish play-wright Jacinto Benavente (Nobel laureate in literature, 1922) recasts the events of *Hamlet* in tragicomic tones in his *El bufón de Hamlet* [*Clown! Hamlet*] (1958), which is a prequel to the Shakespearean tragedy in which the young Hamlet engages in a power struggle with Claudius.[47] As such, *Shamlet* participates in the global discourse of metatheatre.

Sinophone Shakespeares

The works examined in this chapter are part of the cultural production of the Sinophone world. Instead of "Chinese-speaking," a term that has sometimes been used to blur the boundaries between an imaginary homeland ("China") and its cultures, I use the term Sinophone to refer to the multilingual, polyphonic, site-specific performance cultures that are in dialogue with one another beyond nationalist contexts and sometimes circumvent "China" altogether. The Sinophone world, to use Shu-mei Shih's inclusive concept, refers to communities that are connected to or are resisting various forms of dominant Sinocentric ideologies.[48] These communities have produced artworks in Mandarin Chinese or other languages in the Sino-Tibetan language family, which comprises four hundred languages that are used in Tibet, China, and other parts of Asia.[49] The Sinitic languages include Cantonese (often the language of choice for Hong Kong performances and films), Hokkien (one of the primary dialects spoken in Singapore), and Hakka and Southern Min (which feature in many performances in Taiwan). As Shih points out, the Sinophone cultural sphere is "multi-local"—consisting of elements from multiple cultural locations—and is not defined by the settler colonial mentality.[50] Examples include Cantonese culture in Hong Kong under British rule (which is distinct from Cantonese culture in Guangzhou) and the Hong Kong Special Administrative Region after 1997; Hakka and Taiwanese cultures in Taiwan; and Tibetan culture in the Tibet Autonomous Region. The Sinophone framework helps us move beyond the limiting scope of national profiling to consider intraregional networks of Shakespearean performances. Sinophone is an equally useful concept for understanding theatre productions, films, and touring productions that wrestle with the idea of a monolithic Chinese culture.

Along with a number of Japanese and western works, Shakespeare's plays and sonnets have played a significant role in the development of Sinophone performance cultures. Several themes recur in Sinophone adaptations. The first approach, adopted by none of the works discussed in this chapter, explores literary universalism. Directors adopting this approach tend to view Shakespeare's plays as works of art with universal appeal. They do not localize the characters, storyline, and setting for domestic audiences. Seeking to preserve usefully foreign aesthetics, these productions draw on visual symbolism in what were perceived to be authoritative classical performances, such as Laurence Olivier's versions. The first Chinese performance of Shakespeare, *The Woman Lawyer*—adapted by Bao Tianxiao from *The Merchant of Venice* and performed by students from Shanghai Eastern Girls' High School in 1913—followed this pattern, as did other early performances of Shakespeare.[51]

A second approach localizes the plot and setting for cultural assimilation and transforms the characters through local performance genres. *The Banquet, Prince of the Himalayas,* and Almereyda's *Hamlet* use *Hamlet* to reframe issues that are meaningful in local contexts. Another example is Huang Zuolin's *The Story of Bloody Hands* (Shanghai, 1986), a *kunqu* opera adaptation of *Macbeth*, with stylistic innovations but thematically recognizable Shakespearean elements. Since the 1980s, performers and their sponsors have increasingly seen the complex idioms of Chinese opera forms as an asset in creating international demand for traditional theatre forms.

The third approach, well represented in cases studied in this chapter, involves pastiche, dramaturgical collage, and extensive, deconstructive rewritings. *Lear Is Here, Shamlet,* and *One Husband Too Many* change the genre of a play by accessing dormant themes that have been marginalized by centuries of Anglocentric criticism and performance traditions. In the program to Lee's *Shamlet* (1992), discussed above, he suggests, tongue in cheek, that his play is a revenge comedy that "has nothing to do with *Hamlet* but something to do with Shakespeare."[52] The irreverent comedy parodies the troupe's investment in the remedial promise of Shakespeare. While many post-1990 adaptations adopt this approach, parody of western works dates back to 1867 when a travesty by Francis Talfourd entitled *Shylock; or, The Merchant of Venice Preserved*, was staged in Hong Kong for British expatriates. The Hong Kong Amateur Dramatic Club revived the production in 1871 because it proved relevant to the social milieu of a trade colony. The title, *The Merchant of Venice Preserved*, echoes Thomas Otway's 1796 play, *Venice Preserved; or, A plot discovered, a tragedy.*[53]

These three themes—universalization, localization, and pastiche— have coexisted throughout the history of the remedial cultural work. Sinophone performances of Shakespeare frequently highlight linguistic differences. Languages serve as markers of ethnic differences in *Chicken Rice War*, a Singaporean film to be discussed in chapter 4, and *Yumei and Tianlai*, a bilingual Taiwanese-Mandarin *Romeo and Juliet* staged at the Shakespeare in Taipei festival in 2003. In *Chicken Rice War*, the parental generation converse in Cantonese, while the younger generation prefers Singlish. In *Yumei and Tianlai*, the Montagues and the Capulets are each assigned a different language. Performance of linguistic difference represents ethnic conflicts beyond visual signs. Multiple languages are used in *Romeo and Zhu Yingtai*, written by Ning Caishen, directed by He Nian and produced by the Shanghai Dramatic Arts Centre (2008). In scenes taken from *Romeo and Juliet* and presented as two plays within a play, characters speak French, Japanese, English, and Mandarin Chinese. In what Ning called "a tragedy told in comic manners," the star-crossed lovers traverse the Shanghai of 1937 and present-day New York in search of new personal and cultural identities.[54]

Conclusion

Since acting channels the pathos of the characters, performances tend to be given a remedial role in the society. Reparative performance is an attractive mode of expression because it amplifies personal messages without putting individuals on the spot, without requiring any individual to engage in uncomfortable, public confessions. Wendy Beth Hyman and Hillary Eklund have argued that when interpretive practices rest on "texts that are themselves sites of contested meaning," such as Shakespeare's plays with malleable meanings, readers use those texts to "reproduce . . . smaller, less risky versions of the struggles present in other aspects of our institutional and social lives."[55] The adaptations examined here both exploit and contest art's remedial function. Each of the two approaches to reparative adaptation carries unique affective labor in their respective contexts.

The place-based myths of Shakespeare in modern culture are partially responsible for the artistic and critical predilection for reparative performances. Myths about the remedial power of Shakespeare depend on the harmonious—or contentious, as the case may be—layering of fictional and geocultural localities upon one another. *Prince of the Himalayas* performs a discourse of redemption and cleansing through the *Hamlet* narrative and through the film's layering of contemporary Chinese politics of antiseparatism onto a fictional Tibetan court in which "something is rotten." *The Banquet* reads Ophelia and Gertrude as "good girl / bad girl" through pop feminism to recuperate the silencing of female characters in *Hamlet.*[56] *Lear Is Here* uses *King Lear* as source material to resolve Wu's identity crisis and to bring innovations to *jingju*. *One Husband Too Many*, in contrast, parodies the idea of remediation: Hsin's earnest belief in the universal appeal of *Romeo and Juliet* comes off as naïve and pitiable in the scenes where the village audiences mob the stage and turn the tragedy into farce. In a similar vein, *Shamlet* deploys the dramatic device of play within a play to problematize unbridled adulation of Shakespeare as an icon.

The remedial cultural uses of Shakespeare's plays in the Sinophone world are informed by a paradigm shift from seeking to claiming authenticity. Case studies here cover a broad spectrum of reparative interpretations of Shakespeare, ranging from transformations of performance genres and autobiographical narratives to parodies of the reparative impulse. Although East Asian films and performances of Anglophone dramas initially developed out of western modes of representation, such as dialogue-based *huaju* theatre, these works are sites of simultaneous, sometimes contradictory meanings that emerge in a process of continuous negotiation. Sinophone Shakespeares have become strangers at home, simultaneously reframing recognizable ideas in innovative genres and articulating new beliefs through familiar forms.

3

An "isle . . . full of noises"
Polyphonic Reception

Encountering intercultural Shakespeares is an experience similar to listening to interweaving parts in a fugue, a contrapuntal musical piece that introduces a melody through one instrument and then develops that same melody through other instruments successively. The concept of polyphony sheds light on adapting Shakespeare as a practice contains and sustains multiple voices of the directors and critics without subordinating any one perspective.[1] Polyphony includes differing and sometimes contradictory voices. Each artistic and political voice has its own trajectory, authority, and weight in the narrative.

This chapter looks at questions related to the politics of production and reception of Shakespeare performances. It considers case studies of South Korean productions in Seoul, London, and Edinburgh. Because directors and adaptors work with echoes between Korean folklores and Shakespearean plays, this chapter also examines artistically constructed parallels between Korean and Shakespearean narratives. How are these echoes produced? How do international audiences respond to echoes among cultures in adaptations? So far in the book we have been moving through a series of concentric circles, beginning with the formalist features of select adaptations, then looking at artists' stories and their deployment of reparative interpretation. Now this chapter uses reception theory to examine the positionality of works within modern cultures and how audiences respond to those works. First, we address artistically constructed echoes in the polyphonic ecosystem whence adaptations emerge. (Adaptations in this initial section were performed in Seoul.)

Shakespeare and East Asia. Alexa Alice Joubin, Oxford University Press (2021). © Alexa Alice Joubin.
DOI: 10.1093/oso/9780198703563.003.0003

Next, reception theory is brought to bear on the international reception of productions that tour to London and Edinburgh.

Productive Echoes: *King Uru*

The Korean narrative "Samgongbonpuri," the core of the grand shamanistic ritual (*keungut*) on Jeju Island, includes a myth about an aging couple who calls in their three daughters one by one to ask them to whom they owe the good fortune of their happy lives. The first and second daughters answer that they owe their happiness to their parents and to heavenly and earthly gods. This answer pleases their parents. The third daughter's honest answer, that they owe their good fortune to heaven ("the vertical line that runs down the middle of the abdomen"), displeases her parents. They disown her. One day the parents trip on their doorsill and lose their eyesight in the fall. They are eventually reduced to wandering beggars. They are reunited with the youngest daughter who happens to have set up a feast for beggars. She forgives her parents and provides for them. She becomes Jeonsangsin, the god of destiny.

In another Korean myth, "Baridegi," also known as "Barigongju" ("The Abandoned Princess"), when Bari is born as the seventh daughter to King Jusanggeummama, the king, who has no sons, abandons her; he wants a male heir. When he becomes gravely ill, his six remaining daughters refuse to retrieve an elixir that will save him. Bari learns of her father's funeral and seeks out the elixir against all odds. Eventually, she returns from the underworld with the cure and revives her father.[2]

In *King Uru* (*Uruwang*), a musical production written and directed by Kim Myung-gon that ran at the National Theater of Korea (NTK) during 2000–2004, Bari, the abandoned princess, learns that her father, King Uru, has been mistreated by her sisters, Gahwa and Yeonhwa.[3] He has gone mad and is roaming aimlessly on a heath. To cure her father, Bari risks her life to retrieve the elixir. As she restores her father to his senses, Bari is stabbed by an assassin sent by a villain named Solji. Unbeknownst to the king, Bari miraculously survives the attack. When they reunite in a later scene, King Uru, full of remorse, asks Bari to forgive him, before he dies, for foolishly abandoning her at birth. Bari's filial piety turns her into a shaman. She sings and dances the Dance of Life and Love to appease the souls of the departed. A key message of the song is that a better world awaits future generations.[4] *King Uru* dramatizes a test of filial love which, as Paul A. Kottman's study of *King Lear* reveals, does not hinge on any "rhetorical test" but on a futurity: whether Lear's daughters will "let him crawl unburdened toward death" and care for his aging body "without being ritually bound to do so."[5]

Each of these three narratives features South Korean shamanism. Each is also an example of the archetype of a forgiving, unlikely heroine. Audiences familiar with Korean folklore would have heard echoes of the two myths when they encountered Shakespeare's *King Lear*, while others may have seen parallels to the Lear narrative in the performance of *King Uru*.[6] Still others see parallels between *King Uru* and the Old Testament. Itzik Giuli, the artistic director of the Israel Festival, has said that "the conflict between Solji [Edmund, the illegitimate son of Gloucester] and Eulji [his brother, Edgar]" reminds him of "the story of Jacob in the Old Testament" because the final scene "cries out [for] peace."[7] While echoes among different cultures are a defining feature of adaptation, theatre critic Kim So-yeon regards the juxtaposition of "Baridegi" and *King Uru* as a drawback. She argues that the splicing together of these two narratives into a condensed, simplified form fails to sustain either narrative, even though she endorses *King Uru*'s *mise en scène*.[8]

Subtitled *A Fantasia of Life and Coexistence*, *King Uru* fuses narrative elements from the shamanistic myth of the abandoned Princess Bari and the figure of Cordelia in *King Lear*. Solji, a villainous character in *King Uru*, is based on Edmund, Gloucester's illegitimate son, and some audiences would identify Gahwa and Yeonhwa as the Goneril and Regan characters, respectively. Kim's *King Uru* also draws upon traditional Korean masked-dance drama (*t'alch'um*), in which the Clown plays the roles of the king's fool and the chorus; the Clown frequently comments on the dramatic action by talking to the audience. In contrast to established interpretations of Lear's pathos, Uru (Lear) sometimes speaks humorously when the situation does not seem to call for it. When Uru confronted Gahwa with the line: "Are you our daughter?" (1.4.216), the Korean-speaking audience laughed because Gahwa's stern reminder to Uru to pay attention to his public image ("father, uphold the dignity of a king!") contrasts sharply with Uru's mannerism of a child at play. This is one of many instances when Uru's daughters take on a motherly role as he descends into confusion and a regressed state of mind.

Kim's script includes echoes of the "Baridegi" text in newly written lines interspersed between direct translations of lines from *Lear*, putting the two pieces in dialogue with each other. For example, one hears both the familiar lines from Lear's speech on the heath (3.2) and new lines for King Uru in the corresponding scene in Kim's play. Kim takes the germ of an idea from Shakespeare and develops it using Korean folklore. This is an example of polyphony:

> KING URU   Blow winds! Rage, blow!
> Tear apart, such a fool I am!
> Thunderbolts that light up the night,
> All-shaking thunder! [*Sound of thunder*]
> Burn the wombs of the bad women that produce ungrateful men!
> Spit fire, spout rain! [*Sound of rainfall*]
> Praise heaven! Spirits in heaven heard my petition!
> You, I know you harbor evil betrayal,
> Pray mercy to the fearsome spirits![9]
> KING LEAR Blow, wind, and crack your cheeks! Rage, blow,
> You cataracts and hurricanoes, spout
> Till you have drenched the steeples, drowned the cocks!
> You sulphurous and thought-executing fires,
> Vaunt-couriers to oak-cleaving thunderbolts,
> Singe my white head; and thou all-shaking thunder,
> Smite flat the thick rotundity of the world,
> Crack nature's mould, all germens spill at once
> That make ingrateful man.   (3.2.1–9)[10]

The sequence of wind, rain, lightning, and thunder is slightly revised in *King Uru*, but both plays suggest some level of human interaction with nature and both invite ecological interpretations. King Uru makes clear that the "spirits in heaven" have answered his petition when the rain starts to fall. In western performances of *Lear*, the king typically calls on wind gods and water spouts (beings who were banished to the edge of early modern world maps) to reclaim and ravage the world. Donald Sinden whispered the lines as a quiet invocation in the 1976 Royal Shakespeare Company (RSC) production directed by Trevor Nunn. Calling for a storm to take place is very different from a frustrated comment on a storm that is already happening. King Uru's invocation for thunder to "burn the wombs . . . that produce ungrateful men" makes the Shakespearean phrase "nature's mould" easier to understand. The line in plain verse has a more direct impact on Korean-speaking audiences. In Shakespeare, the Latinate word "germens" refers to seeds ("germ-") of "the female reproductive element, in opposition to *sperm-*" (*Oxford English Dictionary*).[11] It suggests that Lear thinks of the world as a womb. King Uru addresses the "womb" more explicitly in his last two lines, which accuse it of harboring evil beings. He orders it to beg the righteous spirits for mercy.

In other instances, echoes among different works can be most faint, or what Kathleen McLuskie has termed "attenuated" allusions.[12] *King Uru* draws energy from its references to Lear's test of and avoidance of particular kinds of love, to Bari's unconditional self-sacrifice, and to the archetypal narrative of ungrateful parent and filial daughter. *Lear* and the Bari myth function dramaturgically as ghosting presences in *King Uru* through attenuated echoes of well-known phrases and motifs. These ghosts—our experiences of a play that are informed by our prior investments in select aspects of it and by previous performances of it—are, as Marvin Carlson puts it, "simultaneously shifted and modified by the processes of recycling and recollection." The polyphony we hear in a performance is symptomatic of the ghosting effect.[13]

In still other instances, the ghosting effect of theatre occurs when a director stages various versions of the same play over his or her career. Ninagawa is well known for his many iterations of *Hamlet*, and Oh Tae-suk has made significant changes to his various stagings of *Romeo and Juliet* over the course of nearly four decades.

The effect of ghosting is evident in the composite figure of Cordelia and Bari in *King Uru*. She prioritizes blood ties to her father even when she is married, though in the Confucian social order she would be expected to prioritize her husband and his family. She is the driving force behind the plot development. She is rewarded for her good deeds in the scene where her father reconciles with her. The final scene depicts her transcending mortality to become a shaman. Shamans, or *mudangs*, occupy a moral high ground. Bari traverses the boundary between the world of the living and the world of the dead. Unlike western sorcerers, shamans are mediators between the worlds of the living and the dead.

In Confucian cultures, shamans are coded feminine because women are typically oppressed, and shamanism is an avenue for female self-expression and empowerment that transcends the social structure.

In imaginative literature, a woman can attain moral agency and political liberation only by becoming a shaman. Traditionally, the myth has been presented as a model of conformity for Korean women, but in *King Uru* the Cordelia-Bari figure gives voice to oppressed women who are silenced under Confucian moral codes. Cordelia-Bari combats the Confucian patriarchy through compassion and perseverance. She still embodies the Confucian female virtues of devotion, resilience, and endurance,[14] but her taking the moral high road calls into question Confucian oppressions of women under the rubric of filial piety. In a similar vein, Bari has been appropriated in modern times as a symbol of political resistance. For example, Korean American writer Nora Okja Keller's novel *Comfort Woman* (1998), built around the figure of Bari, chronicles the ordeals of Beccah and her Korean mother Soon Hyo, who is renamed Akiko and forced into sexual slavery by Japanese soldiers during World War II. Korean writer Hwang Sokyong's 2007 novel *Baridegi* (translated into English as *Princess Bari* in 2015) draws parallels between the myth of Bari and a North Korean girl named Bari who escapes to China and eventually stows away on a ship to London. Both novels thus feature the Bari figure who rises above injustice and trying circumstances.

Though *King Uru* is not as well known outside South Korea as the more widely toured works of Oh Tae-suk or Yang Jung-ung, its long domestic run in Seoul (2000–2004, while Kim was president of the NTK) is a sign of its success. The production, which featured Park Aeri as Bari and Wang Ki-suk as King Uru, was favorably received. Notably, *King Uru* was among the first Korean Shakespeare productions to tour abroad before Yang's acclaimed *A Midsummer Night's Dream* and *Hamlet* (Yohangza Company). *King Uru* toured to multiple festivals and venues in Japan (Osaka, 2002), Israel (Jerusalem, 2002), Colombia (Festival Iberoamericano de Teatro de Bogotá, 2002), Turkey (Tantalya, 2003), and Tunisia (International Carthage Festival, 2004). The international reputation and reception of a work partly depends on its tour itineraries. Unlike Yang's *Midsummer* and Oh's *The Tempest* and *Romeo and Juliet*, Kim's *King Uru* has not been staged in key Anglophone metropolitan centers and venues such as the Barbican or the Globe in London. To view the full video of Yang's 2006 *Midsummer*, please visit globalshakespeares. mit.edu/midsummer-nights-dream-yang-jung-ung-2006/ Yang's 2009

Hamlet is available at globalshakespeares.mit.edu/hamlet-yang-jung-ung-2009/ and 2010 *Hamlet* (Adelaide Festival) at globalshakespeares.mit.edu/hamlet-yang-jung-ung-2010/

Intercultural theatre and cinema follow a bespoke path from the periphery to metropolitan centers—usually Anglophone—and outward to the rest of the world. Informed by Pierre Bourdieu's sociological theory of cultural capital, Pascale Casanova posits in *The World Republic of Letters* that the cultural space for world literature is politically constructed. As it circulates and acquires prestige, a work's path to fame or literary consecration always leads to Paris, "the world capital of literature."[15] A similar economy of prestige and cultural logic of influence govern the reception of adaptations of Shakespeare, with London and New York as the gateways to global endorsement.

In tandem with the politics of touring, art and culture are nurtured by competing and even conflicting voices within and between systems of signification. Structuralist criticism, for example, would identify Cordelia and Bari as symbolizing both the unlikely heroine and an ideal of female self-sacrifice, reconciliation, and filial piety. "Baridegi," *King Uru*, and *King Lear* cross their respective centuries of creation to thrive in intertextual and transhistorical contexts. Audience members may hear echoes from both the Korean shamanistic myth and *King Lear*, depending on their reading habits and theatregoing history.

Echoing Ophelia: *The King and the Clown*

The 1988 Summer Olympics in Seoul and the first democratic presidential election (of Kim Young-sam) in 1992 were landmark events in the reformation and globalization of South Korea's theatre and cinema. Touring Shakespeare from South Korea and the increasingly vibrant film industry were seen as two areas for projecting soft power for a country known, until then, mainly for its production of automobiles and electronics by Hyundai, Kia, LG, and Samsung.[16] To change the image of South Korea abroad, the government in the late 1990s began sponsoring the production of films and theatre works that were seen to have the potential to capture some international markets.

Within this context of the democratization of South Korea, political and academic feminism flourished in the 1990s. South Korean feminism of the time rethought the position of Korean women through

"Marxist-socialist feminism."[17] Inspired by feminist voices, several adaptations of *Hamlet* recast Ophelia as a shaman who, similar to Bari, serves as a medium to console the dead and guide the living. Because female shamans exist outside the Confucian social structure, they have greater agency. In some instances, a shamanistic Ophelia figure frames the entire play.

The use of shamanism as a dramatic device creates a pathway to agency through ghosts. Kim Kwang-bo's production of Jo Kwang-hwa's *Ophelia: Sister, Come to My Bed* (Cheong-u Ensemble, 1995) opens with Ophelia's funeral. Ophelia is caught between the incestuous love of Laertes and the romantic love of Hamlet. Eventually, both men abandon her: Laertes has no future with her, and Hamlet must carry out his revenge mission. Possessed by the dead king's spirit, Ophelia conveys the story of his murder and urges Hamlet to avenge his death. When the ghost of Old Hamlet appears in the form of a large puppet operated by three monks, Ophelia moves in unison with the ghost and changes her voice to that of an old man. The effect is unsettling.

Another type of echo in adaptation occurs in the narrative itself, rather than in parallels between the arcs of character development. Although Ophelia has often been appropriated as a feminist symbol, she is also a site of contestations over gender identities and cross-gender performance practices. The 2005 South Korean blockbuster *The King and the Clown* (dir. Lee Joon-ik)[18] echoes several themes and characters of Shakespeare's plays, including the revenge plot in *Hamlet*, the device of a bawdy play-within-a-play in *Taming of the Shrew*, and the love triangle among Viola (dressed as Cesario), Duke Orsino, and Countess Olivia in *Twelfth Night*. The film is not a straightforward adaptation, nor does it advertise itself as having any relationship to Shakespeare (unlike previously discussed works); however, Adele Lee has argued that it can be seen as a retelling of *Hamlet* "from the perspective of the traveling players," turning the Shakespearean tragedy inside out.[19] Set in the fifteenth-century Joseon Dynasty, the film is part of the New Korean Wave cinema (2007–12), which blends various genres and modes of representation.[20] *The King and the Clown* depicts the erotic entanglements among the King (Yeon-san) and two acrobat street performers: the macho Jang-saeng, who plays male roles, and the trans-feminine Gong-gil, who plays *yodongmo* (queen) roles.

An Ophelia figure, Gong-gil presents as feminine onstage and off. Having fallen in love with Gong-gil (played by Lee Joon-gi, who rose to fame because of this film), the king recruits the vagabond traveling players to be entertainers in the royal court. The film suggests that Jang-saeng also harbors an erotic interest in Gong-gil and as a result uncharacteristically opposes their manager's plan to pimp Gong-gil to a male audience member, even though historically prostitution was common in all-male vagabond troupes.

Like Kurosawa's uses of traditional Japanese theatrical elements in his films, *The King and the Clown* draws attention to Korean theatrical traditions by frequently emphasizing the stage rather than the screen as a more effective medium of expression. The film thrives on the tension between theatrical presentation (the traveling actors stage a play within a play in the genre of *namsadang nori* [lit.: "all-male vagabond clown theatre"]) and cinematic narrative. The camerawork is dispassionate and documentary in nature, but Jang-saeng and Gong-gil's satiric theatre acts are sympathetic to women's stories in a male-dominated society and critique class- and gender-based oppressions. Tapping into theatre's power, the king asks the players to help him appeal to the conscience of corrupt court officials by staging an equivalent to the play-within-a-play that Hamlet designs to "catch the conscience" of the murderer of Hamlet's father (2.2.605). The king, long suspicious of his courtiers, investigates their involvement in his mother's deposition and mysterious death.

Our reading of Gong-gil depends on the literary archetypes and character types into which we fit them. For the purpose of identifying cross-cultural echoes here, I read *The King and the Clown* through the lens of transgender and gender-fluid period drama films and the K-pop phenomenon of "flower boys" (*kkonminam*, typically seen in boy bands, such as H.O.T.), although it would be equally productive to situate Gong-gil in other contexts, such as the gay movement, gender nonconformity, theatrical and cinematic gender presentations, the *jingju* (Beijing opera) female "impersonator" Cheng Dieyi (Leslie Cheung) in *Farewell My Concubine* (dir. Chen Kaige, Tomson Films, 1993), Japan's all-male Kabuki theatre, or all-female Takarazuka theatre. Jeeyoung Shin believes, for instance, that the film's anachronistic integration of *jingju* references the male bonding and homosexuality in a *jingju* troupe in *Farewell My Concubine*. Shin sees *The King and the*

Clown as an example of Korean–Chinese echoes.[21] Adele Lees argues that the trope of *jingju* in *The King and the Clown* "signifies an attempt to link *namsadang nori* with a more elite and better-known art form" that is part of South Korea's effort to "build a stronger economic relationship [with China] in 2005."[22] Among the many echoes surrounding Gong-gil, I isolate the particular ones from *Hamlet*.

Of special interest is how the narrative revolves around Gong-gil, an Ophelia-like figure, whose presence propels the plot. While Gong-gil may be marginalized, they are not socially alienated. They are accepted as a feminine person by characters of high and low social status except for a concubine and a eunuch in scenes in the royal court. However, most characters use masculine pronouns to misgender Gong-gil. Reviews and studies in Korean and English also misgender Gong-gil. I use gender-neutral pronouns out of respect of who the character is.

Ophelia and Gong-gil share several personality traits: they are soft-spoken and unable to express themselves, lack inner direction, and their paths in life are determined by men around them. In one scene, Gong-gil is found lying in a pool of their blood after a suicide attempt, evoking the image of a drowning woman. In another scene, Gong-gil wears a *jingju* headdress made of flowers in a protracted play within the film, where the flowers on their head call to mind not only Ophelia's garland and the flower she picks, but also the figure of gender-fluid flower boy which will be discussed in the following pages. The innocence of Gong-gil–Ophelia, the titular clown, contrasts with the intrigues of characters around them, although that innocence also turns them into an object of what Laura Mulvey theorizes as the voyeuristic, "determining male gaze."[23]

Gong-gil is a trans woman who shares visual and narratological echoes of Ophelia, but Anglophone mainstream media tend to categorize *The King and the Clown* as a gay film, ignoring the transgender performance. Writing for the *New York Times*, Norimitsu Onishi compared the success of *The King and the Clown* to that of *Brokeback Mountain* (dir. Ang Lee, Focus Features, 2005).[24] The tendency to read the love triangle as a gay relationship is understandable, for the film appeared one year after homosexuality was removed from the Youth Protection Commission's list of socially unacceptable acts in 2004. Audiences tend to map what is perceived to be uncategorizable

(Gong-gil's identity) onto what they already know (the gay rights movement). However, the presentation of gender nonconformity and even the king's kiss of an unconscious Gong-gil do not mean the *King and the Clown* should be categorized as a gay-themed film. The film's queer valences and its enthusiastic reception in South Korea (where 12 million people—a quarter of Korean population—saw it and it grossed as much as *Titanic*) mark a significant milestone in transgender cinema in Korea.

Gong-gil's trans femininity is articulated through the trope of flower boys. Distinct from drag queens, "flower boys" are typically effeminate singers or actors whose gender is fluidly androgynous. In contemporary Japanese and South Korean subcultures of flower boys, cis female fans live vicariously through beautiful, often androgynous characters without fear of being stigmatized as being promiscuous.[25] The desire and sexuality of the female fans are complex. The fans may have lesbian tendencies, or they may be desiring ideal heterosexual men who rarely exist in reality. Jeeyoung Shin has identified these subcultures as "an alternative to the patriarchal mainstream culture," where homosexuality remains controversial and female sexuality is confined to "the biological function of reproduction within marriage."[26] *The King and the Clown* used its connection with flower boys to market fantasies about idealized male partners to young women audiences. Two weeks before the film's release, a promotional interview with Lee Joon-gi highlighted his feminine beauty and androgyny, which Jeeyoung Shin sees as a "conscious effort to attract female audiences . . . who would willingly consume a . . . film with a stunning *kkonminam* character."[27]

The film might also be read as a political thriller. As King Yeon-san (reign: 1494–1506), a composite of Hamlet and Claudius, indulges Gong-gil with doting attention and even an official title in the court, one of the king's consorts, Jang Nok-su, becomes jealous of Gong-gil. Gong-gil's longtime street-performance partner, Jang-saeng, also grows resentful over Gong-gil's special status at court. The king is clearly drawn to Gong-gil's appearance as an exotic object, and Gong-gil seems to have sympathy for the unhappy king. The king frequently asks Gong-gil to put on private finger-puppet shows in his chamber. As time passes, the king becomes enamored not only of Gong-gil's appearance but also their generosity, qualities that are rare among the consorts and courtiers. The king goes back and forth between Nok-su and Gong-gil. The king's emotional needs are unclear. In one intimate scene, he displays symptoms of an Oedipal complex when Nok-su says "come to mama; poor baby wants mama's milk," reenacting the bonding between a surrogate mother and son.[28] Having grown up without a mother, the king rests his head on her lap, paralleling Hamlet's foreplay with Ophelia before the players perform (3.2). In contrast to Nok-su, who functions as mother and lover, Gong-gil serves as an innocent figure who is not versed in court politics.

While it is undeniable that the trans character Gong-gil is gendered for the male gaze, the film keeps fluid the sexuality of the male characters around Gong-gil. At one point, Jang Nok-su storms in on the king and Gong-gil and taunts Gong-gil about their "real" gender. She tries to undress Gong-gil in front of the king, creating a great deal of tension. Gong-gil does not say a word and seems rather docile in this moment, when one would expect them to respond to Nok-su's pent-up anger. Nok-su is as frustrated by Gong-gil's version of femininity as she is jealous of the newcomer who is replacing her as the king's favorite subject. The act of peeling the robes off Gong-gil is symbolic of her desire to authenticate embodied identities, as if to up the ante in the competition. Nok-su's fetishization of "what lies beneath" contrasts frequent, eroticized close-up shots of Gong-gil's curves and smooth skin throughout the film. This scene may also reveal Nok-su's anxiety about the king's sexuality. Presumably Nok-su's dramatic act of "gender reveal" is to expose Gong-gil's alleged physical deficiencies as a trans woman and thereby dissuade the king from bestowing further favors on them (Fig. 3.1). The scene subjects Gong-gil, a trans woman, to the society's collective, voyeuristic desires that are anchored in anatomy's putative indexicality for gender identities. A device of exposure, such "reveal" scenes are a common trope in transgender films. While Ophelia is silenced by a patriarchal system of gendered roles, Gong-gil is a victim of a pervasive surveillance system that threatens public humiliation based on supposed bodily truth.

To view video clips of the film, visit the page I curated on MIT Global Shakespeares: globalshakespeares.mit.edu/the-king-and-the-clown-lee-joon-ik-2005/

Unlike Ophelia who is silenced throughout the play except when she sings, Gong-gil presents two contrasting versions of femininity. In

Fig. 3.1 *The King and the Clown*. Jang Nok-su (Kang Sung-yeon) presses the king (Junng Jin-young) on Gong-gil's (Lee Joon-gi) gender identity.

the opening scene, Gong-gil plays a shrewish coquette walking the tightrope who taunts Jang-saeng's character on the ground with provocative postures. Jang-saeng's manhandling of Gong-gil parallels the misogynist Petruchio's psychological torment of Katherine in *The Taming of the Shrew*. As part of its critique of the gender binary, the film draws on the metatheatrical parody of gender roles in *Shrew*, which is an elaborate play-within-a-play designed to mock the drunken peddler Christopher Sly. The caricatures of stereotypes of heterosexual femininity contrast with Gong-gil's trans femininity off-stage. The camerawork (Dutch angle, close ups of spectators' eyes) frames the rowdy audiences as the butt of the joke whose worldviews are being parodied. The transgression of ideal femininity onstage gives way to Gong-gil's feminine identity as a restorative force off stage. In the scene where the pair arrives jubilantly in the capital city Hanyang (modern-day Seoul), they sample street food as they stroll along (00:17:24). A tracking shot showing Jang-saeng and Gong-gil side by side highlights the difference between their mannerisms in off-stage life. Jang-saeng remains consistent with his on-stage, virile persona, but Gong-gil handles food in a delicate fashion. On stage, Gong-gil's character lifts her skirt, opens her legs, and speaks of checking out the manhood of Jang-saeng for size. Off stage, Gong-gil is reserved and sexually exploited. Gong-gil remains feminine even though they present different versions of femininity according to context. Overall, Gong-gil's persona during street and court performances is much more than just a stage role, because they remain in the gored skirt, wears a bowtie on their hairdo, and uses feminine mannerisms in their private life.

The echoes between *The King and the Clown* and the Elizabethan convention of featuring boy actors raise further questions about the gender identity of Gong-gil. The concept of drag does not apply here, as Gong-gil presents as female in daily life, not just onstage. This calls to mind the careers of early modern English boy actors. There are multiple cases of successful boy actors, such as Richard Robinson (1595–1648) and Edward Kynaston (1643–1712), who played female roles onstage before puberty. However, as adult actors, they continued to perform feminine or androgynous roles. These actors presented boyhood as androgynous and gender fluid, but as Simone Chess notes, they carried a "trans residue" with them into male adulthood. Kynaston is probably the best-known example in modern times thanks to Samuel Pepys's diary (August 1660) and the feature film *Stage Beauty* (dir. Richard Eyre, 2004), which depicts Kynaston as presenting as female offstage in his personal life.[29] Gong-gil's gender and sexuality remain ambiguous, but the character's presence provides a powerful framing to the idea of the artificiality of performance—of gender, of history, and of genre.

One important element distinguishes *The King and the Clown* from other transgender films. Gong-gil is not in drag, struggling with gender transition, or attempting to cross-dress. Unlike Trevor Nunn's *Twelfth Night* (Renaissance Films, 1996) and Andy Fickman's *She's the Man* (DreamWorks, 2006) that detail Viola's (Imogen Stubbs and Amanda Bynes respectively) transformation and moments of close calls, *The King and the Clown* does not present gender transformation scenes or dramatize the pains of transition. The film takes Gong-gil's trans feminine identity at face value without scare quotes. Gong-gil is not dysphoric or in struggle to "perform" their gender. Instead, they seem at ease and desirable. Neither does *The King and the Clown* privilege heterosexual norms in romantic love as reparative of queer desires. *The King and the Clown* stands out in LGBTQ cinema for its non-judgmental narrative arc.

The polyphony of distinct and conflicting voices in *King Uru* and *The King and the Clown* do not merge into a singular voice, which is why they are open to contrasting interpretations. While some critics have suggested that intercultural Shakespeare is a site where Koreanness is being constructed and claimed,[30] Korean and Shakespearean voices hold equal weight in these works, each voice presenting its own validity and perspective.

Reception Theory

For intercultural films and stage works, there is often a gap between artistic intent and audience response, or what Umberto Eco has called *aberrant decoding*—the phenomenon where the receiver interprets a message differently from the intention of the sender.[31] American audiences familiar with *Brokeback Mountain* may interpret *The King and the Clown* as predominantly a film about a gay relationship—as shown by the *New York Times* article cited above—rather than as a film marketed to South Korean female fans of the flower boys genre.

Aberrant decoding rarely occurs in culturally homogenous settings, but it becomes a norm in intercultural contexts, where artists and audiences do not share the same cultural heritage. Some directors find these accidental meanings productive, whereas others resist being pigeonholed or profiled on the basis of their cultural origins. Aberrant decoding can produce the artistically positive effects of flipping stereotypes and offering an alternative pathway into a classic work with established interpretations (for example, postcolonial interpretations of *The Tempest*).

Although reception theory and the study of audience response have been important areas of performance studies, measures and metrics that fully gauge every audience's reaction remain elusive.[32] A number of patterns have emerged over the decades. A popular approach extrapolates generalizable patterns from structured conversations with a few audience members or from conversations overheard after a performance.[33] The method relies on anecdotes. Performance criticism runs the risk of channeling the diverse voices of audiences through the critic's own voice, thereby flattening the class, race, gender, and ability heterogeneity of audiences, among other factors. Another approach is to collect quantitative and qualitative data from scholarly surveys of audiences. Theatre companies glean key data points from pre- and postshow questionnaires, and film studios use focus groups to understand the target audience's responses. Ayanna Thompson questions the validity of such company-led surveys, particularly in terms of capturing audience responses to nontraditional casting and "race in/as performance."[34] Similar to customer surveys with unexamined assumptions, surveys designed by a company's marketing and educational departments may precipitate certain kinds of response.

The current consensus is that there is still neither a perfect methodology nor effective metrics for capturing the spectrum of audience reactions. Both oral histories and published histories of cultural events are susceptible to inaccurate, partial, and twisted processes of recollection. Similar to the limitations of the reader-response theory that German theorist Hans Robert Jauss initiated,[35] reception studies cannot measure individual "cultural reference points, political beliefs, sexual preferences, personal histories, and immediate preoccupations."[36] Writing on memories of live performances, theatre historian Dennis Kennedy asks whether there is "an objective standard for remembering [performances]." He candidly notes that in his own experience of reviewing productions, "the more the performance moved or excited me, the less likely my memory of it is completely accurate" because "my heightened . . . memory of specific details may well have caused me to create a context for those moments that is independent of what actually occurred." One choreographs a "dream performance" when playing it back in memory. Kennedy notes that the observer's self is often the focal point of performance memory, for the person recalling a performance is "the constant protagonist of . . . remembered spectation."[37] Each spectator remembers or chooses to remember different parts of it. Peter Holland muses that, unlike a high school student who might focus on remembering the plot of a performance of *Romeo and Juliet*, he, as a professional spectator who "do [es] not watch Shakespeare productions for plot," puts less energy into the "construction of narrative as memory" and instead remembers eclectic details of the *mise en scène*.[38] But Holland concedes that even his memory would not be an objective record of a performance.

There are some more caveats to be noted. Our sense of reception history can be skewed by the prejudices of journalists; by the varying priorities of archivists, or what I have called archival silences—the purging or exclusion of materials from collections that are deemed unworthy or too sensitive; and by what Stephen O'Neill terms the "accidental archive" of collective memory—user-generated videos on YouTube.[39] In the age of instant but ephemeral digital communications, collective memory can be accidental and haphazard, depending on whether a meme or a video goes viral, the timing of the circulation of an opinion, or the international accessibility of the platform (BBC videos may not be available outside the UK due to country-specific restrictions; YouTube has been blocked in China since 2009; and Japan and Korea have their own popular video-sharing platforms rivaling YouTube).[40]

The necessarily selective processes of archiving can have a silencing effect, as can the editorial and publishing processes of performance reviews. Gaps exist in the archive and in reviews of productions because they are selective, inadequate repositories of memories. Beyond the selective process of archiving and publishing reviews, scholars may not have full access to sensitive or restricted archives. Even when scholars are able to locate performances of *Hamlet* in post-Arab Spring Egypt or during anti-extradition bill protests in Hong Kong, they may not be able to discuss the politically sensitive materials in public because of concerns for the safety of their collaborators and interviewees who are still living in those countries. They may not be able to publish their findings because they are concerned that they will be banned from entering those countries on future research trips or will not receive funding from those governments. The condition of preservation can create another obstacle. Libraries and archives may clear out materials deemed less valuable in order to make space for new collections. Some audio and visual records of performances may deteriorate over time, or become obsolete—incompatible with new computer systems. Further, silences in historical records may be caused by theatre companies' policies. Some companies, such as the Ninagawa Studio, resist the concept of digitally accessible archives, because they wish to preserve the production value of their live, ephemeral performances. In contrast, the National Theatre (UK) maintains an on-site archive of videos, rehearsal and production photographs, programs, prompt scripts, costume designs, and other materials. The London Globe films, with multiple cameras from varying angles, their productions into DVDs and now digital videos that can be purchased and streamed online.

Another kind of archival silence relates to collective international valuation of a work. Some works are not considered archive-worthy and therefore lack a full record of reception because they are not yet on the map. Take, for example, the Finnish film *8 Days to Premiere* (*8 päivää ensi-iltaan*, dir. Perttu Leppä, 2008), a romantic comedy about a theatrical production of *Romeo and Juliet*. As Nely Keinänen has shown, Finnish critics felt that the film did not offer enough elements of Shakespeare.[41] The film is virtually unknown outside Finland because Finnish is neither part of the English or World Englishes communities, nor part of cultures that are more diametrically opposed to the west. This kind of archival silence exacerbates the invisibility of minority cultures.

Though the power of intercultural performance over individuals is less predictable than collective, journalistic responses, it can become influential once channels of cross-cultural communication are established. A case in point is the intra-Asian and global influence of the filmic language of Kurosawa. Intercultural works can be received in disparate ways. An example is the contrast between the Japanese and foreign reception of Ninagawa's "cherry blossom" *Macbeth*, a production featuring a huge cherry tree whose petals fall in many scenes. Audiences at Japanese and international venues see it alternatively as a samurai story infused with Buddhist rituals; a stage work with Kurosawa-inspired cinematic qualities; an innovative Kabuki performance; a relatively conservative interpretation of the universal morals of *Macbeth*; a self-serving, self-Orientalizing production that appropriates Japanese traditions out of their local context; and sometimes all of the above. Self-Orientalization refers to a tendency of "Oriental" artists—themselves typically the object of western appropriation—to frame their works in stereotypical, Oriental tones, such as *chinoserie* or *japonisme*, to meet the expectations of the western gaze. The concept featured prominently in Rey Chow's study of fifth-generation filmmakers of China.[42]

The reception of Ninagawa's *Macbeth* is an example of aberrant decoding. The production (discussed in Chapter 1) mixes Kabuki-style witches with the un-Kabuki-like vocal work of Komaki Kurihara's Lady Macbeth, Christian with Buddhist symbols, and hybrid acting styles and cinematic blocking (nobles move like samurais, while warriors engage in stylized fight sequences). Ninagawa's conception of the cherry blossoms as "dialogues with the dead" and his decision to use a direct translation of Shakespeare's *Macbeth*, rather than a localized adaptation of the script, introduced unfamiliar narrative patterns to both the Japanese and British audiences. This is why in Tokyo the production smacked of Occidentalism but was accused of Orientalism when it was on tour in Britain. The production acquired divergent meanings depending on venue: for audiences at the Nissay Theatre in Tokyo in 1980, the cherry blossoms symbolized beauty, death, and the repose of the soul; Edinburgh audiences in 1985 and London audiences in 1987 saw the cherry blossoms as a gateway to Japanese aesthetics. Scholars and directors have variously praised Ninagawa's Occidentalism as a form of empowerment and criticized his visual Orientalism as a form of selling out.[43] Director Hideki Noda thinks that Ninagawa has a tendency to pander to the penchant for exoticism.[44] Scholars Tetsuo Kishi and Graham Bradshaw are also critical of Ninagawa's emphasis on visual stylization, because it does not solve "the problem of the linguistic difficulty which is essentially aural."[45] Ninagawa's internationally touring works sometimes bear the mark of *japonisme*, a cause for both celebration and contestation. Regardless of directorial intentions and Ninagawa's own statements, it is worth noting that there is a pattern: many of Ninagawa's productions in Japan feature western (or modern Japanese) sets and costumes, such as his production of *Othello* at the Saitama Arts Theatre outside Tokyo in 2010, but his internationally touring productions often feature costumes and sets that evoke premodern Japan. As Dennis Kennedy notes, "the spectator of interculturalism is both inside and outside the scene." While touring productions that cater to festival audiences tend to be "set in a beautiful no place, . . . indicative of the cultural indeterminacy of the performance,"[46] other adaptations use localization as a strategy to blend universes to create a new cultural realm for characters that are at once familiar and alien.

Intercultural performances thrive on the parallel and conflicting voices they foster. My focus here is on reviews of films and theatre works, not because they are necessarily the most accurate or authoritative but because they are often responsible for bringing to the public's attention a touring foreign-language work that is assumed to be too exotic to be of interest. I eschew anecdotal reception histories—on-site audience reactions one overhears. Although published and formal histories of reception in the form of reviews (in English and Korean languages) provide only a cross-section or even just a sliver of global reactions to a performance, they record formal circuits of the formation of public opinion and the subsequent international valuation of a work that helps determine the scope and magnitude of its touring itineraries. This paper trail is useful for our understanding of intercultural touring performances, whose reception may be difficult to gauge.

Oh Tae-suk's *Romeo and Juliet* in London

Oh Tae-suk's *Romeo and Juliet*, one of the earliest mainstream South Korean productions of Shakespeare to tour to the United Kingdom, is a landmark in the history of post-1990 Korean Shakespeares. An earlier version of Oh's Koreanized *Romeo and Juliet* made headlines at the Bermer Shakespeare Festival in Germany in 2001, where the *Weser Kurier* (one of the major daily newspapers in Bremen) compared the production to an unrolling beautiful "picture scroll."[47] This focus on postcard-perfect, visual exoticism is a classic reaction in western media to touring Asian performances. Examples include the foregoing section on the contrasting receptions of Ninagawa's *Macbeth*, Ninagawa's career in the UK (see Chapter 1), and Wu's *Lear* in Paris (see Chapter 2). In the fall of 2006, Oh's 90-minute, highly compact *Romeo and Juliet*, which depicted the feud between the clans of Mun (Montague) and Kun (Capulet), was staged in the Pit, a small venue at the Barbican Centre in London. Korean critics took great pride in seeing one of the most prolific contemporary Korean playwrights represented at a prestigious British venue. They hailed the production's arrival in "the Shakespeare kingdom," where it faced "the descendants of a Shakespearean audience," as "a historical event in Korean theatre . . . and the zenith of the Shakespearean boom" in South Korea.[48] The British reception of Oh's *Romeo and Juliet* was mixed. The polyphony of reception is exemplified by the ways in which German critics responded to the visual aesthetics, Korean critics focused on national pride (rather than qualities of the production itself), and British newspapers compared it to other non-English-language stage works. A closer look at what drew the critics' attention sheds light on the range of meanings Asian Shakespeares hold. To view the full video of the 2006 production, please visit globalshakespeares.mit.edu/romeo-and-juliet-oh-tae-suk-2006/

Oh's production has its own three-and-a-half decades of history of polyphony. His first production of *Romeo and Juliet*, in 1972, featured classical western costumes and a set that imitated the Globe. In 1995, after he had founded the Mokhwa Repertory Company in 1984, Oh returned to the play using a new script in colloquial Korean but keeping the western costumes and the set that brings to mind the Globe Theatre.[49] In his 2001, 2002, 2005, and 2006 productions, Oh localized the characters and setting, combining Korean and western modes of presentation. These productions featured characters with Korean names in a Korean setting and quasi-traditional Korean costumes filled with color symbolism (one clan wore brown, the other green). For audiences who followed Oh's shows, the evolution must have been striking. Perhaps not coincidentally, 2001 was the year that his *Romeo and Juliet* began its international touring career. While the 2001 version was far more localized, it still featured a hybrid set with Young Mun (Romeo) in a black jacket and Nurse on a bicycle. Kim Moran identifies the juxtaposition of disparate cultural elements and "intended discords" as a characteristic of Oh's theatre.[50] Oh's 2006 version, which was full of symbolically colorful costumes, was set against a minimalist backdrop that Lee Hyon-u has described as a "meditative and transparent stage" that evoked a scroll painting and "a limpid white porcelain" bowl.[51] The highly stylized production was characterized by an aesthetics of self-restraint; it prioritized stillness over dramatic explosions of emotions. Dance and stylized fight scenes replaced *shingŭk* (new, modern theatre) and Stanislavski-inspired psychological and dialogue-based realism. After the conflict between the heads of the two families in the opening scene, a martial dance expressed their mutual hostility without words. Juliet's pining for Romeo after their meeting at the masked ball was articulated as a sword dance. When actors did speak, they delivered their lines with low and quieter voices, staying aloof rather than diving into the emotional world of their characters. This arc of development of increasing localization to augment a production's "exchange value" on the international cultural market is not dissimilar to the thematic contrast between Ninagawa's domestic and internationally touring productions mentioned above.

The production was also notable for a generally comedic vibe that contrasted strongly with its ominous and tragic opening and final scenes. The combination of humor and tragic narrative tripped audiences up. The scene of Romeo in Juliet's bedroom played out with a heightened sense of frustration. The stage was covered with a gigantic white sheet, and Romeo spent a good part of the scene hunting down Juliet as she scurried under the cover. He never successfully undressed Juliet and "struggled historically to [even] remove Juliet's white socks" even when she lay supine, willingly offering her feet.[52] Sam Marlowe found this scene bewildering because the comedy "obliterated any sense of romantic or tragic power."[53] His analysis that everything is "lost in translation" overlooks the fact that Shakespearean drama is nurtured by a hybrid tragicomic mode of expression. *Romeo and Juliet* itself is peppered with fast-paced, improbable plot developments that are closer to fables. In contrast, Luke Jennings, in a review titled "Less Really Is More," appreciated the "genuine" tragedy that contrasted starkly with the comedic moments.[54] Eve-Marie Oesterlen called it "comically grotesque."[55] Others were unsure if Oh's production was a "convergence or collision of cultural traditions."[56]

One memorable feature of the adaptation is its inclusion of the audience in the world of the play, drawing on the murky boundary between performance and spectatorship in traditional Korean theatre. One might say that the production is self-aware as its characters move across the fourth wall. This feature echoes a similar element of Shakespeare's tragedy. Multiple scenes in *Romeo and Juliet* demonstrate that theatrical performance is on the characters' minds, such as Juliet's comment on having their "true love acted" on a "love-performing night."

The metatheatricality in Oh's production echoes a number of traditional Korean performance styles. In *p'ansori*, for example, both the audiences and the drummer verbally cheer on the singer (the storyteller), thereby integrating themselves into the narration. Audience participation could mean a number of things: encouraging the singer, voicing surprise or disagreement, or signaling approval, similar to the tradition of shouting for encores. Characters in Oh's *Romeo and Juliet* move fluidly through audiences, confess to or speak to them, and encourage them to participate verbally in the dramatic action. Though audiences remain seated, they are folded seamlessly into the world of the play. During the masked ball, Romeo and Juliet talk to each other "through" the audience: Romeo is downstage looking into the audience as he addresses Juliet upstage. In this intimate scene between Romeo and Juliet, although the lovers do look at each other, they always turn to look at the audience when they speak, even if their words are intended for each other. Audiences stand in between the couple physically and metaphorically.

In the important "balcony" scene in which Juliet is obsessed with names and the speech act of naming ("What's in a name? That which we call a rose / By any other word would smell as sweet"; 2.1.85–86), the two characters have no names. They are known only as a maiden and a bachelor. Romeo and Juliet represent Everyman as Oh turns Shakespeare's play into a story of irreconcilable enmity. The three-way dialogue between characters through the audience goes against post-Victorian theatrical naturalism, which may be a source of confusion for reviewers. The technique works to bring audiences into the fold of the fabula of the Korean narrative, and in the Pit at the Barbican Centre, it effectively expanded the small stage in an intimate venue.

In other instances, characters address the audience directly before engaging other characters in the play. Newly in love with Juliet but confronted by Tybalt (Ku Hyeon in the production), Oh's Romeo (Young Mun) shares with the audience his deliberation process in an aside: "To him shall I confess now we are brothers-in-law? I can't. It'll cause a riot in both families." Only then does Romeo turn to Tybalt to tell him, "I can't help loving you."[57] It appears that Romeo, armed with the audience's approval, finds the courage for a second confession of love, this time for Tybalt.

The final scene of Juliet's suicide also departs from the more conventional aestheticization of the couple's suffering and martyrdom. Juliet is clearly in agony as she runs Romeo's dagger into her stomach, creating an ironic distance from the euphemism "happy dagger" (5.3.168). Surprise gives way to regret as she exclaims "my stomach hurts." And in this production, her collapse did not result in a choreographed landing on Romeo.

While the audience is invited to be the privileged party between two feuding clans, it has also been co-opted into a form of complicity: the audience witnesses and even tacitly enables the feud. British critics did not fail to note the "un-English" stylization, although they did not necessarily attribute it to the vocabulary of Korean styles. Peter Smith noted how actors frequently spoke downstage to the audience rather than addressing each other, "as though [the audience] reflected their speeches onto each other."[58] In Oh's opening scene of direct confrontations between the heads of the two clans (rather than between their servants, as in Shakespeare), Montague and Capulet face the audience throughout their dialogue and their synchronized martial dance.

The interplay between the narrative of enmity in Oh's adaptation and the narrative of "love" in Shakespeare's *Romeo and Juliet* created both resonances and discord. Will Sharpe felt that the adaptation "reflects current political realities" in "Korea . . . a country at war with itself."[59] The critics' focus on Oh's *Romeo and Juliet* as a political allegory is justified, given the clear agenda of the adaptation and Oh's account, in the program, of the abduction of his father. Jason Best wrote in *The Stage* that "the bitter divisions between North and South Korea" inform the feuding clans, but he quickly and dismissively pointed out that "countless other productions around the world can claim similar weight."[60] The facts that the Capulets and Montagues fail to reconcile and the entire set collapses in rain and thunder make Oh's *Romeo and Juliet* a persuasive analogy for the irreconcilable relationship between North and South Korea.[61]

Not all works by Oh take the same trajectory. Although his statement in the program for *Romeo and Juliet* linked his own experience of North–South political antagonism with his vision for a play about enmity, Oh Tae-suk would break away from the tendency to interpret *The Tempest* as a political allegory when he brought it to Edinburgh in 2011.

Oh Tae-suk's *The Tempest* in Edinburgh

Written during the dawn of British colonialism and inspired by "the wreck of a ship bound for Virginia,"[62] *The Tempest* has been appropriated as an allegory of the natives' struggle, though scholars debate whether it is to be taken as an enactment of, or precolonial "prophetic" allusion to, the consequences of colonial conquests.[63] With a liberal sprinkling of physical humor, Oh's version of *The Tempest* shifts the focus away from the almost de rigueur postcolonial approach to Caliban's struggles against Prospero and toward the tension between Prospero and Miranda. This Prospero seems more interested in moral and artistic agency and harmonious domestic affairs than in regaining political power. Oh's 2006 *Romeo and Juliet* had concluded with all of the key characters dead, including the friar: no one was spared, but at least the feud would not be passed down to the next generation. Oh's 90-minute *Tempest*, however, is concerned with reconciliation and forgiveness. When it toured, the western media's unanimous perception of Oh's productions serving as political allegories of North and South Korea was worthy of critical attention.

Performance histories show that *The Tempest* has often been interpreted through a postcolonial lens. Buoyed by postcolonial critical traditions and such prominent works as Aimé Césaire's *Une Tempête* (1969), *The Tempest* has been institutionalized as a de facto postcolonial intervention and has become one of the most widely deployed canonical plays in revisionist allegories of local empowerment and anticolonial narratives. Examples include Caliban as a mud-covered figure in Julie Taymor's 1986 production for the Classic Stage Company and her 2010 film version (Touchstone Pictures).[64] There are, of course exceptions. The Dhaka Theatre production at the London Globe in 2012 focused on the comedic aspects of *The Tempest*. In the RSC's 2016 production (dir. Gregory Doran) in collaboration with Intel and the Imaginarium Studios, Simon Russell Beale played Prospero as a "sorrowing mentor [to Caliban]" rather than a "colonial tyrant."[65] The pot-bellied Caliban (Joe Dixon) was decidedly more comic and monstrous, calling to mind Gollum (Andy Serkis) in *The Lord of the Rings: The Return of the King* and *The Lord of the Rings: The Two Towers* (dir. Peter Jackson, New Line Cinema, 2002 and 2003). Beyond Anglophone performances, Caliban's words ("You taught me language, and my profit on't / Is I know how to curse," 1.2.365–66) become even more powerful when the play is redacted in different languages, some of which have closer ties to western colonial practices (such as Spanish) or Asian colonialism (such as Japanese) than others (such as Mandarin Chinese).

The overworked allegory loses its power. An example is the 2009 pan-African *Tempest* coproduced by the RSC and Cape Town's Baxter Theatre Centre, directed by Janice Honeyman. In this allegory of colonialism, Antony Sher's white, dominant Prospero had John Kani's black Caliban—who bears traces of a South African shaman—on a tether, but in the final scene, Prospero delivers the epilogue to Caliban as an acknowledgment of his crimes. Anston Bosman argues that the production "signaled the exhaustion of *The Tempest* as a vehicle for that allegory and the urgent need for South African theater, now fifteen years into democracy, to appropriate Shakespeare in freshly imaginative ways." Bosman mused that the tired allegory notwithstanding, the production, with its dramatis personae precisely keyed to "the complex ethnic patterns of South African society," could "easily be the winner of a competition whose challenge was to create the perfect specimen of a 'glocal' Shakespeare production."[66] However, when this production went on tour on the "global stage," it received favorable reviews in Britain. The politically correct allegory about the Third World was recruited to help British critics justify enjoyment of the African carnival. Kate Bassett found the production "universally poignant," and Michael Billington was struck by how the performance's combination of "racial politics with visual playfulness" liberated "this all-too-familiar play" from dullness and turned it into "a deeply moving cry for forgiveness of the colonial past." [67] In his analysis of the divergent British and South African responses to Honeyman's production, Bosman locates the overseas success of the performance in its apolitical nature: the production is "political only in the most predictable sense—as a call for anticolonial insurrection and indigenous self-governance—which, in 2009, is no longer very political at all."[68] Such polyphonic, location-specific receptions are the blessing and curse of touring theatre. In this context, Oh's departure from the postcolonial perspective is remarkable.

Similar to *King Uru*, Oh Tae-suk's production reimagined the play in the vein of a Korean narrative, specifically the twelfth-century epic *The Chronicles of the Three Kingdoms* (*Samguk Sagi*), one of the most canonical narratives about fifth-century Korea.[69] The production is set in a fictional ancient Korea, creating a past that is open-ended. Oh recast Prospero as a vexed character who was capable of recognizing his own limitations. He was often challenged by a spiky-haired Miranda and worked closely with Ariel, a shaman, to manage domestic affairs. Ariel sometimes assumed a motherly role to augment the aging father's tenuous relationship with his teenage daughter.

The performance ended on a high note. Instead of a staff and books ("I'll break my staff . . . I'll drown my book" 5.1.55–57)—symbols of authority and the source of archived knowledge—Prospero carried a folding bamboo fan (*hapjukseon*)—a symbol of artistry and intellectualism—when he was not at his large, upright, single-headed barrel drum, or *jeolgo*, which was used in royal court music in the Joseon era.[70] The folding fan was an integral part of a gentleman's accessories and is a more versatile prop than a staff. It is also a more powerful symbol than a book. It can be used not only to create a cool breeze but also as a screen to hide its holder's face, as a daggerlike weapon, and as an important prop in the single-singer *p'ansori* music theatre. In the final scene, Chung Jin-gak's Prospero was alone onstage. He folded his fan and asked the audience tentatively whether the "magic [he had] made with this fan [had] given [them] happiness."[71] When the audience clapped in approval, he descended from the stage and handed his fan to an audience member. A single father who happens to be an artist, Prospero was eager to pass on his "magic." Outside the dramatic context, the fan served as a gesture of the company's good will and as a mnemonic device.

The production, which premiered in Seoul in 2010, was defined by minimalism. When the curtain rose at the King's Theatre in Edinburgh on August 14, 2011 (it would receive a Herald Angel Award), it revealed a bare stage with minimal props. As the lights came up, a group of white-robed sailors were caught in a meticulously choreographed storm, dancing to the mesmerizing beats of a master drummer upstage. The performers' costumes echoed traditional Korean *hanbok* attire, and their acting style incorporated *t'alch'um* masked-dance drama techniques. Since the masked-dance theatre traditionally portrays themes of exorcism and social ills, it is an appropriate vehicle for adapting *The Tempest*. The costumes were designed to be minimalist but versatile under different lighting schemes. Their long white sleeves flapped and swayed in sync with their movements. Color symbolism was important in this production. Engulfed in stagewide sapphire and then crimson lighting, their sleeves were transformed from symbols of violent wind and waves to raging fire on board a ship approaching a world where, as Gonzalo aptly summarized, "no man was his own" (5.1.211). With Prospero (King Zilzi) revealed as the drummer upstage and Ariel dancing in the midst of the unfortunate sailors, the storm scene—one of the longest renditions of the "direful spectacle" (1.2.26) in the global performance history of *The Tempest*—served as an anchor to the tragicomic narrative about the self and the other. For a fleeting moment, Prospero gave the impression of being a drillmaster at the helm.[72] To view the full video of the 2011 production in Edinburgh, please visit the page curated by Alexa Alice Joubin on the *MIT Global Shakespeares*: globalshakespeares.mit.edu/tempest-oh-tae-suk-2011

The drumming patterns and the kinetic energy from the opening scene carried over to the rest of the play. As was the case with Oh's *Romeo and Juliet*, a ritualistic visual language governed his *Tempest*. As the play unfolded, the stage was transformed into a rice field symbolized by six broomsticks. Set on an island located off the medieval Korean shore, the production depics a space inhabited by animals and indigenous creatures. The actors' bodies were coded Asian through their mannerisms, stylizations, and costumes. Like the disoriented Viola, washed ashore in act 1, scene 2 of *Twelfth Night*, we are compelled to ask: "What country, friends, is this?" (1.2.2). In the comedy, the captain provides a seemingly straightforward answer: "This is Illyria, lady," referring to an ancient region in the Balkans along the Adriatic coast. There are no such easy answers for touring productions that use transhistorical and evolving cultural locations, both imaginary and real. While Oh's *Tempest* costumes were Korean, the production was set in a no place that seems fitting for Shakespeare's fictional island, one located in both the Mediterranean and the Bermuda Triangle.

Polyphonic Reception of Touring Theatre

How does Shakespeare make Asian theatre legible in the British context? What roles have polyphonic performance styles played in the rise of Shakespearean theatre as a "global" genre and with regard to postimperial British identity in the world?

The context of touring is noteworthy. As one of the three prominent Asian performances of Shakespeare at that year's Edinburgh International Festival (EIF), Oh's *Tempest* raised important issues of non-western directors' agency and the western media's tendency to read Asian Shakespeares as political allegory. The EIF featured several

134 Shakespeare and East Asia

genres of Asian performing arts, ranging from theatre to ballet, including works by the Seoul Philharmonic and the Yogyakarta Palace Gamelan Orchestra, the Shanghai Peking Opera Troupe's production of *The Revenge of Prince Zi Dan* (based on *Hamlet*), the Contemporary Legend Theatre of Taiwan's production of Wu Hsing-kuo's *Lear Is Here* (see Chapter 2), the National Ballet of China's production of *The Peony Pavilion*, and Haruki Murakami's *The Wind-Up Bird Chronicle* in English and Japanese, adapted from the novel and directed by Stephen Earnhart. Why did critics judge Oh's *Tempest* to be a successful piece of touring theatre, while other adaptations of the western canon—which were no less high-profile in their Asian contexts, such as Wu Hsing-kuo's solo *Lear*—did not receive similarly positive reviews? Theatrical transnationalism often collapses temporal and spatial dimensions of artworks—in this instance fifth-century and twenty-first-century narratives, the Korean Peninsula, and the British Isles, according to EIF director Jonathan Mills.[73] Oh's *Tempest*—despite the director's insistence on a non-postcolonial reading of the play—fed into Edinburgh audiences' mapping of the tension between North and South Koreas onto the figure of two-headed Caliban; the conjoined twins ask Prospero to free them from their misery by sawing them apart. As a result, it garnered more attention and success than Wu's autobiographical solo performance. At the 2011 Edinburgh International Festival, Asia's economic prowess did not quite translate into cultural prestige or meaningful ways to intervene in western cultural hegemony.

Adaptations of Shakespeare on tour outside their immediate cultural circles of references often receive polyphonic receptions. Spectators find themselves both insiders and outsiders, picking up some attenuated allusions while missing other cultural references. As works that sustain multiple voices, intercultural performances may prove challenging or alienating to even the most cosmopolitan audiences. Some critics choose to stay aloof and distrust intercultural ventures, deeming them inevitably fraught with a colonial mentality, as Rustom Bharucha does in his criticism of intercultural theatre practice.[74] However, I suggest that the alienating experience serves important sociocultural and aesthetic functions. Such experiences can help us move from narratives driven by political geographies to histories informed by theatrical localities—the varied locations embodied by touring performances. Global cultural flows are an organized and intensified cluster of activities that thrive on multidirectionality. As Fredric Jameson puts it, globalization has become "an untotalizable totality which intensifies binary relations between its parts."[75] Kala-mandalam Padmanabhan Nair's *kathakali* performance of Lear (London Globe, 1999) epitomizes these dynamics. On the one hand, the temple-driven genre of *kathakali* typically portrays "non-worldly" or nonhuman characters drawn from the Indian epics. The humanist concerns in *King Lear* made it challenging for adaptors. On the other hand, the Shakespearean motifs of betrayal and loss were fused seamlessly to classical *kathakali* forms of Malayalam lyrics and corresponding *mudra* (hand gestures). The French director-choreographer Annette Leday and Australian playwright David McRuvie who co-produced the *Kathakali Lear* drew attention to their meticulous preservation of *kathakali* conventions in their adaptation.[76] Encountering the *kathakali King Lear* alienates both audiences who are familiar with the Indian genre or with Shakespeare's tragedy, and that alienating experience creates a productive polyphony.

The European tour of Oh's production of *The Tempest* encapsulates two recurring themes in the reception of touring performances. First, the cultural and political conditions of a venue or a production can affect a work's reception and undercut a director's artistic intent. Second, when Shakespeare productions that feature changed cultural settings go on tour, they do not always correspond to the cultural affiliations of audiences. Changed cultural settings and compressed timelines engender variegated, layered subject positions.

Invariably directors from dominant cultures enjoy more privilege and do not have to cater to international audiences' tastes. Although they are seen as representatives of Korean theatre when touring outside South Korea, Oh's works are anything but typically Korean in style and theme. Other directors also make revisions to accommodate the space and audiences of international festivals. Feng Gang, who wrote *The Revenge of Prince Zi Dan*, a Beijing opera adaptation of *Hamlet*, told the *Daily Telegraph* that he and his colleagues "designed this play for foreign audiences." While it would be ideal to take traditional *jingju* plays overseas, he added, they would be "incomprehensible to foreigners" no matter how "eye-catching" the performance might be.[77] In contrast, the Royal Shakespeare Company—which occupies a more privileged position in the Shakespearean circle—does not usually localize its productions when it tours internationally; an example is Loveday Ingram's *The Merchant of Venice*, which toured in Beijing and Shanghai in 2002.[78]

These issues of international politics and performed cultural affiliations informed the polyphonic reception of Oh's *Tempest*. The production was able to create a sense of wonder because Oh created an ancient Korea that had nostalgic value but was unfamiliar to everyone in the audience at Edinburgh—Korean expatriates, UK audiences, and people from other parts of the world who attended the festival. The energy of its musical and physical expressions of a wide spectrum of emotions effectively bridged the gap between this Korean production and an audience that was accustomed to a more Anglo-European performance routine. While the production's emphasis on visual signifiers may seem at first to be a strategic move, the abbreviated phrases that omitted verbs or nouns were in fact necessitated by the acting style. The actors wore masks to perform physically demanding dance pieces and movements and could not speak full lines simultaneously. However, English surtitles offered deceivingly complete speeches that had been translated and rewritten to serve an international audience. The spoken language (Korean) and the company's use of English surtitles demarcated the actors' and audiences' discrete linguistic communities. As I argued in chapter 1, subtitles and surtitles are powerful heuristic devices that reveal as much as they filter key messages.

As was mentioned in the foregoing section, one of the most refreshing features of the production was its attempt to create an enchanted isle full of noise but not politics. One option for a South Korean company would have been using the play to launch topical discourses about the not-so-distant history of Japanese colonial rule of Korea (1910–45) and the complicated emotional and political relationships between contemporary Korea and Japan. After all, the traditional *ch'anggŭk* (Korean opera theatre) and the national history of Korea tend to draw their energy from a plot structure and a narrative that depict resistance to colonial powers. One might think that a play such as *The Tempest* would work well for Oh's project of constructing and popularizing a coherent Korean identity based on traditional cultural values.[79] However, Oh Tae-suk's *Tempest* took a different approach to questions of agency and coloniality. Oh focused on the revitalization of traditional Korean aesthetics, a process that does not tend to interest casual western theatregoers. Oh began writing plays in 1968. His first venture into adaptations of western drama began with his *madang kuk* (outdoor performance)-style production of Molière's *Les Fourberies de Scapin* in 1972. Oh's more than sixty original plays are rooted in Korea's cultural archetypes. He employs *shingŭk* or a hybrid form of *shingŭk* and traditional Korean styles to counter the "theatrical realism" that is prevalent in South Korea.[80] He has established a unique theatre methodology based on traditional Korean aesthetics, language, and expressions.

Like Ninagawa, Oh's extensive international touring experience has given him a unique vantage point in his *mise en scène* for audiences at international festivals. Opening with the music of the *taegŭm*, a transverse (horizontal) Korean bamboo flute, Oh's production of *The Tempest* evoked Korean myth and music and the Confucian tradition. Throughout the storm scene, music that drew on rural Korean percussion styles provided the rhythmic foundation for the actions, and some characters, such as the spirits, took on animal roles, echoing the fantastical creatures in *t'alch'um* masked-dance drama.

Oh also transformed *The Tempest* into a romantic comedy. While the Daoist magician King Zilzi orchestrates the shipwreck as an act of revenge, he also brings the sailors to his island partly because it is high time his 15-year-old daughter met someone. The Korean Miranda later reminds her suitor that the question about her purity is preposterous; after all, she has grown up in isolation on an island. Combining the large-scale opera *ch'anggŭk* and the masked-dance drama *t'alch'um*, the production shows a new path through both Shakespeare's material and *The Chronicles of the Three Kingdoms* that restores the comedic elements with a sense of "lightness and wit."[81] Oh is more interested in establishing a space of his own in the teeming global cultural marketplace than he is in speaking on behalf of nations. Another Asian *Tempest* that toured to Britain, during the 2012 World Shakespeare Festival at the London Globe, adopted a similar strategy. Nasir Uddin Yousuff's Bengali adaptation steered clear of postcolonial angst to embrace a colorful and vibrant comedy. Folk dance and Bangladeshi songs framed much of the action, and Prospero's charms were evoked by Manipuri drummers with double-headed hand drums.[82]

For good reason, western critics are often more attentive to works that criticize global inequalities, but the European premiere of Oh's *Tempest* demonstrates that productions critical of the geopolitical status quo represent but one approach to the play. Some theatre critics could not resist the urge to imagine political agendas in these works. Toward the end of the production, the spirits ask Prospero to liberate them from years of servitude and (in a surprising turn) add that they wish to be turned into ducks so they can "go sightseeing in the north." Given the *Chronicles*' teleological view of an eventually unified kingdom of Korea and the fact that Oh's company comes from South Korea, reviewers have interpreted this line as a hint as to Oh's political stance toward the question of a divided Korean Peninsula. Craig Singer mentioned the idea of a unified Korea, and Paul Gent sees echoes between the two-headed Caliban and a divided Korean Peninsula: "Caliban is a monster with two heads in constant disagreement. In the final scenes, Prospero grants them their freedom by splitting them—undoubtedly a reference to North and South Korea."[83] The conjoined twins share one body but have conflicting mentalities. However, Oh made it clear during a postshow discussion that he did not have North Korea or the conflicts between North and South Korea in mind.[84]

To be fair, in other instances, Oh invested in the capacity of drama to comment on history. He has distinguished himself as a playwright of historical drama; his works *Bicycle* and *Lifecord*, for example, are based on events in Korean history. He is deeply interested in retrieving a "Korean ethos" and the root of "Koreanness."[85] He takes a pessimistic view of modern Korean history, including the collapse of the 500-year-old Joseon Dynasty, Japan's annexation of Korea, the Korean War, the division of the Korean Peninsula, militarily dictatorship, and South Korea's rocky process of democratization in the 1990s.[86]

However, what is in play in the reviews I've mentioned is cultural profiling: western reviewers of intercultural performance tend to read contemporary Asian arts in political ways. The patterns in the reception history of touring productions also point toward a lingering ideological investment in fixed notions of cultural authenticity. Critics do not have a rich enough context for understanding touring productions, and as a result, receptions of touring works follow the pattern of aligning cultural production with regional politics. While in-depth studies of national Shakespeares exist, the same cannot be said of the history of performances imported from one region into another.[87]

Stories on Asia in western media converge on the notion that politics in Asia dictate cultural life, a notion that leads commentators, critics, and observers to routinely praise works with a dissident tone. Western critics also expect subversive or political undertones in Asian film and theatre. Some Asian performances do strive to tell stories of oppression. However, other cultural stories must also be told. Admittedly Oh's comedic presentation also poses some obstacles. In his otherwise positive review, Mark Fisher wrote condescendingly that the "playful" adaptation is better for its lack of depth because it is "the kind of thing you can imagine appealing to the groundlings in the Globe."[88] Other critics go through a laundry list of parallels and departures from Shakespeare, noting that it is "hard for a British audience not to feel that Shakespeare's play has been diminished" and that the "greatest loss . . . is the word-magic." Many of the reviews of the play and interviews with Oh focused on how the thematic parallels and transhistorical connections suggest a compatibility between Shakespeare's and Oh's visions of dramatic spontaneity, a vision that creates more with less by inviting the audience to "deck [their] kings" with their thoughts (*Henry V*, Prol., 29). Paul Gent reverted to the crude idea that performances of Shakespeare in English must necessarily be more effective. He wrote that "the poignant and troubled relationship between Prospero and Ariel . . . goes for nothing" in the Korean rewriting. He is right that the acting style of "one-note declamation"—a departure from psychological realism—may take some getting used to, but his reaction to the production as a whole suggests that, when confronted with unfamiliar works, critics often use parochial cultural ownership as anchor points.[89]

Critics compartmentalized the politics and aesthetics of Oh's production of *The Tempest* in racialized terms based on nation and culture, constructing these articulations of difference and sameness in terms drawn from Anglophone theatre historiography. This geopolitically situated reception reveals unequal power relations that are naturalized by values associated with the western canon. To combat stereotypes, Oh used Shakespeare to revive a sense of traditional Korea that is distant even to his hometown audience, as well as to polish his signature style of bringing contemporary sensibilities to bear on traditional aesthetics. His production of *The Tempest* not only sharpened but also expanded our auditory sense of the Shakespearean and Korean texts at work.

Conclusion

Postcolonial theorists such as Dennis Kennedy, Martin Orkin, and Ania Loomba have posited that in South Asia and Africa, Shakespeare arrives "in the baggage of empire" and that as a result, the meanings of his plays are entangled in the establishment of and resistance to colonial authority.[90] In East Asia, Shakespearean motifs did not always arrive with Anglophone cultural imperialism, and the baggage of colonialism is routed through other sites—South Korea in relation to the Japanese Empire; Taiwan in relation to Japanese colonization and the contemporary threat from the People's Republic of China; and Hong Kong in relation to the United Kingdom and then to China. Shakespeare's works and celebrity biography were largely filtered through Japan into the Sinophone world as Chinese students who were studying abroad translated and appropriated select plays in an effort to establish a new theatre style when they returned to China. The influence of Japanese westernization and modernization is visible in East Asia.[91] Later, during the Japanese annexation of Korea, the outsider status of Shakespeare and the western values his plays represented became useful in Korea's fight for emancipation. Unlike countries colonized by western powers, Korea's anticolonial movement recruited Shakespeare—unfiltered by Japanese culture—as a neutral and external authority for countering Japanese rule. There is a degree of malleability in Shakespeare, Greek tragedy, and other classics that allows audiences to tell their own stories and thereby to shape their knowledge base of world cultures. However, the range of voices an archive preserves may be curated, censored, and distorted by native informants and global producers, or otherwise filtered by financial circumstances or ideological preferences.

Works such as Oh's *Romeo and Juliet* and *The Tempest* travel farther than others—such as Lee's *The King and the Clown* and Kim's *King Uru*—and as a result populate more archives because they are seen or marketed as politically relevant. Some works, such as *The King and the Clown*, challenge audiences with their polyphony of distinct voices (echoes of Ophelia and transgender figures) that simply do not form a singular voice. Other productions are seen as unified statements of opposition to Anglophone globalization, even though they may have been intended as opposition to colonialism in the Korean-Japanese context rather than to globalization. There are of course critical voices that beg to differ, and not all Korean adaptations express opposition to Japanese colonialism. Lee Youn-taek's shamanistic *Hamlet* (Street Theatre Troupe, 1996 onward), for instance, has been regarded positively as a work "for a globalised world" that is not culturally "essentialistic, but rather interculturally accessible."[92] It has also been judged negatively as a specimen of Korean bardolatry in search of an authentically English Shakespeare, an "exotic commodit[y] for the Western gaze" with "the aspiration to reach universality through Shakespeare."[93] I suggest that it is not a zero-sum game. Intercultural works are governed by polyphony and thrive on hybridity in a third space, a communal space that is distinct from the place of origin ("home") and touring space ("work"). As Hyunjung Lee's study of Lee's *Hamlet* shows, the local does not always need to be the antithesis of the global.[94]

Whether East Asian Shakespeares are co-opted by western expectations or constitute a postcolonial act of "talking back," there is an undeniable level of instrumentality of repurposed cultural signs ranging from *t'alch'um* theatre to *jidai-geki* films. As the chapters so far have shown, such works innovate performance genres, function to remedy social problems, and/or disrupt established interpretations of Shakespearean drama. Contradictory voices in the reception of these works testify to their richness. The next chapter examines multilingual Shakespearean adaptations that originate in multicultural spaces.

4

"Divided in three our kingdom"
Multilingualism and Diaspora

> You speak a language I understand not.
>
> —*The Winter's Tale* (3.2.78)

Hermione uses the word "language" capaciously to describe and refute the tyrannical jealousy and rage of her husband, King Leontes, when he accuses her of having an affair with King Polixenes of Bohemia, who is a guest at his court. It is striking that "language" is used to refer not only to *parole* (words organized by grammatical rules) but also to thought patterns, mannerisms, and body language. After entreating, unsuccessfully, Polixenes to extend his stay, Leontes asks his pregnant wife to help change Polixenes's mind, a task in which she succeeds (1.2.38–89). Her noncompliance would have put her in a difficult position, but now Leontes is suspicious of her success. The capacious concept of "language" points, as Michael Saenger theorizes, to the fundamental instability of languages as systems of communication that are historically in flux.[1] Embodied performances, in any verbal language, rely on this translingual property—when phrases mean similar but not the same things across languages and when lacunae emerge across how phrases are articulated (see the Prologue). This chapter returns to the question of verbal language and embodiment.

One example of words that demand to be unpacked in multiple ways through performance is Cordelia's famous answer, "Nothing," to King Lear's demand of public affirmation of familial bond and political allegiance ("Which of you shall we say doth love us most?," 1.1.50) during the tense conference to divide his kingdom: "What can you say

Shakespeare and East Asia. Alexa Alice Joubin, Oxford University Press (2021). © Alexa Alice Joubin.
DOI: 10.1093/oso/9780198703563.003.0004

to draw / A third more opulent than your sisters?" (1.1.87–88). She carries out a great deal of affective labor by saying "Nothing" (1.1.89). The choice of word, "nothing," means everything from genuine care for Lear's well-being and rejection of Goneril's and Regan's rhetoric, fraught with economic terms of exchange, to a political gesture of defiance against the patriarchal system—protest by abstaining from the family ritual. Key questions for interpreting *Lear* hinge on our understanding of Cordelia's actions in this opening scene. Does Cordelia's eventual hanging enhance the tragic pathos surrounding her journey to self-recognition, or does it help to highlight the aestheticized male suffering? Are Lear's daughters implicated as a source of the tragedy that has been said to be coded masculine? How does *Lear* speak to cultures far removed politically and historically from early modern England, and make certain themes of contemporary cultural life more legible, such as filial piety, loyalty, and the generational gap crystallized by the catchphrase "OK boomer," which went viral after being used as a pejorative retort in 2019 by Chlöe Swarbrick, a member of the New Zealand Parliament in response to heckling from another member?

In a Chinese–English bilingual production of *King Lear* in Stratford-upon-Avon, a British-Chinese Cordelia says *meiyou* (nothing), the only Chinese word at her disposal because, having grown up in Great Britain, she does not speak her father's language, Mandarin. She literally has "nothing" to say to her father, who demands a response in Mandarin despite knowing her situation. Her use of the word is due to both linguistic deprivation and protestation of Lear's test of love. This 2006 production—a collaboration between the Hong Kong-British director David Tse Ka-shing's Yellow Earth Theatre (London) and Shanghai Dramatic Arts Centre—toured China and the United Kingdom and was staged during the Royal Shakespeare Company's Complete Works Festival.

Set in 2020 against the backdrop of cosmopolitan Shanghai, this *Lear* reframes the epistemological gap between Lear (Zhou Yemang) and Cordelia (Nina Kwok) in terms of linguistic difference. Lear's test of love in the division-of-the-kingdom scene is framed within the context of diasporic communication and Confucianism. Lear, a business tycoon, solicits affirmations of love from his three daughters during a board meeting. The Confucian values implicate family roles into the social hierarchy, and Lear, located in Shanghai, insists on respect from his children at home and in business settings. The system of hierarchy seeks to fix and render immobile something that is inherently mobile: the language of love. This scene portrays the failure of such a fantasy. Residing in Shanghai close to their father, Regan (Xie Li) and Goneril (Zhang Lu) are fluent in Mandarin and are ever so articulate as they convince their father of their unconditional love of him. Cordelia, on the contrary, is both honest and linguistically challenged. She is unwilling, or perhaps unable, to follow her sisters' example. She is also physically distant. A member of the Chinese diaspora in London, Cordelia participates in this important family and business meeting via video link. In the tense exchange between Cordelia and Lear, the word "nothing" looms large as Chinese characters are projected onto the screen panels behind which Cordelia stands. Her silence, therefore, takes on new meanings. In its Stratford performance, where the majority of the audience did not know Chinese, the word *meiyou* created a hollow space that embodied "nothingness," key to the conflict in this scene and to Lear's Buddhist redemption later in the play. The Chinese script, foreign to Cordelia, is superimposed on her face, symbolizing a form of linguistic imposition, violation, and violence. Uninterested in the ontological or lexical significance of nothing, Lear urges Cordelia to give him something. As the poster for the production makes abundantly clear, this *King Lear* focuses on the questions of heritage and filial piety. The tag line, in Mandarin and English, reads, "Which of you shall we say doth love us most?" (1.1.50).

Each of the characters has a primary language: English or Mandarin; for most of the actors, it happens to be their native tongue. The script mixes the First Folio version with phrases and lines from Zhu Shenghao's (1912–44) widely performed Chinese translation. Thus whether in the United Kingdom or in China, the majority of audience members could follow only one part of the dialogue with ease, and had to switch between watching the action onstage and reading the bilingual supertitles. Sometimes, the actors alternated between the two languages in the same block of lines or even mid-sentence. In some scenes, the bilingualism generated comic effects or highlighted English words that do not have Mandarin equivalents. When the British actors, such as Daniel York's Edgar, switched to Chinese, or vice versa, as for He Ju's Kent, their diction became unclear; this served as a constant reminder to the audience members—even bilingual ones—of the contingency of language as a fragmented cultural process. A video of the full production is available on the *MIT Global Shakespeares* at globalshakespeares.mit.edu/king-lear-tse-david-2006/

So far, this book has examined appropriations of Shakespeare in a range of genres, styles, and languages through a variety of lenses and genealogies, though the case studies have focused on monolingual performances. The Prologue theorizes the ways in which the translingual property of drama makes all performances of Shakespeare inherently translational. This chapter comes full circle by analyzing multilingual and diasporic performances. Tse's production of *King Lear* followed on the award-winning, multilingual Singaporean comedy film *Chicken Rice War* (dir. Chee Kong Cheah [CheeK], Mediacorp Raintree Pictures, 2000) and Singaporean director Ong Keng Sen's internationally acclaimed, supertitled, multilingual production, *Lear* (1997). Bringing together multiple East Asian languages and traditions, these polyphonic works are fitting subjects for this final chapter on multilingualism and diaspora, as they compel us to ask: What do we gain from experiencing a classic play through sub– or supertitles (Shakespearean lines used for their indexical value or translations back into English of the screenplay or script in a foreign language)? In what ways might CheeK's and Ong's multilingual works differ from the globetrotting Yukio Ninagawa's Japanese-language Kabuki-style *Macbeth* (Chapter 1)?

Multilingual theatre and cinema encompass not simply works that use two or more languages but also those that dramatize the necessity for and failure of translation among languages. Every performance, to quote Ian Balfour and Atom Egoyan's study of subtitles, is a foreign work, "foreign to some audience somewhere, and not simply in terms of language."[2] Unlike works examined in previous chapters, some of which might be categorized as "national" Shakespeares on display in London (in the sense of compulsory realpolitik; see Prologue), such as Oh Tae-suk's *Romeo and Juliet* (Chapter 3) and Ninagawa's *Macbeth* (Chapter 1), diasporic multilingual Shakespeares compress time and space even more radically, recreating their places of origin as the works evolve. They do not, and are often loath to, represent any particular performance tradition in essentialist terms. These works are designed for diasporic communities by incorporating elements from more than two cultures, as evidenced by Ong's Shakespeare trilogy—*Lear*, *Desdemona* (2000), and *Search: Hamlet* (2002)—which is informed by his diasporic position. These performance events dramatize movements of people and ideas across borders and between imagined locations. In fact, for Ong's works, international stagings outnumber "hometown" performances.

Diaspora is an ancient phenomenon that is usually associated with the plight of involuntarily dispersed people.[3] In early modern times, the movement of populations and goods across the globe led to trade wars and colonial conquests. In modern times, diaspora includes a wide range of movements, including voluntary immigration and expatriate culture. The diaspora of Shakespeare's works and their attendant cultural values resulted in an elevated status of Shakespeare as a cultural institution. "Diaspora" as a critical concept has become useful in the study of late twentieth– and early twenty-first-century performances because it refocuses attention on multilingual processes of signification. Distinct from the diaspora of peoples, the global diaspora of Shakespeare is an exilic and nostalgic relocation of ideas from one cultural "homeland" to another—"in states unborn and accents yet unknown" (*Julius Caesar* 3.1.114). While the migration of peoples may conform to the political logic of imperialism, the diaspora of Shakespearean materials today veers closer to the cultural logic of global capitalism, even as it is influenced by the colonial vocabulary.

When performances lay bare the processes of linguistic transaction, they demonstrate why cultural ownership and prescriptive linguistic purity are a fiction, for, as Jacques Derrida writes, "every culture institutes itself through the unilateral imposition of some 'politics' of language." While French is Derrida's native language, its "source, norms, rules and law were situated elsewhere." It is impossible for even a native speaker to "own" a language.[4] Tse's *Lear* exemplifies productions that create interstitial spaces through multilingualism and mobilize linguistically coded differences and alliances. This type of adaptation often emerges in the diaspora, as it speaks to artists and audiences who maintain links, but are unable to communicate fully, with their compatriots residing in their home countries. It also highlights to "hometown" audiences the contingency of native languages.

Even the notion of home is being negotiated on the fly, as members of diaspora communities feel neither here nor there. In some instances, they regard their present cultural location as their new home. Ong, one of the most widely toured avant-garde directors from Asia, counters cultural profiling and compulsory realpolitik in international festivals. Diasporic, multilingual Shakespeares capitalize on the presence of two or more cultures and the gap between them. They embody the realities of globalization through translation as a metaphor. As such, they employ forms of metatheatre and metacinema as a dramatic device and a tool of empowerment.

Screening Multilingualism: *Chicken Rice War*

Cinematic depictions of the tension between the stage and the screen are not unique to *Throne of Blood* (Chapter 1), *One Husband Too Many* (Chapter 2), and *The King and the Clown* (Chapter 3). *Chicken Rice War* (*Jiyuan qiaohe*) brings linguistically coded positionality to enrich metatheatre and metacinema. Whereas the works analyzed so far deploy a culturally hybrid aesthetic, pit the contingency of live performance against film as a more fixed, editorialized medium, and develop a recuperative arc, *Chicken Rice War* depicts the promises and pitfalls of a multilingual universe. In the film, multilingualism is both a dramatic device and a political metaphor. Supported by the Singapore Film Commission (SFC) and shot as a mockumentary with MTV-style rapid cuts and whooshing camerawork, the comedy is Mediacorp Raintree Picture's first movie primarily in English and the first feature-length work by CheeK, editorial director of MTV Asia (headquartered in Singapore). It trivializes the feud in *Romeo and Juliet* by reducing the generations-old dispute between the aristocratic Montague and Capulet families, leading to bloodshed, to the rivalry between the Wong and Chan families, who own competing chicken rice stalls next to each other in a hawker center (semi-open-air food court) in the prosperous city-state. Both narratives are deeply location specific. In Shakespeare, the conflicts confine themselves within the walls of Verona. After all, "there is no world without Verona walls" (3.3.17), as Romeo says of the pain of his exile. In CheeK, the conflicts are confined to the hawker center in Singapore.

The rivalry between the two families—manifested as mutual sabotage (such as planting roaches and mice in each other's kitchens before a hygiene inspection), elaborate efforts to guard secret family recipes (by speaking in code words), competing sponsorship of the Hungry Ghost Festival, and regular brawls—deeply affects Fenson Wong (Pierre Png) and Audrey Chan (May Yee Lam), who end up dating as they play the titular characters in their college production of Shakespeare's play. The film reads *Romeo and Juliet* through the dual framing devices of the college production and the protagonists' life offstage.

Built around the conceit of a multilingual television documentary, the film "screens multilingualism" in two senses: projecting its dream of cultural unity and concealing its pitfalls. The director intersperses the narrative with short interviews in which the subjects speak directly into the camera. Nearly all the characters appear in some form of interview at some point. Although we never see or hear the interviewer, his presence is assumed. Connecting these interviews are shots more typical of narrative films, in which characters show no awareness of the camera's presence.

In fact, the reflexive role of the Chorus in *Romeo and Juliet* is split among the English-speaking newscaster (Paul Tan), who opens the film; the Cantonese-speaking Malay character Fat Lady (Zalina Abdul Hamid), whom the film and characters never identify with a name (Muscle Mike [Gary Loh] is another character with a descriptive, pejorative name) and who sings a version of the Prologue as Cantonese opera at her beverage stall; and two "outsider" characters who frequent the hawker center and comment directly (in interviews) and indirectly (in unsolicited direct addresses to the camera) on the dramatic action. These latter two are Ahmad (Alias Kadir), who is Malay, and Muthiah (Mohan Sachden), who is Indian; they do not interact with the other characters, as they seem to exist outside the principal narrative. The film fails to use people-first language.

Seen against the backdrop of Singapore's policy of multilingualism, this polyphonic and heteroglossic hawker center serves to highlight differences articulated through class, ethnicity, acquired tastes in food, and, most important, linguistic diversity. Hawker centers were set up by the government as a measure to regulate mobile, outdoor hawkers, or street-food vendors. Located near or on the premises of public-housing blocks, the permanent stalls in hawker centers boast more sanitary dining options and have become a signature of Singaporean culture. Public-housing projects were designed to prevent racially motivated conflicts by breaking down ethnic "ghettos" and encouraging all communities to mingle. In short, the hawker center is an ethnically mixed space by design. While both the Chans and the Wongs earn their livelihood by selling chicken rice, the Chans—at least according to their boastful daughter Audrey, cast as a stereotypical "material girl"—are much better off than the Wongs. The two families may belong to the same commercial space and class, as defined by their line of work, but they do not belong to the same social space.

Spaces and habitats are structured along class, ethnic, and linguistic boundaries. The elder and younger generations each have their preferred language and space where they feel at home, whether it's the traditional hawker center in Ang Mo Kio (Bridge Ang Mo—though, ironically, the characters tear down rather than build bridges); the university auditorium; a parking garage (where the experimental, modern-dress *Romeo and Juliet* is eventually staged); a Tiffany jewelry store (depicted as a mecca where heterosexual romance is initiated); and modern and well-lit branches of Kentucky Fried Chicken (seditious Audrey's food of choice). Each space is demarcated by languages spoken within its bounds.

The film's playful Cantonese title creates a rupture with a more established language of romance and with expectations of how *Romeo and Juliet* will play out. This rupture informs the thematic concerns of the film, and it is embedded in the syntax of the title itself. Punning on the words "opportunity" (*ji*, 機) and "fate" (*yuan*, 緣) and "coincidence" (*qiaohe* 巧合), the title replaces the Chinese character *ji* (機) in "opportunity" with the homophonous character *ji* (chicken, 雞), turning the phrase into "coincidental meetings of opportunist or fateful chickens." In the context of the film, chicken (*ji*) refers to the signature dish of both of the feuding families' restaurants, Hainenese chicken rice, a key dramatic device and a MacGuffin that propels the plot and serves as a metaphor for becoming what you eat. Hainanese chicken (Chicken of the South China Sea), or poached chicken over seasoned rice, is often said to be Singapore's national dish. The title advertises a nonchalant attitude. The coincidentally parodic replacement of *ji* 機 with *ji* 雞, itself a symptom of translingual practices in a multilingual space, is one of the key themes of the film. The newscaster in the opening scene harps on the hostility around chicken rice, stating that, in an unprecedented case, the administration of the hawker center in the Ang Mo Kio neighborhood has assigned two chicken rice stalls next to each other. Responding during an interview, presumably to questions about the arrangement, the manager, Mr. Tan, states emphatically and with a straight face that, despite the coincidental assignment, the two stalls have coexisted in peace and the owners "are very happy." His interview follows on the heels of an extended sequence of brawls between the Chans and the Wongs.

In a film where characters are skeptical of one another's motives and recipes, Chan's and Wong's Hainanese chicken rice dishes are bound to be contested—and replaced. Audrey makes it abundantly clear that she despises her father's chicken rice, or any traditional dish for that matter, and that her preferred chicken is Kentucky Fried (KFC). Her replacing her family's secret recipe with American fried chicken parallels the comical act of replacement of the character *ji* in the film's title. In one scene, Audrey explains in Singlish (a colloquial creole) to her sidekick and loyal follower, Cheryl Bryle (Jo Jo Struys), the "art of seduction": with KFC spread across their table, Audrey demonstrates a trick to seduce men by "sucking" on her French fries. The medium shot of Audrey holding a single fry delicately sets up a stark contrast with extreme close-ups of gluttonous, dialect-speaking mouths devouring Hainan chicken at the hawker center, both in terms of approaches to food (savoring versus devouring) and of worldviews (living to eat versus eating to live). Audrey disrupts the making and consumption of Hainanese chicken rice.

Likewise, chickens abruptly disrupt the dancing of Hugo A Go Goh (Jonathan Lim), the vendor who supplies chickens to both families. "Uncle Hugo," as Fenson and his brother call him, is introduced, like many other characters, through a short sequence of his going about his daily life, followed by a vignette consisting of a freeze-frame and onscreen texts characterizing his profession and personality. The character card—an appropriation of title cards—for Hugo reads in English: "sleazy businessman, all round [*sic*] bad guy; likes young girls and *a go go* [dance]." Hugo's dance in a disco club with two scantily dressed women as his sidekicks and support dancers, moving in unison, is disrupted by cackling chickens that materialize out of nowhere. Chicken feathers fly in his face. The disco music is replaced by the cackling as the women flee, and Hugo stands all by himself, frustrated under a sole disco glitter ball. It appears that selling chickens is just a necessary distraction for Hugo, whose main focus in life is dancing. Like Friar Lawrence in *Romeo and Juliet*, Hugo plays key roles of instigator and mediator in propelling the plot. Ironically, it is Hugo who brings peace. Despite charging both families exorbitant prices—under the guise of supplying each with the best chickens in order to shortchange the other—Hugo sells them deceased chickens for their banquets during the Hungry Ghost Festival, which leads to food poisoning of festivalgoers. The Chans and the Wongs unite to accuse Hugo. Exiting the court, Hugo tells the interviewer, proudly and quite rightly, that "because of me, the Chans and Wongs are now good friends," though he laments that he has been unfairly cast as "the bad guy."

Despite the allusion to *qiaohe* (coincidence) in the title, the metalepsis—when a narrator intrudes upon the world being narrated and when words are substituted metonymically for words in a previous trope—in the film is anything but coincidental. Disruptions of speech, romance, and rituals are another running theme of *Chicken Rice War*, and these are often articulated through multilingual conflicts of ideology, class, and identity. A notable case of disrupted speech is during the performance of *Romeo and Juliet*, in a parking garage, to which all the students' families are invited. The college production reflects the reality of the actors' offstage life by having the macho and low-ranking characters—such as Tybalt, Benvolio, and the guards—speak in Cantonese, while Romeo and Juliet speak mostly in English. As Fenson and Audrey, in a mix of English and Cantonese, perform the "balcony" scene, in which Romeo and Juliet meet after the masked ball, their offstage parents become more and more impatient with their public display of affection, not understanding the boundary between play making and playgoing, between theatre and life. The older, parental generation is emotionally detached from and intellectually excluded by the younger generation's Anglophone education, symbolized by their enactment of Shakespeare. A 1987 reader's letter in *The Straits Times* reveals a humorous precedent to the situation portrayed in *Chicken Rice War*:

Once I was doing a project on Shakespeare's works. I came home late from the National Library and grandmother was angry. She asked where had I been and with whom. Exhausted, I told her that I had been with William Shakespeare. She said angrily: "Who is this William Shakespeare? I forbid you to go out with him in future."[5]

Seated at the performance in two separate sections across an aisle, as arranged by the chicken supplier Hugo, the two families initially attempt to maintain civility. The seating arrangement initially calls to mind that at a wedding, with the bride's and groom's families on either side of the aisle. As the play goes on, the parents' unsolicited interventions range from questions among themselves about the validity of using dialects to outspoken objections to Fenson and Audrey kissing. With dialects and languages being deployed as important identity signifiers, the bilingualism onstage does not go unnoticed. In one scene, one family member murmurs that the actors are "supposed to speak in English." As the scene progresses, both sets of parents grow increasingly annoyed and disruptive. The parents' behaviors mirror those of Romeo's and Juliet's parents. Not unlike the unsophisticated rural audiences who storm the stage during a performance of *Romeo and Juliet* in *One Husband Too Many* (Chapter 2), members of both families, their pent-up frustration eventually bursting into a full-blown argument, stand up and interrupt the performance. Audrey's father Vincent Chan (Gary Yuen) and Fenson's mother Madame Wong (Catherine Sng)—known as Wong Ku colloquially in Cantonese, with *ku* referring to a middle-aged woman—take turns insulting the appearance of Fenson and Audrey. The insertion of lines that are extratextual to *Romeo and Juliet* creates a polyphony and additional layers of meanings. As Fenson's Romeo tells Juliet that his lips, "two blushing pilgrims," are ready to "smooth that rough touch [of his forwardness and their families' hatred of each other] with a tender kiss" (1.5.94–95), Vincent Chan interjects: "He is so ugly. How can he be Romeo?" That invites misogynist body shaming from the Wongs: "Your daughter's chest is [flat] like a washing board, and she is such a bad actress." Intruding upon the fictional universe onstage, their snickering comments, growing in volume, evolve from monologues and asides into a full-blown dialogue across the aisle as each parent picks up from where the other leaves off. Wong Ku tells the Chans that "even if you sent this washing board [Audrey] right up to our door step, my son won't be the least interested." The religious cleansing encoded in the Shakespearean scene fails to wash away the mutual hatred of the Wongs and the Chans. The soundtrack of the actors' lines fades out, giving way to the parents' comments from the margin outside the frame of the camera. Romeo and Juliet remain front and center in the shot, but they become inaudible. Upon their first kiss, Vincent Chan interjects with a metaphor that is, ironically, well aligned with the discourse of knightly self-debasement in courtly literature, comparing Fenson Wong to an unworthy "skinny toad lurking after a swan." Their running commentary—similar to that of film commentator on YouTube, a Vimeo viewer's comments and ratings, live tweets during a film watch party, or the commentary track on a DVD—develops into an increasingly prominent soundtrack in this "fugue" of dual discourses that pit romance against antiromance.

Ever so pragmatically minded, like the government of Singapore, the parents take greater offense from what they imagine to be a tactic of corporate espionage—to access their secret family recipes for financial gain—than from the actual romance playing out onstage. Wong Ku makes it explicit that she thinks Audrey is trying to seduce her son with the sole purpose of obtaining her chicken recipe. The chicken vendor Hugo, who at the beginning of this scene stands between the two families "to keep peace," joins the commotion to calm everyone down, reiterating in English that "you cannot argue here, we are dressed very high class at a very high-class play." Hugo fails to bring the audience for the play back to the playing space, and the spectators' space invades and takes over the stage action. Eventually, the Wongs' and Chans' argument moves away from objections to Fenson and Audrey's on– and offstage romance to which family's chicken rice tastes better. The reversal of playing space and spectator space is complete when the actors freeze in horror, stopped in their tracks, and watch the two families fight it out at their seats, with Hugo in the middle trying in vain to separate them. The parents steal the show, and Fenson accuses them of having done so.

The parents' interjections may seem asinine, but their asides and lines interspersed between Romeo and Juliet's conversation transform what has become a "rhetorical set-piece" into a live, unscripted dialogue.[6] By not knowing better to wait their turn, as one would at a play reading, the parents insert themselves into the midst of a fictional dramatic dialogue. Their actions turn the otherwise romantic balcony scene upside-down into what Sujata Iyengar has theorized as an "anti-balcony scene," an appropriation of the iconic scene that is anti-romantic and suspicious of the idealization of heterosexual pursuits. "Anti-balcony scenes" render the pursuit instantly recognizable as "a wooing gone awry." She argues that the balcony scenes in *Romeo and Juliet*, *The Two Gentlemen of Verona*, *The Merchant of Venice*, and *Antony and Cleopatra* feature lovers who are separated by "vertical distance . . . and engage in a kind of duet." The nature of such balcony scenes establishes these "enclosed spaces as prisons from which lovers . . . require rescue."[7] The liberation of the characters Romeo and Juliet from clichés in *Chicken Rice War* takes the form of disruption and simultaneous dual dialogues in two languages.

Ruptures energize the comedy. Another example of disrupted cere-monial speech is the film's opening sequence. The film begins with a whooshing shot. The camera then trains on a calm television news anchor, microphone in hand, in the style of a traditional evening-news framing that shows the anchor center screen from chest up, reporting on site. Other than his voice, there is no soundtrack. His reporting begins with echoes of the first five lines of the Prologue of *Romeo and Juliet*, with local twists but retaining its metaphorical language:

> Two families, both alike in dignity and profession,
> in fair Ang Mo Kio where we lay our scene.
> From ancient grudge break to new mutiny,
> where civil blood makes civil hands unclean.
> From forth the fatal loins of these two foes,
> a pair of star-crossed lovers choose their chicken rice.

The liberal sprinkling of location– and situation-specific qualifiers sets up this Prologue for laughs. The lovers are not compelled to "take their life" in a comedy where only chickens' lives are at stake. Instead, they are compelled to compare their families' secret recipes. In the scenes that follow, the camera lingers with extreme close-ups on hands that are chopping up whole chickens on cutting boards. The hands contrast with close-ups of chopsticks sending chicken into various mouths that are devouring the food savagely. The visualization of unclean "civil hands" brings irony to a low-stakes *Romeo and Juliet*-esque universe where the hands of the Chans and Wongs become "unclean" not because of civil blood but from chicken blood. No character dies, and no blood is spilled other than that of poultry.

The newscaster's creative repurposing of the Prologue is interrupted by his supervisor, who exclaims, "What are you saying?" invoking projected failed communication as a reason of her objection. She asks rhetorically, "Do you think [manager] Mr Tan in Ang Mo Kio can understand you?" The film audience would infer that this is not the news anchor's first attempt. The supervisor goes on to accuse him of going too far: "When I told you not to speak in Singlish, I didn't ask you to sound like Shakespeare!" Her comment sets up Shakespeare as a symbol of "good English" and high culture, primed to be lampooned in the comedy tuned in to linguistic difference. She also pits Shake-spearean English against Singlish on a multilingual terrain. The news-caster's false start is followed by another attempt in a different register and with pragmatic details in Singlish rather than metaphoric lan-guage in English: "How and why we do not know. By a freak stroke of Hawker Authority of Singapore's planning, two chicken rice stalls have been situated next to each other." The camerawork and soundtrack—drummed up for excitement—evolve to suit his more impromptu and lively tone. The camera zooms in on his mouth as he speaks and cuts, in MTV style, to the conflicts between the Chans and the Wongs as the reporting continues. This is followed by an impromptu Cantonese opera aria sung by the Fat Lady that attempts to delineate the origin of the feud (Fig. 4.2). She concludes that Vincent Chan doesn't know, his sworn enemy Wong Ku doesn't know, the Fat Lady herself doesn't know, and nobody really knows the origin of the feud. As the camera pans from her beverage stall to the scene of conflict, the operatic percussion beats underline the fights.

This transition from emotionally detached reporting to reality-TV voyeurism parallels the opening sequence of *William Shakespeare's Romeo + Juliet* (dir. Baz Luhrmann, Twentieth Century Fox, 1996). In that film (starring Leonardo DiCaprio and Claire Danes), after the composed, dispassionate, deliberately old-fashioned script reading by a female TV news anchor framed by an antiquated television set, a whooshing shot "sucks" the film audience through the mouth of the announcer into a second iteration of the Prologue in "fair Verona" in full action, complete with monochrome footage from police helicop-ters (Fig. 4.1). *Chicken Rice War*'s Prologue too features zooming in to

Fig. 4.1 *William Shakespeare's Romeo + Juliet* (dir. Baz Luhrmann). A TV news anchor (Edwina Moore) framed by an antiquated television set delivering the Prologue.

Fig. 4.2 *Chicken Rice War*. The Cantonese-speaking Malay character Fat Lady (Zalina Abdul Hamid) sings an alternative version of the Prologue.

the moving mouth of the newscaster, and CheeK dramatizes the Prologue, as Luhrmann does on three occasions: first, in a detached tone by a female news anchor, before a neutral background, reading from a script without nondiegetic music; second, by the voice of a male announcer in a low, overly dramatic, ominous but solemn tone against live-action shots and operatic music; and third, as a print medium in which key words of the Prologue appear as headlines.

The heteroglossic multimedia delivery of the Prologue in *William Shakespeare's Romeo + Juliet* is as remarkable as the film's multilingual, nondiegetic sound environment. Like *Chicken Rice War*, which sets out to parody it, Luhrmann's own campy film is itself an aurally rich space. A soundtrack of Craig Armstrong's "O Verona" accompanies the live-action shots in "fair Verona" in the second iteration of the Prologue. In terms of the operatic soundtrack in the MTV-like sequence with a male announcer, "O Verona" was inspired by Carl Orff's musical setting of the medieval poem "O Fortuna" (as part of his cantata *Carmina Burana*). "O Fortuna" was not available for licensing, and "O Verona," replete with echoes of the motif of "O Fortuna," served as a stand-in. "O Verona" is a spin-off and possibly a parody of "O Fortuna" for both pragmatic and metacinematic reasons. Equally significant is the fact that the choir sings the Prologue in Latin, interspersed with the announcer's purposeful, methodic, and measured delivery of the Prologue in English. From the 1980s through the early 1990s, "O Fortuna" was used and abused in count-less films, such as *Excalibur* (dir. John Boorman, Orion Pictures, 1981), and trailers of period, fantasy, and action films. Due to its overuse, it became a cliché and began to take on ironic meanings. Starting in the mid-1990s, "O Fortuna" has appeared in such parodies as the trailer of *South Park: Bigger, Longer & Uncut* (dir. Trey Parker, Paramount Pictures, 1999).[8] Similar to the ending of *William Shakespeare's Romeo + Juliet*, the news anchor returns at the end of *Chicken Rice War* to deliver his final verdict: "And thus ends the saga of the Chans and the Wongs. Two families torn apart by hatred and anger, yet ironically joined together by hatred and anger." He makes an appearance, too, in the middle of the film after the failed college production, latching on to the catchphrase "in fair Ang Mo Kio" as he reports: "And thus the scene is set for a final showdown between two proud families. In fair Ang Mo Kio, where we lay our scene . . . "

In CheeK's and Luhrmann's films, Shakespearean syntactical features emerge in contrast to Latin, Singlish, Cantonese, and modern standard English in rich sonic landscapes.

As such, *Chicken Rice War* contains attenuated and explicit references to other films, in and beyond Asia, from the golden age of Shakespeare on film, and from the renaissance of the Singaporean film industry, including the whooshing camerawork of an important Singaporean predecessor, *Money No Enough* (*Qian bugou yong*, dir. Tay Teck-Lock, JSP Group, 1998), of *Shakespeare in Love* (dir. John Madden, Universal Pictures, 1998), and of *William Shakespeare's Romeo + Juliet*. It parodies Hollywood rhetoric and global teen culture by drawing attention to the multilingual space its characters inhabit. Executive producer Daniel Yun pitched the film as "a very Singaporean experience. You can call it Singapore's take on *Shakespeare in Love* [which dramatizes the offstage love stories of some characters]. Or rather *Romeo and Juliet* at the hawker center."[9]

Beyond simply constructing attenuated references for the ideological purchase of a parody, *Chicken Rice War* in fact succeeds in other areas not mentioned by the producer: notably its treatment of multilingualism as a source of anxiety and comic relief, and its productive flipping of the romantic balcony scene in *Romeo and Juliet*. In an early scene where the college students rehearse *Romeo and Juliet*, a stuttering Fenson Wong asks his drama coach, Mr. Pillay (Edmund L. Smith), if he can play Romeo. True to the spirit of a teen flick, Fenson is depicted as being motivated less by any devotion to Shakespeare and more by his adoration of Audrey Chan, the young lady playing Juliet. Audrey rolls her eyes and challenges her classmate in an ableist comment: "What makes you think that you can play Romeo? You don't have the looks, and you can't even speak properly." She is quick to point out that the student originally cast for the male lead— her then-boyfriend, Nick Carter (Randall Tan)—is eminently more qualified, even if he cannot remember his lines: "Nick, on the other hand, looks like Leonardo DiCaprio. That's why he's Romeo." Audrey's follower and protégé Cheryl Bryle promptly supports her cause ("yes I agree") and leaves the aspiring thespian Fenson speechless. Audrey's gaze here bears significance. As Richard Dryer writes, "looking and being looked at reproduce racial power relations."[10] The teen girl's adoration of whiteness epitomizes a form of internalized racial hierarchy in postcolonial Singapore, but it also reveals the power of the white male gaze.

To watch video clips of this film, visit the page I curated on MIT Global Shakespeares, globalshakespeares.mit.edu/chicken-rice-war-cheah-ck-2000/

Fenson's stuttering may be symptomatic not of a speech impediment but of intimidation by both Audrey and Shakespeare. Offstage, Fenson does not stutter. But Shakespearean language does play a therapeutic role here. Even though Nick is Eurasian, and his features, such as a tall nose, are deemed more attractive, Fenson eventually gets the role via brute memorization because Nick cannot remember his lines. Both Fenson and Nick stumble over Shakespearean English, which has been constructed as social shorthand for a particular class. The contrast between Fenson and Nick goes beyond fluency in standard English or dialects. While Fenson is cast as a dialect-speaking "local boy," son of working-class parents, Nick, a native English speaker, is aligned with western modernity. Fenson, vying for Audrey's hand, receives advice from his best friend and sidekick, Leon Deli (Kevin Murphy), to buy something from Tiffany & Co., for that is "what a [modern] girl like Audrey would want." Purchasing the gift and reciting Romeo's lines seem to have cured his stutter and given him courage to approach Audrey.

Sonic Ethnic Lines

Race and ethnicity are not only visible and palpable but also audible in the multilingual film. The aural genealogy in *Chicken Rice War* evokes larger questions about ethnocentrism and accents. The copresence of Singlish, English, Malay, Mandarin, Cantonese, and a range of Chinese dialects rub against the ongoing "Speak Good English" campaign backed by the state and the government's slogan that Singapore is the "New Asia." Mandarin has historically been codified to be the only acceptable Chinese dialect, because Han Chinese are the single largest ethnic group. Consistent with the film's agenda, *no* character in the film speaks Mandarin, or at least Mandarin with the standard accent. Listening to the incidental music and sounds of other cultures, as Chapter 1 delineates, is an integral component of intercultural understanding. Directors such as Ninagawa and Kurosawa fuse incidental music with contrasting cultural motifs to disassociate sounds from exclusive cultural origins. The present chapter has shown that actively and unconsciously listening for accents enacts racialization as much as the visualization of linguistic differences, for, as Jennifer Lynn Stoever theorizes, "listening operates as an organ of racial discernment, categorization, and resistance."[11] Different dialects and accents operate in the overdetermined aural landscape of *Chicken Rice War* as a repository of ethnic identities in formation and contestation. Among Shakespearean English, Singlish, Cantonese, Mandarin, and other sonic registers, characters find their dominant listening habits challenged. They listen attentively and selectively when someone speaks with their preferred accent, and they filter out or mishear what the ethnic Others have to say.

Though recitation of Shakespearean passages seems to have "cured" Fenson of his personality and speech deficiencies, other scenes expose the instability of any illusion about Shakespeare's universal utility. As Mark Thornton Burnett posits, the film demolishes "the illusion that Shakespeare constitutes a universal language."[12] The text of *Romeo and Juliet* haunts, informs, and structures *Chicken Rice War*, not only because rehearsals and the final performance of key scenes of the play parallel the offstage life of the characters, but also because these reenactments serve as reminders of the film's investment in critiquing the popular belief that enacting Anglo-European civilization and speaking standard English are staples of global progressive modernity. The stylized language of *Romeo and Juliet* is recruited by *Chicken Rice War* to create an ironic distance to the hierarchically articulated colloquial multilingualism in the film and in Singapore, in which standard English is regarded as superior to Singlish, which, in turn, is superior to other languages and dialects.

The film is replete with features that both comment on and are designed for multilingual audiences, such as frequent freeze-frame vignettes with texts in English. These character cards introduce characters' names, professions, personalities, and even Chinese zodiac signs (Audrey, for example, is a Tiger). Parallel texts in standard English and Mandarin also appear over selected scenes as extended subtitles to explain Singlish and slangs in dialects. The use of Cantonese creates a parallel universe to the Singaporean film audiences' daily life, where Hokkien is the most commonly spoken local dialect.

The translations that fly onscreen indicate that the film is self-conscious about its own multilingual universe and its multilingual audiences. The texts translate anything between local colloquialisms and verbalized vulgarities in toned-down form. They translate both Singlish—as if it were a foreign language—and Cantonese, a dialect spoken by a small local community, putting Singlish and Cantonese on equal footing. As such, multilingualism serves political, aesthetic, and heuristic purposes.

CheeK's film is designed to ironize and trivialize the "feud" between the Chans and the Wongs. *Chicken Rice War* traverses a complex multilingual terrain where linguistically coded differences define the dynamics of many scenes. Despite the commercial rivalry between the parents of Audrey Chan and Fenson Wong, they are ironically united by their preferred language: Cantonese (although Audrey's father, Vincent, mixes Singlish with Cantonese from time to time). The parental generation converses in Cantonese, while the younger generation speaks mostly Singlish. Marked linguistically, the feud between the two families appears both arbitrary and historically rooted, given the roles of Britain and Malaysia in Singapore's colonial past. The parents' feud is arbitrary, since they speak the same dialect. As a result, they are aligned against the younger generation in terms of linguistic difference. English, Singlish, and Cantonese serve as reminders of biases embedded in both the "Global West" and "New Asia" that Singapore self-consciously embodies—the latter of which is part of the government's slogan for tourism development. The characters are self-aware of the cultural crossroads where they stand and where Singapore finds itself. The familiar trope of "star-crossed lovers" is turned inside out in this tragedy-turned-parody. Contrary to *The King and the Clown* (Chapter 3), the tension between the stage and the screen as media of expression in *Chicken Rice War* leads to a comedy of incongruity and mismatched identities onstage and off.

Multilingualism as practiced in Singapore and as portrayed in the film creates a heteroglossic social space where conflicting voices coexist. The city-state's propaganda emphasizes commercial cosmopolitanism and transnational histories of immigration in the service of economic growth. *Chicken Rice War* brackets the government's promise that the four official languages—Malay, English, Mandarin, and Tamil—are equal. English is repeatedly demonstrated to be the preferred language that conveys authority and power, both in the framing device featuring a television newscaster reporting on, and conducting interviews about, the conflicts between the Wong and Chan families, and in scenes that align English—even with a Singaporean accent—with global, modern culture. It is bad enough for characters whose primary language is not English. It is even worse, in terms of their social standing, for those who cannot code switch or do not speak even one of the four official languages, such as the parents. Many characters, including the newscaster in the opening scene (before being chastised by his supervisor), speak Singlish, a creole used colloquially that is based on vernacular English, Malay, and Mandarin. Complete with its own syntax and slangs and governed by a topic-prominent structure, Singlish features sentences that are interspersed with mood particles and that often end in sentence-final particles, such as *la*. These sentence-final particles convey information on linguistic modality or register to qualify the preceding phrase; they do not carry referential meaning. Multiracialism, backed by state-endorsed multilingualism, has been a distinctive feature of Singapore's nation-building project since independence. In promoting coexistence—and cohabitation in public-housing projects—the government seeks to downplay the more threatening, heterogeneous cultures of the various ethnicities in favor of a "four races model": the "multiracial CIMO (Chinese, Malay, Indian and Others) quadratomy."[13] For example, Tamil Muslims are not included in this quadratomy.

In the festival scene, parts of this quadratomy are singled out for their diametrically opposed cultural values and performance genres defined temporally and spatially: traditional Cantonese opera and modern, American-style, pop concert. The Chans' and Wongs' decisions to sponsor each performance at the Hungry Ghost Festival reflect their outlooks, as the traditional theatre in a dialect is coded as a symbol of backward mentality, whereas the modern pop concert is cast as youthful and progressive. The Malay Fat Lady gets her big break at the festival by performing scenes from Cantonese operas. Her big night does not seem to attract a large audience or much applause; it is primarily a fulfillment of her dream to be onstage. Her identity as an overweight Malay woman attempting to embody Chinese cultural heritage feeds into what Kenneth Paul Tan has called a "racial fantasy of cultural superiority" on the part of the Han Chinese majority in Singapore.[14] At the same time, with the Fat Lady being an under-appreciated character, the film also questions the racialized fantasy of the seamless assimilation of minorities into Singapore's dominant culture.

Despite the two families' emotional investments in the relative merits of their genres of choice, other characters do not seem to make a distinction in this multigenre and multilingual environment. Ng Chee Kong, a hawker center board member, tells us that he supports both families because having two concerts would make "the gods twice as happy." Ahmad and Muthiah, the two "outsider" characters who frequently make comments from the sidelines, also say that they fully support the two concerts despite their perceived incongruity. Here the filmmaker does bracket the reactions of Ng and the "Chorus" as disingenuous. Their body language betrays that they are delivering a standard response because they are on camera. After reaffirming that the two concerts are for "all races" to enjoy, Ahmad and Muthiah even launch into comedic, exaggerated chanting of government slogans that, through such a multilingual Hungry Ghost Festival, "we can become One People, One Nation, One Singapore." They are carried away by repeating the refrain in unison and start singing it. Unlike the Fool in Shakespearean drama, who speaks truth to power, Ahmad and Muthiah act cowardly and comment unintelligently on events. Their motivation for leaking the date of the hygiene inspection to both families is the preservation of both stalls, so that they can continue to have a space to hang out. Commenting on the incongruent arrangement to hold both an opera and a pop concert, they regurgitate the national slogans that Singapore "is home where all races can enjoy." Showing how a Malay buffoon and an Indian bumbler turn propaganda of nation building into slapstick comedy puts pressure on the national narrative of Singapore's independence or secession, depending on viewpoints, from Malaysia.

This is but one of many instances where the film problematizes and mocks slogans of superficial multilingualism at the expense of fostering meaningful diversity. The film transacts in character stereotypes fueled by multilingualism. While the idea of sponsoring a Cantonese opera comes from Fenson Wong's father, Sydney (Kelvin Ng), the proposal for a pop concert comes from Audrey Chan's younger sister,

Penelope (Su Ching Teh). She suggests to her father early in the film that instead of working hard cooking chicken, they could make bigger and easier money by trademarking their recipe and franchising "Chans' Hainan Chicken Rice." Penelope, who is more anchored in her local, Cantonese-speaking community, serves as a foil to Audrey, who is cast as a stereotypical westernized, English-speaking, materialistic Chinese Singaporean. Characters describe Audrey as sexually attractive, but multiple scenes frame her in a negative light: disingenuous and shallow. Audrey confesses to Fenson—who symbolizes a bona fide "local boy"—that so far almost all her friends are Eurasians and Caucasians. Audrey comments rather condescendingly that she never thought "Chinese boys" could share her love of Shakespeare, as they are only "geeky" and into math and science. There is a strong thread of commercialized ethnic deculturalization—the replacement of Singaporean Chinese heritage by Anglophone culture of the dominant group. In contrast to Audrey, dialect-speaking characters are depicted as crude; they, for example, have never been to a play, and they rush, like animals, for food at the Hungry Ghost Festival.

The intermingling of different languages and the social code-switching create a multilingual space for the mysterious feud in Shakespeare's play. Multilingualism in the film is not part of cosmopolitan imaginations of hybridity or harmony. Quite the contrary, it serves to highlight social tensions. For the younger generation in the film, performing *Romeo and Juliet* becomes part of their quest for self-identities in their formative years. The clash of stratified linguistic spaces enables identity creation and contestation. Singaporean theatre, as scholars point out, is a space for constructing imaginative geographies, notions of citizenship, and voices from the margins.[15]

Chicken Not So Well Received

It is important to recognize the linguistic landscape of Singaporean cinema around the time *Chicken Rice War* was filmed. The film emerged on the heels of the success of *Money No Enough*, which paved the way for other films featuring both dialects and Singlish.[16] In fact, both films employ the same styles of camerawork and editing, notably whooshing shots, rapid cuts, short sequences, MTV-style singing, and vignettes introducing key characters. Written by Jack

Neo and directed by Tay Teck-Lock in 1998, *Money No Enough* was the first film almost entirely in Hokkien, one of the dialects in Singapore, to pass the review of the Media Development Authority. At that time, the Films Act of 1981 dictated that films in dialects (Hong Kong films in Cantonese, for example) be dubbed in Mandarin for commercial release in Singapore. The success of the film led to a sequel, *Money No Enough II* (dir. Jack Neo, 2008).

A local hit (S$5.84 million in box-office return in four months on a budget of S$850,000), *Money No Enough* parodies Singapore's money-obsessed culture through its comic depiction of the financial woes of three friends—reflecting the serious financial collapse during the Asian economic crisis (1997–99). The success of *Money* drew investors to more film projects the following year, but none—including *Chicken Rice War*—turned out to be as successful. *Money No Enough* and *Chicken Rice War*—regardless of their box-office returns—did break new ground in multilingual home productions without enforced dubbing. *Money No Enough*'s use of Hokkien indicates that the film targets local Singaporean audiences; the prevalence of Cantonese in *Chicken Rice War* suggests that it is more ambitious in targeting the Hong Kong market and the Cantonese-speaking diaspora worldwide.

Multilingualism has functioned as a form of contestation and experimentation in film and theatre. In Singapore, a city-state of 5.5 million residents separated from Malaysia by the Johor Strait, multilingualism carries with it the historical gravity of British colonization, Malaysian rule, and eventually Singaporean independence. The race riots in Singapore in 1964 led to the Malaysian parliament's vote in 1965 to expel Singapore from its federation. Linguistically coded differences remain pertinent, despite the official rhetoric of multilingual harmony. One example is the notorious hostility against Filipinos. Expatriate Filipinos planned to celebrate the Philippines' Independence Day in 2014, only to be forced by racist opposition online to cancel their plans.[17] Another example is the general election of 2011, hailed as a political landmark, in which the ruling People's Action Party (PAP) received its lowest percentage of the popular vote in its more than four decades of history since independence in 1965. The opposition parties, which enjoyed relative success in this election, have long claimed that the electoral system is unfair to ethnic minorities who disagree with the Chinese-dominated PAP.[18] Even though the 1965 Proclamation of Singapore affirms the people's "inalienable right . . . to be free and independent," self-determination remains elusive.[19] As Jothie Rajah writes, Singapore "has adopted the colonial legal regime in a manner that renders the nation-state a neo-colonising entity, subordinating and infantilising citizen-subjects."[20] The shift of tides in the 2011 election is therefore a watershed event. Multilingualism, a political tool in Singapore's nation-building project to deemphasize differences among local communities, may be headed toward a new model of equality built on the acknowledgment of differences.

In terms of local and international reception, *Chicken Rice War* exemplifies films that succeed intellectually but not commercially in the local box office. After playing for three weeks in Singapore, the film, with a budget of S$800,000, managed to recoup only S$400,000 via the box office. With a S$250,000 investment from the Singapore Film Commission, *Chicken Rice War* was the first project to be sponsored by the SFC.[21] The establishment of the SFC in 1998 was part of the government's project to develop a national film industry after having attained economic prosperity. The government, ever pragmatic and sensitive to commercial prospects, began pegging economic value to artistic production when, in the 1990s, it decided to transform Singapore from a "cultural desert" into "a vibrant global city of the arts."[22] *Chicken Rice War* rode this wave of government-backed local filmmaking, though it also exhibits some traits of films set and shot in Singapore from this era: outlandish plots, uneven performances, repetitive styles, predictable subjects, and a shoestring budget.

Though the film is not available in high-resolution versions on DVD and is not in wide circulation beyond Asia in the VCD (video compact disc) format, it did have an impact locally and was screened at international film festivals. It received the Discovery Award at the Toronto International Film Festival (2001) and the Special Jury Award at the Miami Film Festival (2002), and was nominated for best film at the Buenos Aires International Festival of Independent Cinema (2002).

CheeK's *Chicken Rice War* is part of a group of Singaporean films that, on one hand, provide audiences with instant gratification by foregrounding and critiquing ethnic stereotypes and, on the other, problematize Singapore's hegemonic, multiracial policies informed by commercial demands and the public discourse of ethnic identities defined by multilingualism. Through the narrative framework of *Romeo and Juliet*, the film encodes cultural difference in a heteroglossic setting. The parody questions the efficacy of the state rhetoric of resolving tensions within "an ethnically diverse population" through harmonious multiracialism.[23]

Multilingual *Lear* and *Desdemona*

Multilingualism in live performances highlights more prominently the discord among performance styles than does multilingualism onscreen. *Chicken Rice War* explores the pitfalls of multilingualism within Singapore, and Ong Keng Sen's theatre works take the debate to the global stage. While Tse's *King Lear*, discussed at the beginning of this chapter, and Wu Hsing-kuo's *Lear Is Here* (Chapter 2) have borne personal significance for their creators to varying extents, Ong Keng Sen's pan-Asian multilingual production of *King Lear* pits linguistically coded alliances against national identities. Tse sees the question of self-identity as fluid in the diaspora; Wu superimposes autobiographical traces onto *Lear Is Here*. Ong, however, brings the amalgamated performance styles from Noh, *pencak silat* (Indonesian martial arts), *jingju* (Beijing opera), and other traditional theatres to personify a "new Asia" that is having an ongoing dialogue with "the old, with traditions, with history."[24] Over the years, Ong created several multilingual and multimedia adaptations that defy easy categorization: *Lear* (1997 and 1999), a multilingual stage work; *Lear Dreaming* (2012), a multimedia musical-theatre piece; *Desdemona* (2000), a multimedia installation and performance event; and *Search: Hamlet* (2002), a site-specific "dance-theater event" designed for Kronborg Castle in Denmark. In 1996, Ong began planning his Shakespearean trilogy around the themes of the individual and family (*King Lear*), the individual and race (*Othello*), and the individual and politics (*Julius Caesar*). He was attracted to the conflict among multiple identities in *King Lear*. However, for financial reasons and artistic considerations, Ong was unable to execute the plan to adapt all three plays. The invitation from the Hamlet Sommer Festival replaced *Julius Caesar* with *Hamlet* as the last piece in Ong's trilogy. These works are diasporic in the sense that although the director is from Singapore, these works can hardly be said to have solely a Singaporean origin. Ong's works are created in fragments in multiple locations, often outside Singapore and in collaboration with a transnational team, and deftly re/assembled, staged, and consumed in site-specific contexts all over the world.

Ong's works deal in symbols rather than linear narratives. English speakers are accustomed to think of stories as narratives whose meanings are governed by sequential events—something that unfolds chronologically (e.g., Lear's gradual descend into madness follows the division of his kingdom). By contrast, works such as Ong's *Lear* and *Lear Dreaming* show dreamlike visions as an apparition, as Lear's shadows. A series of symbols evoke discrete thematic and plot elements of *King Lear*. Therefore, these works contain a penumbra of Shakespeare's and other adaptations of *King Lear*. Historical productions of Shakespeare are akin to an opaque object that casts a shadow with a partially shaded outer region around Ong's adaptations of *Lear*. Judith Buchanan theorizes that adaptations contain a "textual penumbra," a body of extra-textual information that is closely associated with the adaptations and that enriches the meanings of the adaptations.[25] An innocuous penumbra could be audiences' awareness of previous works by the artist. A more intrusive penumbra could be directors' statements on record or the significance of the venue (such as the Kronborg Castle for Ong's *Search: Hamlet*).

A multilingual penumbra would include conflicting voices and styles of speech within the same narrative. In his pan-Asian *Lear*, an allegorical work, a character named the Old Man, played by Naohiko Umewaka, appears downstage, walking slowly in the solemn style of Japanese Noh theatre. He chants, "Who am I?" in Japanese. A character named the Older Daughter approaches him and answers in Mandarin in a stylized high-pitched voice typical of *jingju*:

OLD MAN   (*in Japanese*) Ware wa namimono nariya [Who am I]?

> Ware wa shi no nemuri o nemurite itaru mono [Sleeping in terror of a nightmare I cannot recall].
> Omoidasenu akumu ni osoware nagara nemurite itaru mono [I was sleeping the sleep of the dead] . . . .
> Inishie ni ware wa nanimono nite arishiya [Who was I long ago]?

OLDER DAUGHTER   (*in Mandarin*) Fuqin. Nin shi wo de fuqin [Father. You are my father].

OLD MAN   (*in Japanese*) Chichi towa nanzoya [What is a father]?
OLDER DAUGHTER   (*in Mandarin*) Fuqin jiushi sheng wo zhi ren [Father is
     the being who created man]. (scene 1)

Their philosophical conversation—carried out in two languages and
two distinct performance styles—is followed by a ritualistic division-
of-the-kingdom scene. Adding to the linguistic discord is Jiang Qihu's
cross-gender performance of the Older Daughter in *jingju* style with a
headdress. The Old Man's questions—"Who am I?" and "What is a
father?"—are far from rhetorical, though the Older Daughter's initial
response evades the real question about their relationship. After
pointing out that a father is the one who creates her "from a drop of
[his] love," the Older Daughter shifts the focus to herself, to the
question of who she is. The Older Daughter defines the patriarchal
role as one that exerts the power to bring a person into being. She
aspires to hold such a position and does not hesitate to make her
thoughts known throughout the play. The Old Man's composure and
measured delivery of his lines echo the Older Daughter's stylized
jingju performance. The Younger Daughter (Cordelia) speaks Thai,
though she remains silent most of the time. In the Older Daughter's
assessment, "she is always silent. Nobody knows what she is scheming
in her mind." The Older Daughter, a composite figure inspired by
Goneril and Regan in *King Lear*, dominates the play. At the end, the
Older Daughter stabs the Old Man and declares herself "a powerful
puppeteer." She soon realizes, however, that "killing you, I become
myself"; she relapses into an undesirable gendered mode of thinking
and existence, becoming the patriarchal figure she wished to eliminate,
and now she has to live with it. In addition to the idea of theatrical
doubles and surrogation, Ong's *Lear* singles out the theme of mis-
communication in *King Lear*.

   The production features four languages (Chinese, Japanese, Thai,
and Indonesian); six nationalities; and the performance styles of *jingju*,
Noh, and *pencak silat*, among others. The assassins sent by the Older
Daughter speak Indonesian, and the list of languages and styles goes
on. Actors and characters search for a new Asian identity through this
multilingual production. The audience members are reminded of their
own limitations when they are confronted by a plethora of familiar and
defamiliarized linguistic and cultural signs in the dialogue between the

Japanese-speaking father and his Mandarin-speaking daughter, along with the supertitles in the dominant language of the city where *Lear* is then being performed.

Lear contains local references that draw their energy from a shared history—pleasant or ugly—among various Asian nations. The confrontation between the Japanese-speaking patriarch and his Mandarin-speaking daughter brings to mind the Sino–Japanese conflicts throughout the twentieth century. The production opens with Lear's probing question about self and other ("Who am I?") and closes with the Older Daughter's question that goes unanswered but for a great silence and a sense of solitude: "Who is behind me?" One might say that a major Japanese funding agency is behind her, or that the entangled national and colonial histories of East and Southeast Asia are behind her. Allegorical in structure (characters are given names similar to those in fables; the Older Daughter has three shadows named Vanity, Unpredictability, and Ambition), Ong's *Lear* builds echoes of Shakespeare's lines in the dialogues and the supertitles to amplify and undermine the power of language, much as *Chicken Rice War* creates a polyphony of accents and registers from Shakespeare, hawker-center slangs, and a college production in Singlish and Cantonese. The reception of Ong's *Lear* has been positive among academics in and beyond Asia. While the Japanese theatre critic Yuji Odajima expected more tension from the presence of so many theatrical styles and languages onstage, William Peterson calls it Singapore's "most singularly ambitious work to date to cross cultural divides," because the lack of reciprocity among different cultural elements actually preserves their distinct identity.[26]

Showcasing the clashes of multiple languages is not the goal of such works. In retrospect, Ong wrote that "after *Lear*, I was dissatisfied with simply directing an Asian production that juxtaposed many different languages and many different traditional forms" and that he wanted to "encourage the intercultural process."[27] Ong and his nonprofit company TheatreWorks (founded in 1985) focus on staging multilingualism as a process. A full video of the 1997 production and the documentary *The Making of Lear* are available at globalshakespeares. mit.edu/lear-ong-keng-sen-1997/

Desdemona continues the same line of inquiry about self-identity but takes the multiplicity of languages and the diachronic adaptive process to a different level. *Lear* is an experiment in the potentially liberating force stemming from the discord among different languages and performance styles competing against one another for stage space and time. *Desdemona* is a bold statement about cultural translation as a capacious notion, wrestling with some ideologies within the text of *Othello*. It puts pressure on the missing pre-history of Desdemona and translates into images and music competing narratives about Desdemona and Othello. In the same vein as Mary Cowden Clarke's nineteenth-century rewriting, "Desdemona: The Magnifico's Child" in the first volume of *The Girlhood of Shakespeare's Heroines*,[28] Ong's *Desdemona* tells the story from Desdemona's perspective and offers the backstory of her life before meeting Othello. Ong's production embellishes the main characters' intertwined histories with image-rich narratives of the suppressed history of Othello's young bride. Like the Older Daughter who kills the Old Man in *Lear*, Desdemona takes action against the parochial colonial power structure. She returns as a ghost to haunt Othello, transforms him into a woman, and enters his body and kills him with her kiss.

Desdemona's story is told through live stage actions and heavily mediatized presentations, including film sequences and live video feeds. She is portrayed by Singaporean Malaysian actress Claire Wong onstage and has an onscreen double named Mona, who never appears onstage. Likewise, Othello—transformed from a mercenary general into a colonizer—is played by a younger Kutiyattam actor and an older Kathakali actress in an androgynous mode. Ong continues to explore imagined and contested originary sites in his other adaptations.

One of the video sequences in *Desdemona* bluntly reminds the audience in no unambiguous terms that "I do not speak your language, and you do not speak mine." This is part of an interview curated for the show by the installation artist Matthew Ngui, who splits his time between Singapore and Australia. The interview sequence documents diverse worldviews of members of the ensemble behind *Desdemona*, and their suspicion and anxiety about the rehearsal process and about one another are laid bare onstage as the action of *Desdemona* continues. Another instance where the audience is granted a sneak peek at the ensemble's thought process is a series of emails seen on monitors. Low Kee Hong—a versatile dancer skilled in ballet, Balinese dance, *butoh*

(Japanese modern dance), and other genres who plays Ambition (one of the Older Daughter's three shadows in *Lear*)—sends a series of candid emails to Mona. Low's probing questions are indicative of the actors' anxiety about the visions of the *Desdemona* project: "Are we simply pawns in Keng Sen's game?" "Do we provide an instant Asia exotic tidbit for the festival market?" Such questions break the fourth wall and bring audiences backstage.

A full video of the 2000 production of *Desdemona* at the Adelaide Festival, the short video projected on stage, and the documentary *The Making of Desdemona* are available at globalshakespeares.mit.edu/desdemona-ong-keng-sen-2000

Through his touring activities, Ong has been sensitized to his own positionality. He asked himself in a reflection piece he wrote after the production, "Are *Lear* and *Desdemona* the new Peter Brook *Mahābhārata*?" (that is, are they examples of western mindless borrowing of Asian materials without reciprocal access to prestige?). "Am I buying Asian art just like Europeans and Americans before, fascinated by otherness?"[29] *Desdemona* did not offer answers to Ong's candid questions, but the anxiety about misappropriation is shared by many theatre makers. While Ong is uncomfortable about being seen as the Asian answer to Peter Brook or Pina Bausch, the spirit of his works compels us to consider his "parallel truths" in a broader context.[30] Ong has every reason to complain that "It's fine when Pina Bausch or Richard Foreman is obscure but good Asian companies should provide an 'ethnic evening out.'" *Desdemona* was his attempt to reveal the biases against the contemporary Asian work, especially when it incorporates but does not simply celebrate traditional performing arts.[31] His works are distinguished from other "foreign" or national Shakespeares by their insistence on the plurality within compartmentalized units of meanings, echoing the postcolonial critic Gayatri Chakravorty Spivak, who is strongly opposed to any attempt to formulate "Asian-ness" as a site of shared heritage or values:

Asia—the entire thing, something of it you can find in the distinction between the Mediterranean and North Africa and the rest of Africa, but it's not as peculiar as the divisions within Asia. That's why it's an impossible interpellation. It's either plural, and you have to live with that plural interpellation, or it's globalized and the name means nothing, except sectorially, or it's completely narcissistic.[32]

Like the Québécois director Robert Lepage, who conceded in 1995 that "if I do Shakespeare, I never really end up doing Shakespeare,"[33] Ong is not concerned with reproducing the valence and plots of Shakespeare's plays for his Singaporean or international audiences. Between 1992 and 1994, Lepage produced a Shakespeare cycle consisting of *Macbeth*, *La Tempête*, and *Coriolan* with "tradaptations" in Québécois by poet Michel Garneau.[34] Both Lepage and Ong are known for their strong directorial concepts and use of distinct, visually oriented metatheatrical frameworks that draw attention to the meaning-making process itself. Ong's trilogy suggests that neither Asia nor Shakespeare has consolidated interests.

The reception of *Desdemona* has been mixed. During a postshow discussion of *Desdemona* in Munich, an audience member commented on how "metatext and framing devices" disrupted his otherwise peaceful enjoyment of "the clear story in the traditional dance/music sequences."[35] Ong is frustrated by this type of response, driven by persistent cultural essentialism. Clearly the stakes are high, and resistance is strong (not least from audiences that insist on cultural purity), for a touring Asian company from a multilingual city-state.

To combat such stereotypes, Ong's *Lear* tackles the notion of linguistic authenticity. It reveals the deeply unsettling yet productive discord behind the veil of multilingual globalism mediated by a dominant language. Taking this one step further, *Desdemona*, or "*Othello* from a female perspective," as the *Hamburger Abendblatt* called it,[36] confronts the authenticity of self-representation through extensive metatheatrical and multimedia scaffolding around gender and the performers' personal identities. In Ong's own words, it is "a cultural study about a group of Asian artists looking at themselves and rethinking the ways in which Asia has been represented on the stage in the past."[37] *Desdemona* is thus both a performance and a laboratory for cross-cultural interactions.

One of the key themes for *Lear* and *Desdemona* is the politics of naming. "Who am I?" asks the Old Man and Othello at the beginning of their respective plays. The characters' names in *Lear* are replaced with generic, relational signifiers (the Old Man versus the Older Daughter), and the Older Daughter conspires throughout the play to take the Old Man's place, to seize all that is signified by the figure of the head of the house. The childless Othello does not seem to have a distinct identity, for both his father and his grandfather (who colonized Desdemona's people) were named Othello. In contrast to Othello's lack of distinct identity, Desdemona does not have a name to begin with: "We used to have names but now we are numbers." Her mother secretly gives her the name Desdemona. In naming her thus, her mother brings her into existence. "Desdemona" names all that is connected to her mother and the feminine. Desdemona later repeats her mother's act of naming. Playing on "words" and its anagram "sword," she tells the slave character that "I will give you a name. Your name is Sword." Naming provides a common ground for a dialogue but also gives palpable shapes to ideas, fear, and love: a spying Othello grows fearful and kills Desdemona. Ong, like many Asian directors before him, had to confront the thorny question of naming his adaptations of Shakespeare. Why *Lear*—naming that which connects the early modern and postmodern playwrights—and not a more distinct, local name for this Asian tale about patricide? Reusing Shakespeare's play title signals a political action, a conscious attempt to reference a common "standard" while exposing each culture's blind spots as they encounter the other. It also symbolizes Ong's possession and repurposing of Shakespeare's play.

Both *Lear* and *Desdemona* are products of the collaborative effort between Ong and the Japanese avant-garde playwright and director Kishida Rio (1950–2003). A leading feminist, Kishida was interested in staging the predicament of women in the modernization process as well as in male-dominated societies.[38] Her play *Thread Hell* (1984) follows a girl who searches for and eventually kills her mother. Ong and Kishida built upon several points of contention in *King Lear* and *Othello*, such as the figures of surrogate mother and failing patriarch, and exerted pressure on those points in their rewritings. Beyond the politics of intralingual space, gender roles and gendered cultural differences are prominent themes in these plays as well. Despite her multiple intra-Asian collaborative productions, Kishida is only known outside Japan for her role in Ong's *Lear*. She is one of the few feminist playwrights in Japan, but unfortunately *Lear* and *Desdemona* have come to be known primarily as Ong's despite her appearance in Ong's documentary *The Making of Lear*.

Multilingual *Search: Hamlet*

The politics of naming also informs Ong's approach to the question about self and other ("Who am I?") in another work in his trilogy. *Search: Hamlet*, a site-specific performance event at "Hamlet's castle," deconstructs unexamined assumptions about authentic localities through an even more ambitious multilingual, transnational cast and styles. It recognizes that languages are often assumed to be connected to "native" sites, where particular languages are spoken. In *Search: Hamlet*, the ideological weight of naming deconstructs the putative authenticity of the performance location. The questions of who Lear is and why *Lear* matters are now replaced by the question of why *Hamlet* in Elsinore (Helsingør)? Commissioned by the Hamlet Sommer Festival in Denmark, the performance highlighted the connections and disjunctions between its sites of origin—Asia, Europe, America—and its performance venue, Kronborg Castle, in order to recast the narratives about originary sites driven by tourism and festivals. The "Hamlet castle" where a festival is held each summer is an authentically fake "historical" site for *Hamlet* that boasts connections to the fictive setting of Shakespeare's play. The castle and the festival organizers capitalize on Kronborg's fictive connection to Shakespeare to attract tourists and festivalgoers. The performance was billed as an indoor and open-air dance-theatre event in which Hamlet is missing yet omnipresent because of his absence. Aptly titled *Search: Hamlet*, the production sent its performers and audience in search of Hamlet and the new meanings of Shakespeare's tragedy when different languages meet in Elsinore.

Search: Hamlet shares some similar features with *Lear*, but it also marks a new beginning in Ong's intercultural engagements. The production premiered at Kronborg Castle (August 16–23, 2002) and then ran for another three nights (September 22–24) at the Edison annex to the Betty Nansen Theatre in Copenhagen. *Search: Hamlet* does not align each culture with its traditional form of expression (e.g., Mandarin with Beijing opera). Revisions in *mise en scène* were made to suit each venue. Ong pointed out that while Kronborg might be foreign to some Asian artists unaccustomed to performing in such a space, the castle is not alien to Ann Crosset, an American dancer-choreographer who has lived in Denmark for many years. What passes as local is defined not by "native" language, race, ethnicity, or cultural heritage but rather by lived experiences.[39]

Search: Hamlet continues the themes of identity formation and identity crises that Ong explored in *Lear* and *Desdemona*. With race-blind casting, Ong intends to avoid "a simple substitution of an Asian face for a European face."[40] It is not the only multilingual production to have been performed at the castle. In 2006, Italian director Eugenio Barba staged *Ur-Hamlet*, a play based on Saxo Grammaticus's *Vita Amlethi* (1200), in the courtyard of Kronborg as part of the Hamlet Sommer Festival. Though similar to Ong's piece in terms of its multicultural framework, Barba's production featured forty-eight Japanese, Indian, Afro-Brazilian, and European performers and musicians, including Balinese *gambuh* dancers, as well as a chorus of forty actors from twenty-five countries. Hamlet was played by the Condomblé (Afro-Brazilian religious) dancer Augusto Omolù with headdress, simultaneously distancing and reproducing the familiar princely figure.

The scenes in *Search: Hamlet* are arranged into five "books," following the style of a Noh play. The first half of the performance began in different rooms in the castle and moved gradually into the courtyard. Due to this logistical complication, the audience members could not have a full view or knowledge of the entire performance. During the first part of *Search: Hamlet*, they could choose to join one of the simultaneous guided tours through the basement or different rooms of the castle, walking past costumes and actors in preparation, similar to the immersive experience of audiences of Punchdrunk's site-specific performance installation, *Sleep No More* (dir. Felix Barrett and Maxine Doyle, London, 2003, New York, 2011, Shanghai, 2016). The second half of the play is a tour de force of the five books, including a prologue and an epilogue: Book of the Ghost, Book of the Warrior (Laertes), Book of the Young Girl (Ophelia), Book of the Mad Woman (Gertrude), and Book of the Demon (Claudius). A short documentary made by the Chinese filmmaker Wu Wenguang, dealing with gay culture in Beijing, was shown during the interval, which reminded the audience of the homemade movie in Michael Almereyda's film *Hamlet* (2000 [Chapter 2]) that replaces the play within a play and provides a self-reflexive moment.

Full videos, the video projected on stage ("Search for Hamlet in China"), interviews, and highlights of different versions of *Search: Hamlet* are available on pages curated by Alexa Alice Joubin in the *MIT Global Shakespeares*: the Kronborg Castle version at globalshakespeares.mit.edu/search-hamlet-ong-keng-sen-2002-two, and the Edison Theatre version at globalshakespeares.mit.edu/search-hamlet-ong-keng-sen-2002/

Pulling this diverse group of characters and actors together is a Noh-style Storyteller, who was performed by Charlotte Engelkes from Sweden. The Storyteller comments with heavy irony that she is "not yet playing Hamlet." She doesn't know where he is, which is "why everybody is looking for him."[41] Following the Danish theatre tradition of commemorating a renowned performer, the Storyteller danced with a spotlight—a "living space," as Ong called it. The spotlight came to represent Hamlet. As a "living space," Hamlet's presence in the end suggested rather than confirmed any "concrete [dramatic] situation."[42]

Search: Hamlet deconstructs the myth about authentic, originary sites. Ong no longer mingles different iconic cultural symbols that align languages and "native" performance styles, as he does in *Lear*. Here he pursues a radical form of multiple narratives in order to drive home the message that everyone is Hamlet and that essentialist, linguistically coded constructions of national identities are simply irrelevant to diasporic cultures. His version of *Hamlet*—featuring Asian, European, and American singers and performers—revolves around tourists' search for sites of origin at the famous but fictional "Hamlet's castle" in Denmark and secondary characters' reflections on *Hamlet*.

By dissolving Hamlet's presence, Ong probes an important theme: Hamlet's disinheritance. In Shakespeare, Claudius' ascension triggers the prince's fear of becoming a dispossessed heir, while Fortinbras, the prince's foil with military prowess, and Laertes, a son resolved to avenge his father, both threaten to further marginalize Hamlet in the court, making the prince invisible and irrelevant as a weak-willed, indecisive son.[43] Ong's production interprets Hamlet's actions as attempts to assuage his fear of dispossession—his fear of having a weak and now absent father, and his fear of becoming his weak father. Ong's approach echoes recent scholarship that has shifted *Hamlet*'s central concern from introspective psychology of interiority—inner life—to international politics. Dynastic anxieties of dispossession and loss of empire emerge as the themes in Margreta de Grazia's analysis of Shakespeare's uses of *Aeneid* as foundational national epic and Peter S. Donaldson's interpretation of the First Player's speech on the death of Priam (2.2.453–500). The "extinction of the royal house of Denmark" parallels the Fall of Troy which the First Player references.[44]

The thematic shift from interiority to international politics is not coincidental. Transnational networks of funding and collaboration were important factors in shaping Ong's trilogy. *Search: Hamlet* was sponsored by a number of private, government, and (trans)national funding agencies, including the Asia-Europe Foundation (ASEF), Danish Centre for Culture and Development (DCCD/CKU), Singapore National Arts Council, Embassy of Japan, Embassy of Indonesia, and Danish Theatre and Music Council. *Lear* and *Desdemona* were supported by myriad transnational funding agencies, including the Japan Foundation Asia Center (JFAC).

The mandates of some of these organizations helped to shape these works. Established in 1972, the Japan Foundation promotes overseas Japanese-language education. In 1995, the Asia Center was formed as a subsidiary organization to promote "the coexistence of different ethnic groups" and "the harmonization of traditional and contemporary culture."[45] The JFAC has an intra-Asian focus, believing that mingling Asian arts and cultures can help tackle various social ills triggered by the rapid development and accumulation of wealth in Asia. Ong's *Lear*, funded by the JFAC, thus took an intra-Asian approach to intercultural performance and to Shakespeare's text. This intraregional focus can also be seen, with revisions, in some of his other works.

Diasporic Subject Positions

Each of the three directors—David Tse Ka-shing, Chee Kong Cheah (CheeK), and Ong Keng Sen—takes a different approach to portraying multilingualism and diaspora. All of them occupy precarious, diasporic positions between cultures and between various places they call home at different points in time. As a member of the British East Asian (BEA) community, one of the three largest ethnic minority groups in the United Kingdom, Hong Kong-British director Tse has worked to raise awareness about the invisible minority group. His Yellow Earth Theatre was the only BEA company supported by box-office income in Great Britain. He speaks of himself as being "bicultural" and finds that critics and artistic managers have treated his "dual heritage" as something that either can "be negotiated with a patronising attitude" or is simply too unpalatable—impossible to understand.[46] His bilingual *Lear* seeks to tackle the dual heritage through two languages and two texts (Shakespearean and Tse's).

A Malaysian-born Singaporean director and producer, CheeK creates works for television and cinema that comment on Singapore's positionality at the crossroads of Southeast Asia and in the world. CheeK's, unlike that of Ong, career has focused on Singapore. In 2015, he was appointed the chief content officer at Mediacorp, a Singaporean broadcast conglomerate. Although *Chicken Rice War* was not released internationally, its palpable impact in Singapore and Malaysia is evidenced by a short documentary video in 2013 produced by *Straits Times* Razor TV.[47] Presented by journalist Shawn Lee Miller, the video, also called "Chicken Rice War," was shot in the style of whooshing camerawork similar to that in CheeK's film. Miller interviews people at eateries to gather their views on the controversy over the origin of two popular dishes. Singaporeans were riled up over the Malaysian tourism minister's claim to cultural ownership of Hainanese chicken rice and chili crab. Dubbed a "chicken rice war" between the two countries, the controversy is presented in the video as a symptom of the ongoing political and cultural tension between Singapore and Malaysia. Interviewees from various ethnic backgrounds respond in Singlish, English, and Mandarin, though we hear the interviewer speak exclusively in English. CheeK's *Chicken Rice War* also inspired a full-length stage adaptation in English in neighboring Malaysia by secondary-school students at SMK Batu Lintang, where Malay is the primary language of instruction. The student production, also titled *Chicken Rice War*, mimicked the *mise en scène* of the film, complete with two mobile kitchenette sets where the Chans and the Wongs prepared their chicken rice dishes; it won second place at the Kuching District English Drama competition in 2018.[48] The intra-Asian circulation of the metaphor of a chicken rice war, created by CheeK, bears regional significance much as

Akira Kurosawa's approach to western classics has influenced other Asian directors.

Ong calls himself "a child of the diaspora" who is inventing "the future and the histories from which [diasporic people] come."[49] He has had more than his fair share of western bias against Asian arts, which is why he refused to serve up an Asia in an "ethnic evening out" that symbolizes the "return to nature" or the "spiritual connection" to transport the "first world . . . away to another time."[50] His parents emigrated to multiethnic Singapore from southern China, and Ong speaks English, Mandarin Chinese, and a southern Chinese dialect. Ethnic Chinese comprised 76.8 percent of Singapore's population, and Malays and Indians 13.9 and 7.9 percent, respectively, in 2000.[51] Ong's multicultural background and Singapore's cultural policy to encourage border-crossing works contributed to his inclination to fuse multiple performance traditions in order to critique the form of multiculturalism at work at various international festivals, as well as in Singapore's slogan of being the "New Asia." Equally significant to his work is that Ong is fluent in English and well versed in the academic vocabulary of postcolonial and intercultural performance; this is one reason some of his works have found a ready home in academia and are better received by academics than by festival audiences. The founding artistic director of TheatreWorks in Singapore, Ong received his training at the Tisch School of the Arts at New York University. Many of TheatreWorks's projects explore the psychological and political dimensions of the acts of departing from and arriving at a location, including migration and cultural otherness.

Ong uses multiple languages, supertitles, and mixed performance styles and media to problematize the assumption that Asian and Anglo-European cultures can be condensed into "East" and "West." He has striven to raise awareness of the politics of the production and consumption of exotic spectacles. At the same time, his work has been described as "highly self-conscious, deeply Asian, and undeniably marketable with its high gloss—even glib—post-modernism."[52] Despite his apparent success at securing funding and international touring invitations, Ong has maintained that marketability should not take over art, because his primary focus is on expanding the meaning of Asia rather than on condensing it for mass consumption. In an interview, he cautioned, "We have to be careful not to stereotype what is meant by 'Asian'—that it has to be traditional or that it has to be filled with history. These definitions of Asian would immediately exclude you [referring to his interviewer] and I [*sic*] in the sense that we are English-speaking and completely contemporary [and urban]."[53] His metropolitan bias notwithstanding, Ong has made important contributions to both Shakespeare's and Asian theatres' current vitality.

Diasporic artists' projects to perform Shakespeare find greater success outside China, Hong Kong, and Singapore. Detached from Singaporean cultures, Ong's *Lear* is designed for international audiences; as a result, it tours successfully outside Singapore. Despite its focus on Singapore, *Chicken Rice War* attracts the attention of more international audiences than Singaporean ones. In Philip Smith's assessment, "Singaporeans . . . preferred to import, rather than produce, Shakespeare" due to "prejudice over accent (as enacted in *Chicken Rice War*) as well as a general tendency to look down upon locally-made works."[54] *Chicken Rice War* fell victim to the cultural attitude it portrays.

Rootlessness and an attitude of at-home-in-the-world are two common features that have come to define the works discussed so far. As the Singaporean scholar Yong Li Lan points out, the multiplicity of languages and cultural signs raises the question of "whether Asia performs Shakespeare, or Shakespeare Asia,"[55] a question that can be answered only when one recognizes one's own geographical or imagined position. With a tense relationship with celebratory polyglot cosmopolitanism, multilingual works deconstruct various conventions of authenticity—signs and practices onstage that are commonly regarded as conveying an authentic slice of a Shakespearean text or a culture.

New Accents and Multilingual Shakespeare

Your accent is something finer than you could purchase in so removed a dwelling.

—*As You Like It* (3.2.334–35)

Multilingual theatre goes all the way back to early modern London, where Shakespeare, Thomas Kyd, and other playwrights flirted with foreign tongues onstage, though contemporary directors and filmmakers have put an extra spin on the genre by dramatizing the promises and perils of the intrinsic mobility of language. The plethora of media and languages in our world has led to Peter Brook's *La Tempête* (1990), with a multiracial cast; Karin Beier's *A Midsummer Night's Dream* (1995), featuring actors speaking a range of European languages and performing in several styles, including *commedia dell'arte*; and Tim Supple's *A Midsummer Night's Dream* (2006–2008), staged in Hindi, Bengali, Malayalam, Marathi, Tamil, Sanskrit, and English with a pan-Asian cast. But unlike these productions, linguistic difference is hardly the only marker of class and identity in CheeK's and Ong's works.

When, where, and for whom is a play by Shakespeare a classical text? What are its cultural affiliations today? How does the Shakespearean canon reorient the relationship between disparate cultures on the move, specifically multilingual diasporic cultures? Multilingual Shakespeares counter the narratives about universal literary experience that are packaged and consumed at international festivals.

As such, they compel us to work with, rather than work out of, the space between languages. In the twenty-first century, Shakespeare's verse is becoming ever more foreign, even to native English speakers, except for a large number of common expressions—for example, "playing fast and loose," being "tongue-tied," recognizing it is "high time"—that circulate out of context (and often not remembered as Shakespearean). Historical distance has led to obfuscation of heterogeneous meanings of these phrases. Subtitled multilingual performances can, on the one hand, erase difference, and, on the other hand, *recognize* difference, with an eye toward equality.

Multilingual performances and Shakespeare with accents have a deterritorializing effect, in the anthropological sense, that unmarks the cultural origins of intercultural productions because they counter assumptions about politically defined geographies in historiography—artificial constraints that no longer speak to the realities of filmmaking and theatre making.[56] For instance, contemporary performances of Shakespeare in England have normalized Northern accents to form some kind of universal, traveling language for productions. One audible, deterritorializing effect of this normalization is that such speech is no longer associated with a region in England but regarded as how Shakespearean language should sound. Onstage, it has the benefits of proceeding apace. Audiences do not have time to process the speech. They would rely on actors' body language to parse the meanings of words. As Carol Chillington Rutter writes,

Northern speech, shortening vowels, hitting consonants, produces a powerful traveling language that, collapsing pronouns and connectives, accelerates the verse line while punching out the nouns and verbs that drive the argument of the speech and the pace of the plays. *With* becomes *w, him, 'em, to do, t'do*. One consequence is that playing times shorten and audiences . . . hear Shakespeare at tempo, hurtling, with no time for second-guessing, through the obstacle courses of his plays.[57]

In response to the dearth of Shakespeare spoken in "the cadences of Singaporean speech" and "a deliberate and sincere Singaporean voice," Philip Smith speculates that the "fast pace, glottal stops, and fully-articulated vowels" of the Singaporean accent offer possibilities for localizing Shakespeare.[58] Accents can connote both a disadvantage and privilege depending on the context. Tuning into accents alerts us to processes of racialization predicated on visual and aural signs. Shilpa S. Davé's research confirms the widespread use of "the performance of accent as a means of representing race . . . beyond visual identification."[59] Global and multilingual Shakespeare performances face an unarticulated bias against non-Anglophone languages and accents. In contrast, Anglophone performers do not seem to shy away from regional accents. As Sonia Massai reveals, UK theatres are increasingly using accents, race, gender and "other crucial markers of social identity" to "challenge a traditional alignment of Shakespeare with cultural elitism."[60]

Beyond new accents, multilingual Shakespeares can obscure the cultural origins of various stage elements. More recently, there has been a shift from an emphasis on essential difference among cultures to a logic of sameness, and Shakespeare's characters and plays are sometimes used as a common ground to mount theatrical experimentation or to market a specific culture abroad. Even though intercultural performance is an obtuse process of signification, we are told by one of South Korea's major newspapers, for example, that a "Korean *Hamlet* Works Well on International Stages" when the production visited Russia, because Shakespeare provides a social shorthand by condensing select aspects of Russian and Korean cultures.[61] Touring productions (Chapter 3) and multilingual and diasporic works (discussed herein) can also reterritorialize the plays as they travel. Performatively defined—rather than geopolitically formulated—locations most effectively describe these works (e.g., a French-Japanese *Richard II* in Paris and on tour; a "culturally neutral" *Richard III* made in Beijing but presented in Berlin). Simplified notions of the universal can be self-deceptive and even self-effacing, as Marvin Carlson points out in his study of Peter Brook and Ariane Mnouchkine, because they "deny the voice of the Other in an attempt to transcend it."[62]

Multilingual Shakespeares put pressure on some of the theoretical models for documenting the western sources of non-western performances. One of the contributions of multilingual Shakespeares is that Viola's question in *Twelfth Night*, "What country, friends, is this?" (1.2.2) when her ship is wrecked ashore, will be asked with increasing urgency and will prompt more reflections on cultural identities that have been taken for granted.

This passage from *King Lear* sums up the nature of cross-cultural appropriation. The banished and disguised Kent tells us, as he approaches the raging King Lear,

> If but as well I other accents borrow,
> That can my speech diffuse, my good intent
> May carry through itself to that full issue
> For which I razed my likeness.　(1.4.1–4)

His statement about borrowed identities, unfamiliar accents, and the ethics of communication echoes the intercultural traffic onscreen and onstage. Performances of Shakespeare have always borrowed other accents—English, American, or otherwise—and the accents we learn from Asian performances help us reexamine familiar and unfamiliar parts of Shakespearean plays and of Asian cultures. As multilingual endeavors work with cultural incompatibilities and limits of translation, Rey Chow urges that "intercultural translation" should treat the "partners in interaction" as "peers" regardless of the number of languages involved.[63] The cases examined in this book show that cross-fertilization and mobility are the norms, not the exceptions.

Appropriating Shakespeare is an act that diffuses the speech and intensifies the vocabulary of performance. Energized by internal divisions and pathways, East Asian Shakespeare in all its forms, from experimental to multilingual, is the prodigal child that ultimately expands the riches of human civilizations.

> He kissed—the last of many doubled kisses—
> This orient pearl.
>
> —*Antony and Cleopatra* (1.5.39–40)

The "doubled kisses" that the messenger tells Cleopatra exemplify the blessing and perils of encounters between premodern and modern cultures. From the perspective of cultural diplomacy, adaptations represent Asia on the world market and are simultaneously the conveyor of Anglophone thought patterns to global audiences. In terms of aesthetics, adaptations trade in dual temporalities and localities between the early modern dramatic universe and the here and now. Part of this duality is encoded in dramatic ambiguity on multiple levels starting with the playtext itself. Some of the best-known examples are the double entendres in Shakespeare. Consider, for example, Macbeth's confession of guilt in the porter scene:

> No; this my hand will rather
> The multitudinous seas incarnadine,
> Making the green one red.
>
> (2.2.57–60)

The use of "incarnadine" and "red" is serendipitous, but the deliberate alternation between words of Latin and Anglo-Saxon roots creates two pathways to Macbeth's guilt in murdering King Duncan. The built-in multilingual redundancy is informed by two perspectives on the world in which he lives.

In other instances, interpreting Shakespeare in a multilingual framework enriches our understanding of words that would have elided attention. In *The Tempest*, what exactly do Prospero and Miranda teach Caliban that the latter should yell, "You taught me language" (1.2.365)? It is often taken to mean his master's language, a symbol of oppression. But it can also mean rhetoric and political speechwriting, a new tool for him to change the world order. Caliban's word, "language," was translated into German as *redden* (speech) by

Christoph Martin Wieland (1766). In Japanese, it is rendered as "human language," as opposed to languages of the animals, or computer language. Take, for example, another word in act 4, scene 1, where Prospero announces that "our revels now are ended" (148). The word "revels" in the Elizabethan context refers to royal festivities and stage entertainments, but it carries different diagnostic significance in translation. Christoph Martin Wieland used *Spiele* (plays) and *Schauspieler* (performer) to refer to Prospero's masque and actors ("unsre Spiele sind nun zu Ende"). Sometimes translators working in the same language have different interpretations. Zhu Shenghao translated it as "carnivals" (1954) to highlight the festive nature of the wedding celebration, but Liang Shiqiu preferred "games" in Mandarin Chinese in 1964, suggesting that Prospero is manipulatively toying with newcomers to the island.

Directors see the multiplicity of meanings as an asset, as "doubled kisses" (*Anthony and Cleopatra* [1.5.39]), because translation is a process that simultaneously defamiliarizes and familiarizes literary works. Global Shakespeares have deconstructed the myth of linguistic purity. Drawing on his own experience as a Maghreb-Algerian and a naturalized citizen of France, Jacques Derrida reminisces that "never was I able to call French . . . 'my mother tongue.'" While French is supposed to be his "maternal" language, he does not create or own its grammar.[1] Perhaps intuitively aware of the benefit of defamiliarization, as instanced by Akira Kurosawa's treatment of *Macbeth* (see Chapter 1), and skeptical of assuming ownership of one's native language, director Peter Brook worked closely with poet Ted Hughes as he conceptualized his film of *King Lear* (Athéna Films, 1971). Hughes rewrote part of the play in his distinctive poetic voice; Brook, having worked with Hughes's "translation," was then able to engage with *Lear* (in Shakespeare's language) from a renewed perspective. Hughes's contribution was recasting the tragedy in language "that could neither roll automatically off the tongue through years of intimate acquaintance nor provoke too much learned reverence," thereby jostling "out of its usual linguistic cadences."[2] In the words of the film's producer, Michael Birkett, this exercise reinvigorates the play's "essential themes."[3] The benefits of the exercise remained stable even when Brook did not film *Lear* using Hughes's lines. Brook's method of finding directions out by indirection is similar to how non-Anglophone directors adapt Shakespeare. Judith Buchanan compares Brook to Kurosawa, observing that both directors enjoy the "luxury . . . of coming fresh . . . to the specific language of a play" in translation.[4] Kenneth Rothwell similarly regards filming Shakespeare in foreign languages as a freedom to reinvent the plays in "purely cinematic terms."[5]

Words Made Flesh

The *translingual* property—when phrases are relevant but may not necessarily mean the same things in different languages—makes all performances of Shakespeare inherently fluid and translational in the dramaturgical and gestural senses.[6] British theatre director Tim Supple elucidates Shakespearean narratives rather than simply reenacts the purportedly untranslatable language of poetic drama. One of Supple's most well-known works is *A Midsummer Night's Dream* with a pan-Asian cast in seven languages (RSC, 2006–2008; see Chapter 4). When audiences of different backgrounds encounter such perform-ances, their horizons of expectation enrich the event, even though not all layers of allusion and wordplay are activated at all times. Unlike pigments that make up a painting or individual notes that constitute a musical work (both of which are often transparent to the audience),[7] non-Anglophone performances of western classics frequently draw attention to their formal features and thereby enable new paths to the cultures being represented, as evidenced by the example of gender discord in the Japanese productions of *Twelfth Night* in the Prologue.

English-language performances, too, constantly seek to carve new paths through plays with dense layers of meanings. A frequently stated myth is that Shakespearean drama is all about its poetic language, and adaptations in another language would violate the "original." The history of performance and reception in and beyond the Anglophone world suggests otherwise. As J. L. Austin theorized in *How to Do Things with Words*, words do not mean in and by themselves, and this is especially true for drama. The force of performance arises in the "terrain between language and its enactment," as W. B. Worthen's analysis of Austin shows.[8] Words—in any language—acquire mean-ing when spoken in context and embodied by actors. Drama gains efficacy through stage behaviors and embodiments. Additionally, audiences would find many scenes confusing without seeing the actors performing them. Some scenes would lose their dramaturgical impact if only read and not performed. Examples include the mock trial in *King Lear* (13.16–52 [Quarto]) where, without modern stage directions, it would not be immediately clear that Lear is speaking to a piece of furniture ("joint-stool"); the appearance of Banquo's ghost at the banquet in *Macbeth* (3.4); and the fifteen characters (eight of whom are in disguise) in *Love's Labour's Lost* (5.2).

Deep Connection

There are, as we've seen, deep connections among Asian and Anglophone performances beyond the translingual property of drama. Peter Brook's production of *Titus Andronicus* (1955) in Stratford-upon-Avon (starring Laurence Olivier and Vivien Leigh) replaced conventional, naturalistic portrayals of horror with Asian-inspired stylization (such as scarlet streamers signifying Lavinia's rape and mutilation) and an abstract, minimalist set. Brook's work anticipated the use of red ribbons to symbolize blood in Yukio Ninagawa's production of the same play in 2006 as part of the Royal Shakespeare Company's Complete Works festival. The Singaporean film *Chicken Rice War* (2000; Chapter 4) pointedly parodies global teen culture in Baz Luhrmann's campy *Romeo + Juliet* (1996). Sherwood Hu's Tibetan film *Prince of the Himalayas* (2006; Chapter 2) contains visual echoes of Millais's iconic Pre-Raphaelite painting *Ophelia* (1851/1852) and creates an Ophelia figure deeply associated with water. Wearing a floral wreath, Odsaluyang (Ophelia) dies giving birth in the sacred Namtso Lake to Hamlet's and her baby; the scene thus alludes not only to Millais's *Ophelia* but also to the cyclical quality of life and death in Tibetan Buddhism. Michael Almereyda appropriates Asian spirituality in his Buddhist-inflected film *Hamlet* (2000; Chapter 2), set in twenty-first-century Manhattan: the Vietnamese monk Thich Nhat Hanh is featured in a spin-off of the "To be or not to be" speech; Ophelia is depicted as interested in Krishnamurti's *On Living and Dying*; and a clip from Ulrike Koch's *The Saltmen of Tibet* (1998) is viewed in Claudius's limousine.

Asian directors, too, have appropriated spirituality as an alternative source of wisdom, though their agenda is not to elucidate Shakespeare but to curate personal voices. Taiwanese *jingju* actor-director Wu Hsing-kuo encodes Buddhism in his solo *Lear Is Here* (2007), which concludes with him circling the stage, dressed in a monastic robe, asking one of the key questions posed by Shakespeare's Lear: "Who is it that can tell me who I am?" (1.4.212). This scene offers a space for reconciliation between Wu's internal conflict as a Taiwanese actor professing a Chinese art form when China is a military threat to Taiwan.

It is important to note that, in some instances, the transhistorical connections between Shakespeare and "us" are articulated not on the epic scale (as in Kurosawa's *Throne of Blood*) but on a personal scale, as in Wu's autobiographical responses to nine of *King Lear*'s characters in his *Lear Is Here*.

Some adaptations are so well received that they have their own afterlives in which performances are not always routed through Shakespeare. Take *Macbeth*, for example. This iconic tragedy has a long and varied history of Asian-style enactments in Japanese, Mandarin Chinese, Korean, English, and Spanish. One of the best-known versions is Kurosawa's samurai film *Throne of Blood* (1957), which has been so successful over the past sixty years that it has been cited as the inspiration for new works in and beyond Asia: Ninagawa's Kabuki-style, "cherry blossom" *Macbeth* (1980); Arne Zaslove's "Wild West" stage production (1982; revived in 1990); Wu Hsing-kuo's Beijing opera *The Kingdom of Desire* (1987); Alwin Bully's Dominican adaptation, *McB* (1997); and Aleta Chappelle's Caribbean film (long in development by Moon Shadow Films since 2013).[9] Wu pays homage to Kurosawa throughout his adaptation of *Macbeth* and, most notably, in his bravura final scene, where soldiers below shoot arrows, made of the wood from the forest, at Macbeth— rendered in the *wusheng* (martial male) role type—on a balcony, a theatrical rendition of the final scene in Kurosawa's epic film. Other Asian-style productions influenced by Kurosawa include Tadashi Suzuki's all-male *The Chronicle of Macbeth* (Japanese, 1991; English 1992), Shōzō Satō and Karen Sunde's *Kabuki Macbeth* (1987–1988), Satō and Sunde's *Kabuki Lady Macbeth* (2005), and Charles Fee's Kabuki-inflected *Macbeth* (2008) (these last three in English). There is even a visually faithful stage production of the film in English, *Throne of Blood* (dir. Ping Chong), staged at the Oregon Shakespeare

Festival in 2010.[10] Another play that recycles visual elements from Kurosawa, notably the witch figure, is John R. Briggs's *Shogun Macbeth* (1985), an English-language adaptation set in twelfth century Honshu (see Chapter 1). *Shogun Macbeth* coincided with Japan's rising economic influence in the United States in the 1980s and American culture's interest in select Japanese cultural tokens, which continued into the new millennium. All these works either map the English imaginary of Scottish incivility onto what are perceived to be equivalent Asian contexts (as Kurosawa's film does with feudal Japan), or create a new performance idiom from amalgamated elements from various traditional Asian styles (as Satō's productions do). It is not uncommon for artists to combine unfamiliar styles of presentation with English texts, including Shakespeare's, of which native English speakers tend to assume ownership.

These rich cross-references, cross-pollinations, and touring activities suggest that adaptations of the western canon have intraregional and global significance. Non-Anglophone Shakespeares are not antithetical to English-language performances; both must negotiate pathways to contingent meanings through transhistorical and cross-cultural axes. All performances, with their unique cultural coordinates, are best understood in a comparative context. A similar framework has recently been deployed in other fields of study, such as American literature, which, Wai Chee Dimock proposes, is best understood as "a crisscrossing set of pathways, open-ended and ever multiplying, weaving in and out of other geographies, other languages and cultures."[11] My rhizomatic understanding of global Shakespeare adds transhistorical and textual–somatic dimensions to comparative literature, that is, actors' embodiment of texts from historical periods as well as their own time. While most students might think they understand what Asian and Shakespeare performances entail, neither Asia nor Shakespeare has an intrinsic, unified identity in any meaningful sense without context. Texts that actors embody include cultural ideologies, playscripts, and screenplays, as well as the legacy of other films and performances.

Adaptations of the western canon in Asia, Latin America, and Africa are sometimes regarded as distinct national projects with little connection among one another. Further, in South Africa, Shakespeare's role in cultural globalization is often characterized as "a conduit for Empire."[12] The story of Shakespeare and East Asia, in contrast, unfolds in a nonlinear, rhizomatic, transgenre network of transcultural flows. There are multiple, nonhierarchical entry points for ideas to flow through disparate cultural spaces and through genres of stage and screen. In the creative fusion of artistry, there are no clear points of origin of "genius." The Royal Shakespeare Company's naturalistic routines are not a universal template for "authentic" Shakespeare; nor are Tang Xianzu's (1550–1616; see Chapter 2) oneiric qualities "authentic" *kunqu* (one of the oldest forms of Chinese opera), nor Chikamatsu Monzaemon's (1653–1725) allegorical frameworks "true" Bunraku and Kabuki. The interactions between Shakespeare and East Asian styles are characterized by a nomadic mode of propagation in which authenticity derives not from national poets but from intrepid contemporary directors and actors. Even the initial introductions of Shakespeare into several East Asian cultures were routed not exclusively through Britain but via Japan and the Soviet Union. European directors have incorporated Asian styles, and Asian directors have drawn on one another's work, creating dense networks of Asian and European motifs in artistic experimentation. Adaptations derive aesthetic and social energy from the collision and fusion of distinct cultural elements in an interstitial space.

Conclusion

What do Asian-style presentations achieve in film and theatre histories? Asian performers and directors have reshaped their genres and Shakespeare to counter the ideological forces of globalization, to critique contemporary national and international politics, and to enrich Asian performance styles through international touring. Directors of Asian Shakespeare performances often emphasize their own cultural contexts and personal styles, rather than the binary mode of East versus West that is favored by popular discourses and the marketing language of international festivals. Their artistic innovation paves the way to a more equitable globalization based on mutual respect of cultural values.

As we enter the third decade of the twenty-first century, performances of Shakespeare have become ever more mobile and agile. The rich and complex history of Asian-themed performances complicates the notion of globalization as necessarily solely global Americanization.[13] For supporters of Taiwanese independence and Hong Kong's cause in the protests against the draconian national security law, the threat of perceived Sinicization (politicocultural affiliation with, or influence by, the People's Republic of China) is much more worrisome than Americanization. Similarly, Japanization is a real threat for Koreans who lived through Japanese colonization, and is therefore a more urgent topic for exploration. These anxieties add distinct local flavors to the performances of Shakespeare's plays.

As cross-cultural and transhistorical works, adaptations promote self-reflexivity on social and personal levels. Artists and audiences become more aware of their cultural positionality. This self-reflexivity enhances the awareness of historical and cultural proximity and distance, of collective cultural memory, and of the theatricalization of difference. The performances are productive in the sense that they are generative: they engender evolving ideas of the Shakespearean canon and Asian modes of expression. These works may pay tribute to Shakespeare or Asia as cultural signifiers, but more important, adaptations actively formulate the meanings of these signifiers.

Notes

PROLOGUE

1. Lorie Brau, "The Women's Theatre of Takarazuka," *TDR* 34.4 (1990): 79–95; 81.
2. Jennifer Robertson's *Takarazuka: Sexual Politics and Popular Culture in Modern Japan* (Berkeley: University of California Press, 1998) remains one of the most thorough studies of the cultural phenomenon of all-female Takarazuka and its female fan base. See also Leonie Stickland's *Gender Gymnastics: Performing and Consuming Japan's Takarazuka Revue* (Melbourne: Trans Pacific Press, 2008).
3. Nobuko Tanaka, "John Caird delivers home truths with *Twelfth Night*: Stage giant bestrides a world of ideas," *The Japan Times*, March 4, 2005, www.japantimes.co.jp/culture/2015/03/04/stage/john-caird-delivers-home-truths-twelfth-night/#.XoOnGtNKgQE, accessed November 1, 2019.
4. Japan: *The Merchant of Venice* as *Sakura-doki zenino yononaka* [It's a world where money counts for everything], 1885. China: *The Merchant of Venice* as *Rou quan* [A bond of flesh], 1913. Korea: *Julius Caesar* by Kyungsong vocational school, 1925. Postcolonial Taiwan: *Othello* as *Yi yun* [Clouds of suspicion], 1949. Taiwan under Japanese colonization: Kawakami Otojiro's *Othello* recasts Taiwan as the outpost of the colonial Japanese empire in the adaptation. Hong Kong: *Shylock, or The Merchant of Venice Preserved*, in English, 1871. Hong Kong: Hong Kong Mummers staged *Twelfth Night* in 1913.
5. Salom Teshale, "Japanese puppeteer returns to campus," an interview, *The Chicago Maroon*, November 6, 2009; www.chicagomaroon.com/article/2009/11/6/japanese-puppeteer-returns-to-campus/, accessed March 30, 2020.
6. D. J. R. Bruckner, "*The Tempest* at New Audience," *New York Times*, March 27, 1986, Section C, Page 15; www.nytimes.com/1986/03/27/theater/stage-the-tempest-at-new-audience.html, accessed March 30, 2020.
7. Scott Hollifield, "The Lionesses and Olive Trees of Meiji-Era Japan: A Consideration of Kenneth Branagh's *As You Like It*," *Borrowers and Lenders: The Journal of Shakespeare and Appropriation* 3.2 (Spring/Summer 2008), http://www.borrowers.uga.edu/781870/show, accessed January 2, 2009.

8. Jonathan Romney, "Jonathan Romney on *Stoker*: Embalming fluid can go a long way," *The Independent*, March 3, 2013, www.independent.co.uk/arts-entertainment/films/reviews/jonathan-romney-on-stoker-embalming-fluid-can-go-a-long-way-8517905.html, accessed March 30, 2020; and Katie Kilkenny, "Trailer critic: Stoker," *Slate*, September 27, 2012; https://slate.com/culture/2012/09/stoker-trailer-park-chan-wooks-english-language-debut-looks-like-brutal-business-as-usual-video.html, accessed March 28, 2020.

9. *Parasite* made Oscar history in 2020 when it won the Academy Award for Best Picture, Directing, International Feature Film, and Writing (Original Screenplay). For reviews that use the label "Shakespearean" describe the film, see Mark Kermode, "*Parasite* review: A gasp-inducing Masterpiece," *The Guardian*, February 10, 2020; www.theguardian.com/film/2020/feb/09/parasite-review-bong-joon-ho-tragicomic-masterpiece, accessed February 10, 2020; and Thessaly La Force, "Why does rage define 'Parasite' and other popular East Asian movies?," *New York Times*, November 26, 2019, www.nytimes.com/2019/11/25/t-magazine/asia-movies-parasite.html, accessed March 15, 2020. Bong's other films include *Okja* (2017) and *Snowpiercer* (2013).

10. Bong Joon-ho, acceptance speech, the 77th Golden Globe Awards, Los Angeles, January 5, 2020.

11. For non-Asian pairings, see Kevin J. Wetmore Jr., *Black Dionysus: Greek Tragedy and African American Theatre* (Jefferson, NC: McFarland, 2003), and *Athenian Sun in an African Sky: Modern African Adaptations of Classical Greek Tragedy* (Jefferson, NC: McFarland, 2002); Toril Moi, *Henrik Ibsen and the Birth of Modernism: Art, Theater, Philosophy* (Oxford: Oxford University Press, 2006); and William Childers, *Transnational Cervantes*, University of Toronto Romance Series (Toronto: University of Toronto Press, 2006).

12. James English, *The Global Future of English Studies* (Malden, MA, and Oxford: Wiley-Blackwell, 2012), 191.

13. Sujata Iyengar and Miriam Jacobson, "Introduction: Shakespearean Appropriation in Inter/national Contexts," *The Routledge Handbook of Shakespeare and Global Appropriation*, ed. Christy Desmet, Sujata Iyengar, and Miriam Jacobson (New York: Routledge, 2019), 2.

14. Sam Wanamaker, "Shakespeare's Globe Reborn," *RSA Journal* 138.5401 (December 1989): 25–34 (Royal Society for the Encouragement of Arts, Manufactures and Commerce). See also, for example, the account of the first years of the reconstructed Globe Theatre on Bankside as a series of heritage exercises that are "deadening and sanitizing what was once alive and radical"; Pauline Kiernan, *Staging Shakespeare at the New Globe* (London: Macmillan, 1999), 3.

15. Peter McCurdy (architect and designer for the Globe Theatre, London), conversation with the author, May 3, 2012. In August 2020, Tom Evans announced the plan to build a replica of the 1614 Globe in Stratford, Connecticut. Anna Bybee-Schler, "Future Of Shakespeare Site Could Be Globe Theatre Replica," *Patch*, August 29, 2020; patch.com/connecticut/stratford/future-shakespeare-site-could-be-globe-theatre-replica?fbclid=IwAR1Pd-VvonSbNLapvtv2YqPDA3CLGVWLL4N7I-hvMKZRm9KteH1ZS60NNTA

16. Joshua Goldstein, *Drama Kings: Players and Publics in the Re-creation of Peking Opera, 1870–1937* (Berkeley: University of California Press, 2007), 270–80; Jonah Salz, "Intercultural Pioneers: Otojiro Kawakami and Sada Yakko," *Journal of Intercultural Studies* 20 (1993): 25–74.

17. Goldstein, *Drama Kings*, 270, 285.

18. Fredric Jameson, "Preface" to *The Cultures of Globalization*, ed. Fredric Jameson and Masao Miyoshi (Durham, NC: Duke University Press, 1998), xi–xvii; xii.

19. Jeffrey R. Wilson, "Why Shakespeare? Irony and Liberalism in Canonization," *Modern Language Quarterly* 81.1 (2020): 33–64; 36.

20. Susan Bennett, "Re-thinking 'Global Shakespeare' for Social Justice" (paper presented at "Shakespeare and Social Justice: Scholarship and Performance in an Unequal World," triennial conference of the Shakespeare Society of Southern Africa, Cape Town, May 16–18, 2019).

21. Peter Holland, *English Shakespeares: Shakespeare on the English Stage in the 1990s* (Cambridge: Cambridge University Press, 1997); Tetsuo Kishi and Graham Bradshaw, *Shakespeare in Japan* (London: Continuum, 2005); Chen Fang, *Shuqing, biaoyan, kua wenhua: dangdai Sha xiqu yanjiu* [Lyricism, performance, and cross-culture: studies in contemporary Xiqu adaptations of Shakespeare] (Taipei: National Taiwan Normal University Press, 2018). There are several edited collections on Shakespeare in Asia, such as Minami Ryuta, Ian Carruthers, and John Gillies, eds., *Performing Shakespeare in Japan* (Cambridge: Cambridge University Press, 2001). Monographs published in more recent years situate adaptations of Shakespeare beyond single-country contexts, though they focus on either film or theatre, such as Katherine Hennessey, *Shakespeare on the Arabian Peninsula*, in Global Shakespeares series ed. Alexa Alice Joubin (New York: Palgrave, 2018); Mark Thornton Burnett, *Shakespeare and World Cinema* (Cambridge: Cambridge University Press, 2013), and *"Hamlet" and World Cinema* (Cambridge: Cambridge University Press, 2019).

22. Rey Chow, "Introduction: On Chineseness as a Theoretical Problem," *Modern Chinese Literary and Cultural Studies in the Age of Theory: Re-imagining a Field*, ed. Rey Chow (Durham, NC: Duke University Press, 2000), 1–25; 3.

23. Ibid. Rey Chow continues: "Hence, whereas it would be acceptable for authors dealing with specific cultures, such as those of Britain, France, the United States...to use generic titles...authors dealing with non-Western cultures are often expected to mark their subject matter with words such as *Chinese, Japanese, Indian, Korean, Vietnamese,* and their like" (3). See also Adele Lee, *The English Renaissance and the Far East: Cross-Cultural Encounters* (Madison, NJ: Fairleigh Dickinson University Press, 2018), 150.

24. Henry Louis Gates Jr., "Talking Black: Critical Signs of the Times," *The Norton Anthology of Theory and Criticism*, ed. Vincent B. Leitch et al. (New York: Norton, 2001), 2424–32; 2428.

25. Siddhartha Deb, "The Rise of the Global Novelist," *New Republic*, April 25, 2017, https://newrepublic.com/article/141676/rise-global-novelist-adam-kirsch-review, accessed September 10, 2019.

26. Tim Parks, "The Dull New Global Novel," *New York Review of Books*, February 9, 2010, www.nybooks.com/daily/2010/02/09/the-dull-new-global-novel, accessed September 1, 2019.

27. Karolina Watroba, "World Literature and Literary Value: Is 'Global' the New 'Lowbrow'?," *Cambridge Journal of Postcolonial Literary Inquiry* 5.1 (2018): 53–68; 53–54. Similar debates take place in other fields, from poetry to film. See, for example, Rebecca L. Walkowitz, *Born Translated: The Contemporary Novel in an Age of World Literature* (New York: Columbia University Press, 2015), 31; Stephen Owen, "The Anxiety of Global Influence: What Is World Poetry?," *New Republic*, November 19, 1990, 28–32; Rey Chow, *Writing Diaspora: Tactics of Intervention in Contemporary Cultural Studies* (Bloomington: Indiana University Press, 1993), 1–5; and David Damrosch, *What Is World Literature?* Translation/Transnation 5 (Princeton, NJ: Princeton University Press, 2003), 18–24.

28. Arjun Appadurai, *Modernity at Large: Cultural Dimensions of Globalization* (Minneapolis: University of Minnesota Press, 1996), 32.

29. Daniel F. Vukovich, *China and Orientalism: Western Knowledge Production and the P. R. C.* (New York: Routledge, 2012), 142–50.

30. Rustom Bharucha, "Foreign Asia/Foreign Shakespeare: Dissenting Notes on New Asian Interculturality, Postcoloniality and Re-colonization," *Shakespeare in Asia: Contemporary Performance*, ed. Dennis Kennedy and Yong Li Lan (Cambridge: Cambridge University Press, 2010), 253–81; quoted in Yong Li Lan's introduction to part IV of that volume, 217–18; 217.

31. Rossella Ferrari, *Transnational Chinese Theatres: Intercultural Performance Networks in East Asia* (Cham, Switzerland: Palgrave, 2020), 10.

32. William A. Callahan, "Sino-speak: Chinese Exceptionalism and the Politics of History," *Journal of Asian Studies* 71.1 (2012): 33–55.

33. "Interview with Gayatri Chakravorty Spivak," in Mark Sanders, *Gayatri Chakravorty Spivak: Live Theory* (London: Continuum, 2006), 104–24; 121.

34. For example, the Edinburgh International Festival was established after World War II in 1947 to "enliven and enrich the cultural life of Europe, Britain and Scotland" and to create "a major new source of tourism revenue" for its host city; Edinburgh International Festival, www.scot land.marylea.me.uk/EdinburghFestival/index.html and http://eif.co.uk/ about, accessed accessed March 20, 2020.

35. Ian Watson, "Introduction: Contexting Barba," *Negotiating Cultures: Eugenio Barba and the Intercultural Debate*, ed. Ian Watson (Manchester: Manchester University Press, 2002), 1–17; 3.

36. Gilles Deleuze and Félix Guattari's approach is parallel to the concept of economic deterritorialization (the phenomenon that some transnational corporations have more financial power than the state), as discussed in their two-volume *Capitalism and Schizophrenia*: *Anti-Oedipus* (vol. 1, 1972), trans. Robert Hurley, Mark Seem, and Helen R. Lane (London: Continuum, 2004), and *A Thousand Plateaus* (vol. 2, 1980), trans. Brian Massumi, Continuum Impacts (London: Continuum, 2004). Originally published as *Mille Plateaux* (Paris: Les Éditions de Minuit, 1980).

37. James Richardson, "A Thing Most Brutish: The Calibanization of the African American Male," *Still Not Equal: Expanding Educational Opportunity in Society*, ed. M. Christopher Brown II (New York: Peter Lang, 2007), 355–66; Ali Farka Touré, quoted in liner notes to Ali Farka Touré and Ry Cooder, *Talking Timbuktu* (Hannibal Records, HNCD 1381, 1994), n.p., http://db55.net/tt.html, accessed March 11, 2020.

38. Deleuze and Guattari, *A Thousand Plateaus*, trans. Brian Massumi, 2 vols, Vol. 2 "Capitalism and Schizophrenia" (London: Continuum, 2004), 7, 16, and 25. Originally published as *Mille Plateaux* (Paris: Les Éditions de Minuit, 1980).

39. J. L. Styan, *The Shakespeare Revolution: Criticism and Performance in the Twentieth Century* (Cambridge: Cambridge University Press, 1977), 5.

40. James C. Bulman. "Introduction: Shakespeare and Performance Theory," *Shakespeare, Theory, and Performance*, ed. James C. Bulman (London: Routledge, 1996), 1–11; 2–3.

41. Barbara Hodgdon, "Introduction: A Kind of History," *A Companion to Shakespeare and Performance*, ed. Barbara Hodgdon and W. B. Worthen (Oxford: Blackwell, 2005), 1–9; 4.

42. Marvin Carlson, *The Haunted Stage: The Theatre as Memory Machine* (Ann Arbor: University of Michigan Press, 2001); Bulman, ed., *Shakespeare, Theory, and Performance*; W. B. Worthen, *Shakespeare and the Authority of Performance* (Cambridge: Cambridge University Press,

1997); Peggy Phelan, *Unmarked: The Politics of Performance* (London: Routledge, 1993).

43. Taiwan is the first and, so far, the only country in East and Southeast Asia to offer national recognition of gay marriage. On May 17, 2019, Taiwan's Executive Yuan and Legislative Yuan passed the "Act for Implementation of Judicial Yuan Interpretation No. 748," and the president signed it into law on May 22. The law allows same-sex couples to marry with almost all the rights of heterosexual married couples under the Civil Code. However, same-sex married couples are allowed to adopt only children genetically related to one of them.

44. Nobuko Anan, "Theatre of Kishida Rio: Towards a Re-Signification of 'Home' for Women in Asia," *Women in Asian Performance: Aesthetics and Politics*, ed. Arya Madhavan (London: Routledge, 2017), 110–23; 120–21.

45. Walter Benjamin, "The Task of the Translator" ["Die Aufgabe des Übersetzers," 1923], *Illuminations: Essays and Reflections*, ed. Hannah Arendt, trans. Harry Zohn (Boston and New York: First Mariner, 2019), 11–25.

CHAPTER I

1. Shin Jeong-ok, *Hangug-eseoui seoyang-yeongeug: 1990 nyeon–1995 nyeonkkaji* [Western Theatre in Korea from 1900 to 1995] (Seoul: Sohwa Press, 1999), 43, cited in Kyounghye Kwon, "The Hilarity of Unhappiness in Oh Tae-suk's *Tempest*: Cross-Cultural Access and Precolonial/Indigenous Aesthetics," *Asian Theatre Journal* 34.1 (2017): 75–96; 75.

2. François Truffaut, "Une Certaine Tendance du cinéma français" ("A certain tendency in French cinema"), *Cahiers du cinéma* 6.31 (1954): 15–29.

3. Geoffrey Reeves, "Shakespeare on Three Screens: Peter Brook Interviewed by Geoffrey Reeves," *Sight and Sound* 34.2 (1965): 66–70; interview with Peter Hall, *The Sunday Times*, January 26, 1969. Peter Brook, CBE, author of the influential *The Empty Space* (1968), is a winner of the Laurence Olivier Award and several Tony and Emmy awards. Sir Peter Hall founded the Royal Shakespeare Company in 1960 and was director of the National Theatre during 1973–88.

4. Stephen Prince, *The Warrior's Camera: The Cinema of Akira Kurosawa*, rev. and exp. ed. (Princeton, NJ: Princeton University Press, 1999), 351–53; 353. Prince further elaborates that Lucas's *Star Wars* takes inspiration from Kurosawa's 1958 *The Hidden Fortress*. Both films feature a dethroned princess and her loyal followers fleeing through enemy territory. The robots R2-D2 and C–3PO in *Star Wars* are transpositions of the feuding peasants Tahei and Matakishi in *The Hidden Fortress*.

5. Aragorn Quinn, "Political Theatre: *The Rise and Fall of Rome* and *The Sword of Freedom*, Two Translations of *Julius Caesar* in Meiji Japan by Kawashima Keizō and Tsubouchi Shōyō," "Shakespeare and Asia," ed. Alexa Huang, special issue, *Asian Theatre Journal* 28.1 (2011): 168–83. For a cover image of the book see Ben-Ami Shillony, *The Jews & the Japanese: The Successful Outsiders* (Rutland, VT and Tokyo: Charles E. Tuttle, 1991), 115.

6. Indra Levy, *Sirens of the Western Shore: The Westernesque Femme Fatale, Translation, and Vernacular Style in Modern Japanese Literature* (New York: Columbia University Press, 2006), 208. The play's title has often been translated into English as "Mercenary Affairs under the Cherry Blossoms."

7. *Brief Sketch of Geo. C. Miln and Some Criticisms on His Dramatic Ability* (Chicago: Fergus Printing Company, 1883), digital copy of the original from Harvard University, 2008; see also Kaori Kobayashi, "Between the East and the West: Tsubouchi Shoyo's Production of *Hamlet* in 1911," *Renaissance Shakespeare: Shakespeare Renaissances: Proceedings of the Ninth World Shakespeare Congress*, ed. Martin Procházka, Michael Dobson, Andreas Höfele, and Hanna Scolnicov (Newark, DE: University of Delaware Press, 2014), 220–28; 225.

8. Masahiko Masumoto, *Yokohama Gēte-za: Meiji Taishō no Seiyō Gekijō* [The Yokohama Gaiety Theatre: The Western-Style Theatre in the Meiji and Taisho Eras], 2nd ed. (Yokohama: Iwasaki Kinen Press, 1989); Kaori Kobayashi, "Touring in Asia: The Miln Company's Shakespeare Productions in Japan," *Shakespeare and His Contemporaries in Performance*, ed. Edward J. Esche (Aldershot: Ashgate, 2000), 53–72.

9. Muri Mitsuya and Nishi Issho, eds., *Engeki-shi to Engeki-riron* [Theatre History and Theory of Drama] (Tokyo: NHK Publishing, 1988), 130.

10. Ryuta Minami, "Chronological Table of Shakespeare Productions in Japan 1866–1994," *Shakespeare and the Japanese Stage*, ed. Takashi Sasayama, J. R. Mulryne, and Margaret Shewring (Cambridge: Cambridge University Press, 1998), 257–331; 258; Yoshiko Kawachi, "*The Merchant of Venice* and Japanese Culture," *Japanese Studies in Shakespeare and His Contemporaries*, ed. Yoshiko Kawachi (Newark, DE: University of Delaware Press, 1998), 46–69; 50–51.

11. Fukuda Tsuneari, "Directing Shakespeare," *Gekijō e no shōtai* [An Invitation to Theatre] (Tokyo: Shincho-sha, 1957), 165–88. Quoted in Tetsuo Kishi and Graham Bradshaw, *Shakespeare in Japan* (London: Continuum Press, 2005), 31–32.

12. Kishi and Bradshaw, *Shakespeare in Japan*, 46–49.

13. For the regional "transculturation" of Japanese literature, see Karen Laura Thornber's *Empire of Texts in Motion: Chinese, Korean, and Taiwanese Transculturations of Japanese Literature* (Cambridge, MA: Harvard University Asia Center, 2009).

14. Engelbert Kaempfer, *De beschryving van Japan*, 3 vols. (Amsterdam: Jan Roman de Jonge, 1733).

15. Dennis C. Washburn, *The Dilemma of the Modern in Japanese Fiction* (New Haven, CT: Yale University Press, 1995); Stephen Vlastos, ed., *Mirror of Modernity: Invented Traditions of Modern Japan* (Berkeley: University of California Press, 1998).

16. Quinn, "Political Theatre," 170.

17. Robert Tierney, "*Othello* in Tokyo: Performing Race and Empire in 1903 Japan," *Shakespeare Quarterly* 62.4 (2011): 514–40.

18. Ayako Kano, *Acting Like a Woman in Modern Japan: Theater, Gender, and Nationalism* (New York: Palgrave Macmillan, 2001), 107.

19. Shoichiro Kawai, "Kabuki *Twelfth Night* and *Kyogen Richard III*: Shakespeare as a Cultural Catalyst," *Shakespeare Survey 64: Shakespeare as Cultural Catalyst*, ed. Peter Holland (Cambridge: Cambridge University Press, 2011), 114–20. "Shakespeare as Cultural Catalyst" had been the theme of the 2010 International Shakespeare Conference in Stratford-upon-Avon, August 8–13.

20. Izumi Kadono, "The Kabuki Version of *Hamlet*: *Hamlet Yamamoto No Nishikie*," *Shakespeare Yearbook 9: Shakespeare in Japan*, ed. Tetsuo Anzai et al. (Lewiston, NY: Edward Mellen, 1999), 105–21; 108–109, 117.

21. Kuniyoshi Munakata Ueda, *Noh Adaptation of Shakespeare: Encounter and Union* (Tokyo: Hokuseido Press, 2001), viii–ix. His *Noh Hamlet* toured as a solo performance to Britain, Sweden, Denmark, and Canada in 1990. I thank Ueda for sharing his knowledge of Noh and for his book.

22. Tadashi Suzuki, "Culture Is the Body," *Interculturalism and Performance: Writings from PAJ*, ed. Bonnie Marranca and Gautam Dasgupta (New York: PAJ Publications, 1991), 241–48. A video of the stomping in *A Tale of Lear* may be viewed at https://globalshakespeares.mit.edu/the-tale-of-lear/#video=the-suzuki-method-stomping.

23. "Interview with Suzuki Tadashi," *Performing Shakespeare in Japan*, ed. Minami Ryuta, Ian Carruthers, and John Gillies (Cambridge: Cambridge University Press, 2001), 196–207; 196–97.

24. Dennis Kennedy, *Looking at Shakespeare: A Visual History of Twentieth-Century Performance*, 2nd ed. (Cambridge: Cambridge University Press, 2002), 314; Minami, "Chronological Table," *Shakespeare and the Japanese Stage*, 328–31.

25. The Tokyo Globe reopened in 2004 under new management and moved away from a Shakespearean repertoire. Michiko Suematsu, "The Tokyo

Globe Years 1988–2002," *Shakespeare in Hollywood, Asia, and Cyberspace*, ed. Alexa Huang and Charles S. Ross (West Lafayette, IN: Purdue University Press, 2009), 121–28; 125.

26. Kishi and Bradshaw, *Shakespeare in Japan*, 90.

27. David Lindley and Bill Barclay, "Introduction," *Shakespeare, Music and Performance*, ed. Bill Barclay and David Lindley (Cambridge: Cambridge University Press, 2017), 1–13; 4.

28. Jacques Derrida, *The Ear of the Other: Otobiography, Transference, Translation*, ed. Christie McDonald, trans. Peggy Kamuf and Avital Ronell (Lincoln: University of Nebraska Press, 1988), 50–51.

29. Derrida, *Ear of the Other*, 51.

30. Derrida, *Ear of the Other*, 35.

31. Marcus Tan, *Acoustic Interculturalism: Listening to Performance* (London: Palgrave, 2012), 21–22.

32. Daniel Gallimore, *Sounding Like Shakespeare: A Study of Prosody in Four Japanese Translations of "A Midsummer Night's Dream"* (Hyōgo: Kwansei Gakuin University Press, 2012), 174.

33. Ramona Wray, "Music in Contemporary Shakespearean Cinema," *Shakespeare, Music and Performance*, 209–22; 209.

34. Melissa Croteau, "Wicked Humans and Weeping Buddhas: (Post)humanism and Hell in Kurosawa's *Ran*," *Shakespeare on Screen: King Lear*, ed. Victoria Bladen, Sarah Hatchuel, and Nathalie Vienne-Guerrin (Cambridge: Cambridge University Press, 2019), 47–61; 47–48; J. M. Shields, "Kurosawa, Akira (1910–1998)," *Encyclopedia of Religion and Film*, ed. Eric Michael Mazur (Santa Barbara: ABC-CLIO, 2011), 279–83; 279.

35. Evelyn Tribble, "'When Every Noise Appalls Me': Sound and Fear in *Macbeth* and Akira Kurosawa's *Throne of Blood*," *Shakespeare* 1.1–2 (2005): 75–90; 85.

36. Mark Thornton Burnett, "Akira Kurosawa," *Welles, Kozintsev, Kurosawa, Zeffirelli*, Great Shakespeareans 17, ed. Mark Thornton Burnett et al. (London: Bloomsbury, 2015), 54–91; 61.

37. Kendra Preston Leonard, *Shakespeare, Madness, and Music: Scoring Insanity in Cinematic Adaptations* (Lanham, MD: Scarecrow Press, 2009), 81–82.

38. Leonard, *Shakespeare, Madness, and Music*, 82.

39. Leonard, *Shakespeare, Madness, and Music*, 82–83.

40. Anthony Dawson, "Cross-Cultural Interpretation: Reading Kurosawa Reading Shakespeare," *A Concise Companion to Shakespeare on Screen*, ed. Diana E. Henderson (Oxford: Blackwell, 2006), 155–75; 167–68.

41. Dawson, "Cross-Cultural Interpretation," 169.

42. Jessica Chiba, "Lost and Found in Translation: Hybridity in Kurosawa's *Ran*," *Shakespeare Bulletin* 36.4 (2018): 599–633; 601.

43. In addition to *ore*, other first-person pronouns include the informal *boku*, typically used by young men, and the more formal but more feminine *watashi*, commonly used by women. Tsuyoshi Ono and Sandra A. Thompson, "Japanese *(w)atashi/ore/boku* 'I': They're Not Just Pronouns," *Cognitive Linguistics* 14.4 (2003): 321–47. I am grateful to Daniel Atherton for sharing his insights on the Japanese pronouns and drawing my attention to their usage in *Throne of Blood*.

44. From time to time, Mitsuha, a high-school girl living in a small mountain town, would inexplicably swap bodies with Taki, a high-school boy in Tokyo. When inhabiting the other's body, they strive to act normal (that is, Mitsuha would have to act and talk like the boy she now embodies, and Taki would have to adopt feminine speech patterns when in Mitsuha's body). Comical scenes ensue when they fail, such as when Mitsuha—waking up and going to school in Taki's body—slips and uses the feminine, singular first-person pronoun.

45. Shoichiro Kawai Shoichiro, "Ninagawa Yukio," *The Routledge Companion to Directors' Shakespeare*, ed. John Russell Brown (London: Routledge, 2008), 269–83; 279–80.

46. "Tempesto: Sadoshima no rehasuru," anonymous interview with Ninagawa, *Marie Claire* (Tokyo), January 1987; translation by J. Thomas Rimer quoted in Kennedy, *Looking at Shakespeare*, 315.

47. Marcus Tan, *Acoustic Interculturalism: Listening to Performance* (London: Palgrave, 2012), 115.

48. Peter Whitebrook, review of *The Ninagawa Macbeth*, *The Scotsman*, August 23, 1985.

49. Michael Ratcliffe, review of *The Ninagawa Macbeth*, *The Observer*, August 25, 1985.

50. Akira Kurosawa, Hideo Oguni, and Ide Masato, *Ran: The Original Screenplay and Storyboards*, trans. Tadashi Shishido (Boston: Shambhala, 1986), scene 67, 46, quoted in Prince, *Warrior's Camera*, 288.

51. Prince, *Warrior's Camera*, 289.

52. Maurice Hindle, *Shakespeare on Film*, 2nd ed. (New York: Palgrave, 2015), v.

53. Quoted in Prince, *Warrior's Camera*, 341, and in Ben Nicholson, "Kurosawa vs Shakespeare," *BFI: Film Forever*, www.bfi.org.uk/news-opinion/news-bfi/features/kurosawa-vs-shakespeare, accessed January 31, 2019.

54. Kennedy, *Looking at Shakespeare*, 12, 5.

55. Prince, *Warrior's Camera*, 142.

56. Hindle, *Shakespeare on Film*, 2nd ed., 124–25; emphasis in the original.

57. Neil Forsyth, *Shakespeare the Illusionist: Magic, Dreams, and the Supernatural on Film* (Athens: Ohio University Press, 2019), 144–45.

58. Brian Parker, "Nature and Society in Akira Kurosawa's *Throne of Blood*," *University of Toronto Quarterly* 66.3 (1997): 508–25; 516.
59. Forsyth, *Shakespeare the Illusionist*, 144.
60. I thank Michael Gnat for drawing my attention to the Greek mythology.
61. Hindle, *Shakespeare on Film*, 126; Neil Forsyth, "Shakespeare the Illusionist: Filming the Supernatural," *Cambridge Companion to Shakespeare on Film*, ed. Russell Jackson (Cambridge: Cambridge University Press, 2000), 280–302; 296; Jack J. Jorgens, *Shakespeare on Film* (Bloomington: Indiana University Press, 1997), 156; Peter S. Donaldson, *Shakespeare Films/Shakespearean Directors* (Boston: Unwin Hyman, 1990), 76.
62. Judith Buchanan, *Shakespeare on Film* (London: Pearson, 2005), 76.
63. Jack J. Jorgens, "Kurosawa's *Throne of Blood*: Washizu and Miki Meet the Forest Spirit," *Literature/Film Quarterly* 11.3 (1983): 167–73, quoted at 172.
64. Buchanan, *Shakespeare on Film*, 79.
65. Tadao Sato, *Kurosawa Akira no sekai* [The World of Akira Kurosawa], Asahi bunko 577 (Tokyo: Asahi shinbunsha, 1986), 253.
66. Buchanan, *Shakespeare on Film*, 78.
67. Peter Brook, *The Shifting Point, 1946–1987* (New York: Harper Collins, 1987), 78.
68. Yukio Ninagawa, *Note 1969–1988* (Tokyo: Kawade Shobō Shinsha, 1989), trans. Ryuta Minami; quoted in Ronnie Mulryne, "From Text to Foreign Stage: Yukio Ninagawa's Cultural Translation of *Macbeth*," *Shakespeare from Text to Stage*, ed. Patricia Kennan and Mariangela Tempera (Bologna: Cooperativa Libraria Universitaria Editrice Bologna, 1992), 131–43; 136.
69. "Interview with Ninagawa Yukio," 212–13.
70. Yukio Ninagawa, program for *The Tempest*, trans. Stefan Kaiser and Sue Henny, Edinburgh International Festival, 1988.
71. Ninagawa, *Note 1969–1988*; quoted in Mulryne, "From Text to Foreign Stage," 141.
72. Ninagawa, *Note 1969–1988*; quoted in Mulryne, "From Text to Foreign Stage," 141.
73. Akihiko Senda, "The Rebirth of Shakespeare in Japan: From the 1960s to the 1990s," trans. Ryuta Minami, in *Shakespeare and the Japanese Stage*, 15–37; 22–23.
74. Huangpu Theatre in Shanghai screened a videotaped version of Ninagawa's 2018 *Macbeth* as "X-Live: Ninagawa x Shakespeare—*Macbeth*" on January 6 and 29, and February 23, 2019.
75. Lyn Gardner, review of *Cymbeline*, *The Guardian*, May 30, 2012; www.theguardian.com/stage/2012/may/30/cymbeline-review-barbican-ninagawa; accessed February 23, 2019.

76. Michiko Suematsu, "Verbal and Visual Representations in Modern Japanese Shakespeare Productions," *The Oxford Handbook of Shakespeare and Performance*, ed. James C. Bulman (Oxford: Oxford University Press, 2017), 584–98; 584.

77. Dennis Kennedy and Yong Li Lan, "Introduction: Why Shakespeare?," *Shakespeare in Asia: Contemporary Performance*, ed. Dennis Kennedy and Yong Li Lan (Cambridge: Cambridge University Press, 2010), 1–23; 17.

78. W. J. T. Mitchell, *Picture Theory: Essays on Verbal and Visual Representation* (Chicago: University of Chicago Press, 1994), 38.

79. Felicia Chan, *Cosmopolitan Cinema: Cross-cultural Encounters in East Asian Film* (London: I. B. Tauris, 2017), 91.

80. John R. Briggs, *Shogun Macbeth* (New York: Samuel French, 1988), 11.

CHAPTER 2

1. Michael Dobson, "Afterword: Shakespeare and Myth," *Local and Global Myths in Shakespearean Performance*, ed. Aneta Mancewicz and Alexa Alice Joubin (London: Palgrave, 2018), 259–65; 262–63.

2. In Fredric Jameson's controversial essay "Third-World Literature in the Era of Multinational Capitalism," which brought modern Chinese writer Lu Xun (1881–1936) to the attention of western readers, Lu Xun's short story "The Diary of a Madman" played a key role in Jameson's argument that "all third-world texts are . . . to be read as . . . national allegories . . . particularly when their forms develop out of predominantly western machineries of representation, such as the novel." Fredric Jameson, "Third-World Literature in the Era of Multinational Capitalism," *Social Text* 15 (Autumn, 1986): 65–88; 69.

3. Fredric Jameson, *Allegory and Ideology* (London: Verso, 2019).

4. I-chun Wang, "Shakespeare's *Cymbeline* in the College English Classroom during the Sunflower Student Movement," *Doing English in Asia: Global Literature and Culture*, ed. Patricia Haseltine and Sheng-mei Ma (Lanham, MD: Lexington Books, 2016), 121–32.

5. Philip Williams, "China's Leader Struts UK Stage," *ABC News (Australia)*, June 26, 2011; www.abc.net.au/news/2011-06-27/chinas-leader-struts-uk-stage/2772846; accessed February 25, 2019.

6. Jill Lawless, "Xi Visits U.K. amid Concerns about China's Influence on British Economy," *Globe and Mail* (Toronto), October 20, 2015; www.theglobeandmail.com/news/world/chinas-xi-jinping-receives-royal-welcome-in-britain/article26883847/; accessed February 25, 2019. Also, "Xi Jinping Visit: UK–China Ties 'Will Be Lifted to New Height,'" *BBC News*, October 25, 2015; www.bbc.com/news/uk-34571436; accessed February 20, 2019.

7. Following Poshek Fu and David Desser's assessment that Hong Kong cinema refracts its status as a former "crown colony with a hybrid culture" and a special administrative region of China under "one government, two systems," Mark Thornton Burnett believes that *One Husband Too Many* embodies the condition of Hong Kong itself. Burnett, *Shakespeare and World Cinema* (Cambridge: Cambridge University Press, 2013), 219. See also Adele Lee, "*One Husband Too Many* and the Problem of Postcolonial Hong Kong," *Shakespeare in Hollywood, Asia, and Cyberspace*, ed. Alexa Huang and Charles S. Ross (West Lafayette, IN: Purdue University Press, 2009), 195–204. Adele Lee, "'Chop-Socky Shakespeare'?! The Bard Onscreen in Hong Kong," *Shakespeare Bulletin* 28.4 (2010): 459–79. Poshek Fu and David Desser, "Introduction," *The Cinema of Hong Kong: History, Arts, Identity*, ed. Poshek Fu and David Desser (Cambridge: Cambridge University Press, 2000), 1–11; 5.

8. Felski develops Paul Ricoeur's theory of a "hermeneutics of suspicion" in European humanistic traditions and what Eve Kosofsky Sedgwick calls "paranoid reading" (151) in her argument about the common symptom of "modernity and the anxieties of the professional class." Informed by a general paranoia about texts never meaning what they say, critics read literature for progressive messages through a "reparative style of criticism" (3). Rita Felski, *The Limits of Critique* (Chicago: University of Chicago Press, 2015), 1–2 and 35.

9. Douglas Lanier, "Shakespeare and the Reparative Turn," paper presented (January 19) at annual conference of La Société française Shakespeare, Paris, January 18–20, 2018, n.p.

10. Fictional film examples of reparative adaptation include *A Midwinter's Tale* (dir. Kenneth Branagh, Castle Rock Entertainment, 1995), *The Last Lear* (dir. Rituparno Ghosh, Planman Motion Pictures, 2007), and *Cesare deve morire* (*Caesar Must Die*) (dir. Paolo Taviani and Vittorio Taviani, Rai Cinema, 2012); documentaries include *A Dream in Hanoi* (dir. Tom Weidlinger, Moira Productions, 2002), *Mickey B* (dir. Tom Magill, esc films, 2007), *The Road to the Globe* (dir. Mike Jonathan, Monsoon Pictures International, 2012), and *The Hobart Shakespeareans* (dir. Mel Stuart, Stuart Productions Inc., 2005).

11. Lanier, "Shakespeare and the Reparative Turn," n.p.

12. Sarah Rose Cavanagh, *The Spark of Learning: Energizing the College Classroom with the Science of Emotion* (Morgantown, WV: West Virginia University Press, 2016), 3.

13. Todd Landon Barnes, *Shakespearean Charity and the Perils of Redemptive Performance* (Cambridge: Cambridge University Press, 2020), 1.

14. Peter Brook, on *South Bank Show*, ITV, January 11, 1987 (season 10, episode 11). The show focused on David Hare's production for the

National Theatre, starring Anthony Hopkins. Regarding Brooks on place, see Macdonald P. Jackson, "Screening the Tragedies: *King Lear*," *The Oxford Handbook of Shakespearean Tragedy*, ed. Michael Neill and David Schalkwyk (Oxford: Oxford University Press, 2016), 607–23; 613.

15. Andrew Bozio, chapter 3, "The Perception of Place in *King Lear*," *Thinking through Place on the Early Modern English Stage* (Oxford: Oxford University Press, 2020), 98–122.

16. Alexa Alice Joubin and Aneta Mancewicz, "Introduction," *Local and Global Myths in Shakespearean Performance*, ed. Mancewicz and Joubin, 1–22; 6–7.

17. Bozio, *Thinking through Place*, 5.

18. *Wuxia* is a cinematic genre associated with nationalist sentiments. Stephen Teo identifies "a cult of the sword" in the genre that is associated with the sword-wielding knights-errant in pursuit of justice. This genre is not to be confused with *kung fu*, which, while sharing similar agendas, emphasizes the hero's fist-fighting skills. Martial arts is an umbrella term encompassing these and other related genres in fiction and cinema. Stephen Teo, *Chinese Martial Arts Cinema: The Wuxia Tradition* (Edinburgh: Edinburgh University Press, 2009), 3–4.

19. Jason McGrath, *Postsocialist Modernity: Chinese Cinema, Literature, and Criticism in the Market Age* (Stanford: Stanford University Press, 2008), 1–24.

20. *Ciyuan* [Chinese dictionary of etymology], rev. ed., ed. Shangwu yinshuguan Editorial Committee (Beijing: Shangwu yinshuguan, 1997), 1823.

21. The Khitans were a nomadic people in northwestern China.

22. The Ophelia Collective consists of female dancers and choreographers. Their *Ophelia Project* is a hybrid stage work of physical theatre and contemporary dance. The work was staged at the Robin Howard Dance Theatre at the Place in London in January, 2011; quotation taken from www.theromanticrevolution.co.uk/, accessed December 1, 2010. See also http://theopheliacollective.blogspot.com/.

23. Felicia Chan, "*Crouching Tiger, Hidden Dragon*: Cultural Migrancy and Translatability," *Chinese Films in Focus: 25 New Takes*, ed. Chris Berry (London: BFI, 2003), 56–64; Fran Martin, "The China Simulacrum: Genre, Feminism, and Pan-Chinese Cultural Politics in *Crouching Tiger, Hidden Dragon*," *Island on the Edge: Taiwan New Cinema and After*, ed. Chris Berry and Lu Feii (Hong Kong: Hong Kong University Press, 2005), 149–59.

24. Pang Bei, ed., *Ximalaya wangzi* [Prince of the Himalayas] (Shanghai: Shanghai People's Publisher, 2006), 54.

25. Jerome Silbergeld, *China into Film: Frames of Reference in Contemporary Chinese Cinema* (London: Reaktion Books, 1999), 175.

26. Silbergeld, *China into Film*, 175.

27. Elaine Showalter, "Representing Ophelia: Women, Madness, and the Responsibilities of Feminist Criticism," *Shakespeare and the Question of Theory*, ed. Geoffrey H. Hartman and Patricia Parker (New York: Routledge, 1986), 92.

28. The impossibility of the singularity of any category has been examined by Rey Chow's *Woman and Chinese Modernity: The Politics of Reading between West and East* (Minneapolis: University of Minnesota Press, 1991) and Gayatri Chakravorty Spivak, "Interview with Gayatri Chakravorty Spivak," in Mark Sanders, *Gayatri Chakravorty Spivak: Live Theory* (London: Continuum, 2006), 104–24; 121.

29. Contemporary Legend Theatre is an intercultural Beijing opera company that Wu founded in 1986 with input from his wife, renowned modern dancer Lin Hsiu-wei.

30. Jacques Lacan, *Écrits: A Selection*, trans. Alan Sheridan (New York: Norton, 1977).

31. James Howe, *A Buddhist's Shakespeare: Affirming Self-Deconstructions* (Cranbury, NJ: [AUP for] Fairleigh Dickinson University Press, 1994).

32. Philip Brockbank, "Upon Such Sacrifices," *Proceedings of the British Academy* 62 (1976): 109–34.

33. Jonathan Dollimore, "*King Lear* (ca. 1605–1606) and Essentialist Humanism," *Radical Tragedy* (Birmingham: Harvester Wheatsheaf, 1984), 189–203.

34. Ernst Kantorowicz, *The King's Two Bodies: A Study in Medieval Political Theology* (Princeton, NJ: Princeton University Press, 1957; 2016), 7. See Bernhard Jussen's assessment of the significance of Kantorowicz's work in "*The King's Two Bodies* Today," *Representations* 106.1 (2009): 102–17.

35. Mary Louise Pratt, "Arts of the Contact Zone," *Profession* (1991): 33–40.

36. W. E. B. Du Bois, *The Souls of Black Folk*, ed. David W. Blight and Robert Gooding-Williams (Boston: Bedford Books, 1997), 12.

37. On Du Bois, see Alexa Alice Joubin and Martin Orkin, *Race* (New York: Routledge, 2019), 210–11.

38. Commenting on post-9/11 secular humanism, Gayatri Chakravorty Spivak calls for the de-transcendentalization of "the radical other (the divine) into figurative instrumentality." Quoted in Srinavas Aravamudan, *Guru English: South Asian Religion in a Cosmopolitan Language* (Princeton, NJ: Princeton University Press, 2006), 20. See also Gayatri Chakravorty Spivak, *An Aesthetic Education in the Era of Globalization*

(Cambridge, MA: Harvard University Press, 2012), 10. On secularism in literature, see Amardeep Singh, *Literary Secularism: Religion and Modernity in Twentieth-Century Fiction* (Newcastle: Cambridge Scholars Press, 2006), 125. I thank Farisa Khalid for drawing my attention to this theory.

39. Mark Thornton Burnett, *Shakespeare and World Cinema* (Cambridge: Cambridge University Press, 2013), 214.

40. Celia R. Daileader, *Eroticism on the Renaissance Stage: Transcendence, Desire, and the Limits of the Visible* (Cambridge: Cambridge University Press, 1998), 41.

41. Zeffirelli's *Romeo and Juliet* has inspired other East Asian adaptations as well, including Takahashi Rumiko's manga and anime works. In one episode of *Urusei Yatsura*, troublemaker Ryoko Mendou invites the series' male protagonist, Ataru Moroboshi, to have a Romeo-and-Juliet-style rendezvous with her. She wears a dress very similar to that of Olivia Hussey's Juliet. In an episode of *Ranma ½*, Ranma Saotome and Akane Tendo are cast as Romeo and Juliet in a high school production. Ranma's and Akane's costumes mimic those of Leonard Whiting's Romeo and Hussey's Juliet in Zeffirelli's film. Episode 21 is titled "Kissing Is Such Sweet Sorrow! The Taking of Akane's Lips."

42. For instance, *Shakespeare Wallah* (dir. James Ivory, Merchant Ivory Productions, 1965); *The Last Lear* (dir. Rituparno Ghosh, Planman Motion Pictures, 2007); and the Italian made-for-television short *Che cosa sono le nuvole* (What Are the Clouds? dir. Pier Paolo Pasolini, Dino De Laurentiis, 1968), a parody of *Othello* in which the peasant audience storms the stage just as Othello is about to strangle Desdemona.

43. John Gillies, "Shakespeare Localized: An Australian Looks at Asian Practice," *Shakespeare Global/Local: The Hong Kong Imaginary in Transcultural Production*, ed. Kwok-kan Tam, Andrew Parkin, and Terry Siu-han Yip (Oxford: Peter Lang, 2002), 101–13; 106.

44. Shu-hua Wang and Perng Ching-hsi, interview with Lee Kuo-hsiu, July 2009.

45. Lee Kuo-hsiu, *Shamuleite* (Taipei: Shulin Publisher, 1992), 48–9; translation mine.

46. Kuo-hsiu, *Shamuleite*, 129; translation mine.

47. Juan F. Cerdá, "European Touring Stars and the Shakespearean Distinction of the Spanish Actor-manager in Madrid and Latin America (1898–1936)," *Shakespeare*, special issue on Global Shakespeares, ed. Alexa Huang, 9.3 (2013): 322–29.

48. Shu-mei Shih, "The Concept of the Sinophone," *PMLA* 126.3 (2011): 709–18.

49. Victor H. Mair, "What Is a Chinese 'Dialect/Topolet'? Reflections on Some Key Sino-English Linguistic Terms," *Sino-Platonic Papers* 29 (September 1991): 1–31.

50. Shu-mei Shih, "Introduction: What Is Sinophone Studies?," *Sinophone Studies: A Critical Reader*, ed. Shu-mei Shih, Chien-hsin Tsai, and Brian Bernards (New York: Columbia University Press, 2013), 1–16; 8.

51. Li Shixue, *Zhongxi wenxue yinyuan* [Sino–western literary relations] (Taipei: Lianjing, 1991), 61.

52. Quoted in Lee, *Shamuleite*, 119.

53. Thomas Otway, *Venice Preserved; or, A plot discovered, a tragedy* (London, 1796); University of Toronto Robarts Library.

54. "Ning Caishen and He Nian's New Play *Romeo and Zhu Yingtai* [Ning Caishen, He Nian xinpai huaju *Luomiou yu Zhu Yingtai*]," *Eastern Morning News* [*Dongfang zaobao*], April 8, 2008; https://yule.sohu.com/20080408/n256157993.shtml, accessed March 29, 2020.

55. Wendy Beth Hyman and Hillary Eklund, "Introduction: Making Meaning and Doing Justice with Early Modern Texts," *Teaching Social Justice through Shakespeare: Why Renaissance Literature Matters Now*, ed. Eklund and Hyman (Edinburgh: Edinburgh University Press, 2019), 1–26; 6.

56. Courtney Lehmann critiques pop feminism in films such as *Shakespeare in Love*. The pop-feminist version of "the bitch," Lehmann writes, "is able to manipulate the virgin/whore binary in a way that serves both business and pleasure, thereby negating the masculinist stereotype of the bitch's default sexual status as either psycho or spinster." The catch, however, is that "the bitch triangulation merely reinstates the line limiting female subjectivity to a precarious choice between virgin and whore, renaming this choice 'good girl/bad girl' as a postmodern variation on a Victorian theme." See "Crouching Tiger, Hidden Agenda: How Shakespeare and the Renaissance Are Taking the Rage Out of Feminism," *Shakespeare Quarterly* 53.2 (2002): 260–79; 261, 266–67.

CHAPTER 3

1. While polyphony is a well-known concept in musicology, it was introduced to literary studies by Mikhail Bakhtin in his analysis of Fyodor Dostoevsky's novels. I use polyphony in literal and metaphorical senses to discuss the synthesis of different voices, accents, body language, and music on stage, as well as contrasting voices in reception of touring productions. M. M. Bakhtin, *Problems of Dostoevsky's Poetics*, trans. Caryl Emerson (Minneapolis: University of Minnesota Press, 1984).

2. Michael J. Pettid, "Late-Chosŏn Society as Reflected in a Shamanistic Narrative: An Analysis of the *Pari kongju muga*," *Korean Studies* 24 (2000): 113–41; 122. Dae-Seok Seo, "The Legend of Princess Paritegi," *Koreana* 13.2 (Summer 1999): 92–95; 95. See also the *Encyclopedia of Korean Folk Literature*, vol. 3: *Folklore and Traditional Culture* (Seoul: National Folk Museum of Korea, 2014).

3. Along with Lee Yung-tack's production *Our Contemporary Lear* (1995)—an imaginary discussion of *King Lear* between Stalin and an actor—and other contemporary South Korean adaptations, *King Uru* testifies to the special place *King Lear* holds in East Asia. *King Lear*'s compelling themes of filial obligation and political allegiance attracts directors and audiences alike. Kim, who is a renowned *p'ansori* performer, is also a screenwriter; he wrote the screenplays for the acclaimed films *Chunhyang* (dir. Im Kwon-taek, Taehung Pictures, 2000) and *Sopyonje* (dir. Im Kwon-taek, Taehung Pictures, 1993). *Sopyonje* depicts the tensions a family of traditional Korean *p'ansori* singers experiences in a modern world that does not care for traditional art.

4. Lee Hyon-u, "Dialectical Progress of Femininity in Korean Shakespeare since 1990," in *Glocalizing Shakespeare in Korea and Beyond*, ed. Lee Hyon-u (Seoul: Dongin Publishing, 2009), 45–74; 50–51.

5. Paul A. Kottman, *Tragic Conditions in Shakespeare: Disinheriting the Globe* (Baltimore: Johns Hokpins University Press, 2009), 92.

6. Kim Gap-sik, "Review: *King Uru*," *Dong-A Ilbo*, December 19, 2000.

7. "Israel Praises *King Uru*," *Maeil Business Newspaper*, May 27, 2002, quoted and translated in Seong-kwan Cho, "Shakespeare and the South Korean Stage" (Ph.D. thesis, University of Warwick, 2014), 91.

8. Kim So-yeon, "Review: *King Uru*," *Chungdae shinmun*, September 3, 2002.

9. Kim Myung-gon, *Uruwang (King Uru: A Fantasia of Life and Coexistence)*, unpublished script, n.p.

10. The Folio Text of *King Lear*, *The Oxford Shakespeare: The Complete Works*, 2nd ed., ed. Stanley Wells and Gary Taylor (Oxford: Oxford University Press, 2005).

11. Stanley Wells, ed., *The History of King Lear*, Oxford World's Classics (Oxford: Oxford University Press, 2000), 181 n. 8.

12. Kathleen McLuskie, "Afterword," *Shakespeare on the Global Stage: Performance and Festivity in the Olympic Year*, ed. Paul Prescott and Erin Sullivan (London: Bloomsbury Arden, 2015), 323–38; 334.

13. Marvin Carlson, *The Haunted Stage: The Theatre as Memory Machine* (Ann Arbor: University of Michigan Press, 2003), 2.

14. Martina Deuchler, "Propagating Female Virtues in Chosŏn Korea," *Women and Confucian Cultures in Premodern China, Korea, and Japan*,

ed. Dorothy Ko, JaHyun Kim Haboush, and Joan R. Piggott (Berkeley: University of California Press, 2003), 142–69.

15. Pascale Casanova, *La République mondiale des lettres* (1999), translated as *The World Republic of Letters* by M. B. DeBevoise (Cambridge, MA: Harvard University Press, 2004), 87.

16. Some of these corporations are controlled by a *chaebol* (family conglomerate). Bae-Gyoon Park, "Politics of Scale and the Globalization of the South Korean Automobile Industry," *Economic Geography* 79.2 (2003): 173–94.

17. Modern South Korean feminism is generally thought to have taken root in academia with the establishment of a reading group in 1993 that eventually developed into the Korean Association of Feminist Philosophy. Heisook Kim, "Feminist Philosophy in Korea: Subjectivity of Korean Women," *Signs* 34.2 (2009): 247–51.

18. Lee Joon-ik, dir., *The King and the Clown* (*Wang-ui namja*) (South Korea: Eagle Pictures, 2005).

19. Adele Lee, "The Player King and Kingly Players: Inverting *Hamlet* in Lee Joon-ik's *King and the Clown* (2005)," *Borrowers and Lenders: The Journal of Shakespeare and Appropriation* 12.1 (2018): 1–18; www.borrowers.uga.edu/784121/show, accessed March 10, 2020.

20. Jin Dal Yong, *New Korean Wave: Transnational Cultural Power in the Age of Social Media* (Urbana: University of Illinois Press, 2016), 68–90.

21. Jeeyoung Shin, "Male Homosexuality in *The King and the Clown*: Hybrid Construction and Contested Meanings," *Journal of Korean Studies* 18.1 (2013): 89–114.

22. Lee, "The Player King and Kingly Players," 7, 6.

23. Laura Mulvey, "Visual Pleasure and Narrative Cinema," *Screen* 16.3 (Autumn 1975): 6–18.

24. Normitisu Onishi, "Gay-Themed Film Gives Closet Door a Tug," *New York Times*, March 31, 2006.

25. Mark J. McLelland, "The Love between 'Beautiful Boys' in Japanese Women's Comics," *Journal of Gender Studies* 9.1 (2000): 13–25.

26. Shin, "Male Homosexuality in *The King and the Clown*," 100.

27. Shin, "Male Homosexuality in *The King and the Clown*," 101. Note that Lee Joon-gi is spelled Yi Chun'gi in the McCune–Reischauer romanization system. Ch'oe Kyŏnghúi, "Chorong tanghal surok sesang ún chúlgŏwŏjinda" [The more ridiculed, the merrier the world becomes], www.movist.com, December 29, 2005, www.movist.com/article/read.asp7type=32&id=11293, accessed February 1, 2019; quoted in English in Shin, "Male Homosexuality in *The King and the Clown*," 101.

28. English subtitles of the film.

29. Simone Chess, "Trans Residue: Nonbinary Affect and Boy Actors' Adult Careers," paper presented at the annual meeting of the Shakespeare Association of America, Washington, DC, April 2019. Samuel Pepys, *The Diary of Samuel Pepys. A New and Complete Transcription*, 11 vols., ed. Robert Latham and William Matthews (London: Bell & Hyman, 1970–1983).

30. Kim Moran, "The Stages 'Occupied by Shakespeare': Intercultural Performances and the Search for 'Korean-ness' in Postcolonial Korea," *Replaying Shakespeare in Asia*, ed. Poonam Trivedi and Minami Ryuta (New York: Routledge, 2010), 200–20; 201.

31. Umberto Eco, "Towards a Semiotic Inquiry into the Television Message," trans. Paola Splendore, *Working Papers in Cultural Studies* 3 (1972): 103–21.

32. Willmar Sauter, "Thirty Years of Reception Studies: Empirical, Methodological and Theoretical Advances," *About Performance* 10 (2010): 241–63.

33. Stephen Purcell, *Shakespeare and Audience in Practice* (Basingstoke, UK: Palgrave Macmillan, 2013).

34. Ayanna Thompson, "(How) Should We Listen to Audiences? Race, Reception, and the Audience Survey," in *The Oxford Handbook of Shakespeare and Performance*, ed. James C. Bulman (Oxford: Oxford University Press, 2017), 157–69; 161.

35. Hans Robert Jauss, *Toward an Aesthetic of Reception*, trans. Timothy Bahti (Minneapolis: Minnesota Press, 1982).

36. Helen Freshwater, *Theatre and Audience* (Basingstoke, UK: Palgrave Macmillan, 2009), 6.

37. Dennis Kennedy, "Memory, Performance and the Idea of the Museum," in *Shakespeare, Memory and Performance*, ed. Peter Holland (Cambridge: Cambridge University Press, 2006), 329–45; 339–40.

38. Peter Holland, "Forgetting Performance," in *The Oxford Handbook of Shakespeare and Performance*, ed. Bulman, 170–83; 176.

39. Alexa Alice Joubin, "Global Shakespeare Criticism beyond the Nation State," in *The Oxford Handbook of Shakespeare and Performance*, ed. Bulman, 423–40; Stephen O'Neill, *Shakespeare and YouTube: New Media Forms of the Bard* (London: Bloomsbury, 2014), 11.

40. For example, a YouTube or BBC video may not be viewable in certain countries or territories depending on the copyright situation.

41. Nely Keinänen, "What's 'Global' about 'Global Shakespeare'? The Case of Perttu Leppä's *8 päivää ensi-iltaan* [*8 Days to Premiere*]," special issue on "Global Shakespeare," ed. Alexa Alice Joubin, *Shakespeare* 9.3 (2013): 330–38.

42. It is a kind of Orientalism that requires a repackaging of the "ethnicity" in glossy images of its own *primitivism*, the resorting to "mythical pictures" to which the "convenient label of otherness" can be easily attached. Rey Chow, *Primitive Passions: Visuality, Sexuality, Ethnography and Contemporary Chinese Cinema* (New York: Columbia University Press, 1995), 170–71.

43. Dennis Kennedy writes, "Turning the tables on Mnouchkine, [Ninagawa] raids Western culture for its tendency to hybrid art, and thereby forges a new eclecticism. . . . Ninagawa may be the ideal director." Occidentalism is seen as "a declaration of interest from an outsider who feels at liberty to appropriate Europe [for his hometown audiences] the way that Europe has traditionally appropriated Japan." Dennis Kennedy, *Looking at Shakespeare: A Visual History of Twentieth-Century Performance*, 2nd ed. (Cambridge: Cambridge University Press, 2001), 315.

44. Kennedy, *Looking at Shakespeare*, 324.

45. See Tetsuo Kishi and Graham Bradshaw, *Shakespeare in Japan* (London: Bloomsbury, 2005), 91.

46. Dennis Kennedy, *The Spectator and the Spectacle: Audiences in Modernity and Postmodernity* (Cambridge: Cambridge University Press, 2009), 116.

47. Alexander Schnackenburg, "Liebe in der Kunst," *Weser Kurier: Tageszeitung für Bremen und Niedersachsen*, April 28, 2001.

48. Lee Hyon-u, "British Responses to Oh Tae-suk's *Romeo and Juliet* at the Barbican Centre," in *Glocalizing Shakespeare in Korea and Beyond*, ed. Lee, 125–54; 125. Kim Jun-young, "Korean Shakespeare on the London Stage: Mokhwa Repertory Company's *Romeo and Juliet* Performed at the Barbican Center," *Korean Theatre Review* 1 (2007): 74–88; 75–76.

49. The word *mokhwa* means raw cotton.

50. Kim, "The Stages 'Occupied by Shakespeare,'" 205.

51. Lee, "British Responses to Oh Tae-suk's *Romeo and Juliet* at the Barbican Centre," 128.

52. Peter S. Smith, Review of *Romeo and Juliet*, in the appendix to Lee, "British Responses to Oh Tae-suk's *Romeo and Juliet* at the Barbican Centre," 145.

53. Sam Marlowe, "*Romeo and Juliet*," *The Times* (London), November 29, 2006.

54. Luke Jennings, "Less Really Is More: Balanchine and a Small-Scale Korean Production Outdo Lavish Sets," *The Observer*, November 25, 2006.

55. Eve-Marie Oesterlen, Review of *Romeo and Juliet*, in the appendix to Lee, "British Responses to Oh Tae-suk's *Romeo and Juliet* at the Barbican Centre," 147.

216 *Notes*

56. Will Sharpe, Review of *Romeo and Juliet*, in the appendix to Lee, "British Responses to Oh Tae-suk's *Romeo and Juliet* at the Barbican Centre," 149.

57. *Romeo and Juliet*, unpublished script, Arko Art Library, Seoul, 2002, 17–18; English translation by Kim, "The Stages 'Occupied by Shakespeare,'" 210.

58. Smith, Review of *Romeo and Juliet*, 144, 146.

59. Sharpe, Review of *Romeo and Juliet*, 152.

60. Jason Best, Review of *Romeo and Juliet* at Barbican Pit London, *The Stage*, November 28, 2006, www.thestage.co.uk/reviews/2006/romeo-and-juliet-review-at-barbican-pit-london/, accessed March 1, 2019.

61. Il-bŏm Chang, "Oh Tae-sŏk Meets Shakespeare," *Auditorium* (October 1995): 184–85; cited in Hyunjung Lee, *Performing the Nation in Global Korea: Transnational Theatre* (London: Palgrave, 2015), 120.

62. Michael Dobson, "Shakespeare and Korea," in playbill of the Mokhwa Repertory Company's *The Tempest*, Edinburgh, August 13–16, 2011.

63. Meredith Anne Skura, "Discourse and the Individual: The Case of Colonialism in *The Tempest*," *Shakespeare Quarterly* 40.1 (1989): 42–69. Stephen Greenblatt, "Learning to Curse: Aspects of Linguistic Colonialism in the Sixteenth Century," Greenblatt's *Learning to Curse* (New York: Routledge, 1990), 22–51.

64. Kevin Quarmby, "Behind the Scenes: Penn & Teller, Taymor and the *Tempest* Divide Shakespeare's Globe, London," *Shakespeare Bulletin* 29.3 (2011): 383–97.

65. Michael Billington, "*The Tempest* review: Beale's superb Prospero haunts hi-tech spectacle," *The Guardian*, November 18, 2016, www.theguardian.com/stage/2016/nov/18/the-tempest-review-simon-russell-beale-rsc, accessed March 10, 2019.

66. Anston Bosman, "Cape of Storms: The Baxter Theatre Centre–RSC *Tempest*, 2009," *Shakespeare Quarterly* 61.1 (2010): 108–17; 109 and 113.

67. Kate Bassett, "*The Tempest*, Courtyard, Stratford; *Othello*, West Yorkshire Playhouse, Leeds," *The Independent*, February 22, 2009, www.independent.co.uk/arts-entertainment/theatre-dance/reviews/the-tempest-courtyard-stratfordbrothello-west-yorkshire-playhouse-leeds-1628609.html, accessed 23 June 2012; Michael Billington, "*The Tempest:* Courtyard, Stratford-upon-Avon," *The Guardian*, 19 February 2009, www.guardian.co.uk/stage/2009/feb/19/review-tempest-stratford-upon-avon, accessed June 23, 2012.

68. Bosman, "Cape of Storms," 114.

69. Kim Pu-sik, *Samguk sagi*, 2 vols., ed. Yi Kang-nae (Seoul: Han'gilsa, 1998).

70. Lee E-Wha, *Korea's Pastimes and Customs: A Social History*, trans. Ju-Hee Park (Paramus, NJ: Homa & Sekey Books, 2006), 205–206.

71. Chung, who received the Dong-A Award for Best Actor in 1993, has appeared in *My Love DMZ, Romeo and Juliet, Macbeth*, and numerous other Korean plays and adaptations. All quotations herein from the English performance text are taken from the surtitles used in Edinburgh.

72. Full videos or highlights of Oh's *Tempest* and other productions discussed in this chapter can be accessed at the Global Shakespeares digital archive, http://globalshakespeares.org/.

73. "Edinburgh International Festival 2011: East Meets West in a Festival Aiming to Build Bridges," *Scotsman*, March 23, 2011.

74. Rustom Bharucha, "Foreign Asia/Foreign Shakespeare: Dissenting Notes on New Asian Interculturality, Postcoloniality, and Recolonization," *Theatre Journal* 56.1 (2004): 1–28.

75. Fredric Jameson, "Preface," *The Cultures of Globalization*, ed. Fredric Jameson and Masao Miyoshi (Durham, NC: Duke University Press, 1998), xi–xvii; xii.

76. Diane Daugherty, "The Pendulum of Intercultural Performance: *Kathakali King Lear* at Shakespeare's Globe," *Asian Theatre Journal* 22.1 (2005): 52–72. Phillip Zarilli, "For Whom Is the King a King? Issues of Intercultural Production, Perception, and Reception in a *Kathakali King Lear*," *Critical Theory and Performance*, ed. Janelle G. Reinelt and Joseph R. Roach (Ann Arbor: University of Michigan Press, 2007), 108–33.

77. Malcolm Moore, "Edinburgh Festival 2011: *The Revenge of Prince Zi Dan*—The Secret of Hamlet in Chinese," *Daily Telegraph*, August 15, 2011.

78. For a general assessment of the RSC's tours to China, see Alfred Hickling, "Sit down and shut up," *The Guardian*, June 11, 2002, www.theguardian.com/stage/2002/jun/12/rsc.artsfeatures, accessed January 15, 2020.

79. Andrew Killick, *In Search of Korean Traditional Opera: Discourses of Ch'angguk* (Honolulu: University of Hawai'i Press, 2010), 173.

80. Ah-jeong Kim and R. B. Graves, "Introduction," *The Metacultural Theater of Oh T'ae-Sŏk: Five Plays from the Korean Avant-Garde*, trans. Kim and Graves (Honolulu: University of Hawai'i Press, 1999), 1–20; 1.

81. Michael Billington, "*The Tempest*—Review: King's, Edinburgh," *The Guardian*, August 15, 2011.

82. Sonia Massai, "*The Tempest*—Directed by Nasir Uddin Yousuff for Dhaka Theatre Company (Dhaka, Bangladesh) at Shakespeare's Globe," *A Year of Shakespeare: Re-living the World Shakespeare Festival*, ed. Paul Edmundson, Paul Prescott, and Erin Sullivan (London: Bloomsbury Arden, 2013); Imogen Tilden, "*The Tempest*—Review: Shakespeare's Globe, London," *The Guardian*, May 8, 2012.

218   *Notes*

83. Paul Gent, "Edinburgh Festival 2011: *The Tempest*, King's Theatre," *The Telegraph*, August 15, 2011. Craig Singer, "*The Tempest* (EIF)," What-sOnStage.com, August 15, 2011, www.whatsonstage.com/reviews/the atre/london/E8831313399539/The+Tempest+%28EIF%29.html, accessed September 20, 2012.

84. The conversation took place during the event entitled "Continental Shifts: All the World's a Stage," with Oh Tae-suk, Michael Billington, and Alexa Alice Joubin, at The Hub on Castlehill, Edinburgh, August 15, 2011.

85. Kim and Graves, "Introduction," 3.

86. Kim and Graves, "Introduction," 3–4.

87. See, for example, Peter Holland, *English Shakespeares: Shakespeare on the English Stage in the 1990s* (Cambridge: Cambridge University Press, 1997); Minami Ryuta, Ian Carruthers, and John Gillies, eds., *Performing Shakespeare in Japan* (Cambridge: Cambridge University Press, 2001); Zdeněk Stříbrný, *Shakespeare and Eastern Europe* (Oxford: Oxford University Press, 2000); and Wilhelm Hortmann, *Shakespeare on the German Stage*, vol. 2: *The Twentieth Century* (Cambridge: Cambridge University Press, 1998).

88. Mark Fisher, "Festival Reviews," *Edinburgh Festivals*, August 21, 2011, www.edinburgh-festivals.com/viewreview.aspx?id=3001, accessed September 20, 2012; scottishtheatre.blogspot.com/2011/09/scotland-on-sunday-theatre-round-up-21.html, accessed March 30, 2020.

89. Gent, "Edinburgh Festival 2011."

90. Dennis Kennedy, "Afterword: Shakespearean Orientalism," in *Foreign Shakespeare: Contemporary Performance*, ed. Kennedy (Cambridge: Cambridge University Press, 1993), 290–303; 291; Ania Loomb and Martin Orkin, "Introduction: Shakespeare and the Post-Colonial Question," in *Post-Colonial Shakespeares*, ed. Loomba and Orkin (London: Routledge, 1998), 1–19; 1.

91. In 1883, Kawasima Keizo translated *Julius Caesar* into Japanese; it was the first Shakespeare play to be translated into that language. Act 3, scene 2, from the play was performed in Korea in 1925, and Yi Gwang-su partially translated the play into Korean in 1926. *Caesar* was popular among Japanese and Korean intellectuals in the late nineteenth and early twentieth centuries. It was used as a vehicle to propagate their political beliefs in the democratization movements. See Akiko Sano, "The First Japanese Translation of *Romeo and Juliet*," the British Shakespeare Association Conference, University of Warwick, August 31—September 2, 2007.

92. Jan Creutzenberg, "To Be or Not to Be (Korean): Lee Youn-taek's *Hamlet* and the Reception of Shakespeare in Korea," *Shakespeare Seminar* 7 (2009): 21–38; 21–22.

93. Yeeyon Im, "The Location of Shakespeare in Korea: Lee Yountaek's *Hamlet* and the Mirage of Interculturality," *Theatre Journal* 60.2 (2008): 257–76; 259–60 and 263.

94. Lee, *Performing the Nation in Global Korea*, 93–126.

CHAPTER 4

1. See Michael Saenger's definition of "interlinguicity," in his introduction to *Interlinguicity, Internationality, and Shakespeare*, ed. Michael Saenger (Montreal: McGill–Queen's University Press, 2014), 3–5.

2. Atom Egoyan and Ian Balfour, "Introduction," *Subtitles: On the Foreignness of Film*, ed. Egoyan and Balfour (Cambridge, MA: MIT Press and Alphabet City, 2004), 21–32; 21.

3. Jana Evans Braziel and Anita Mannur, "Nation, Migration, Globalization: Points of Contention in Diaspora Studies," in *Theorizing Diaspora: A Reader*, ed. Evans Braziel and Mannur (Oxford: Blackwell, 2003), 1–22.

4. Jacques Derrida, *Monolingualism of the Other; or, The Prosthesis of Origin*, trans. Patrick Mensah, Cultural Memory in the Present (Stanford: Stanford University Press, 1998), 39, 41, 25.

5. Eric Koch, in "Why Study Shakespeare?," *Straits Times* (Singapore), April 14, 1987, 1.

6. Oliver Morgan promotes a new linguistic approach to rethink "speech" in Shakespearean drama, in *Turn-Taking in Shakespeare*, Oxford Textual Perspectives (Oxford: Oxford University Press, 2019), 3. The text following a character's name, according to Morgan, should be read as a "turn at talk" and part of an ongoing dialogue.

7. Sujata Iyengar, "Shakespeare's Anti-Balcony Scene," *Arrêt sur scène/Scene Focus* 6 (2017): 135–45; 137, 139.

8. Trailer for *South Park: Bigger, Longer & Uncut*, posted April 10, 2010, www.youtube.com/watch?v=aes3Iz8QPgA&list=PLL-px6wjLfGsVaHoo SfAIZ0GmbEpId8VA&index=4&t=0s, accessed October 21, 2019.

9. Quoted in Yong Li Lan, "Romeos and Juliets, Local/Global," in *Shakespeare's Local Habitations*, ed. Krystyna Courtney and R. S. White (Lodz: Lodz University Press, 2007), 135–54; 141.

10. Richard Dryer, *White* (London: Routledge, 1997), 45.

11. Jennifer Lynn Stoever, *The Sonic Color Line: Race and the Cultural Politics of Listening* (New York: New York University Press, 2016), 4.

12. Mark Thornton Burnett, *Shakespeare and World Cinema* (Cambridge: Cambridge University Press, 2013), 134.

13. Netina Tan, "Multiracialism and Politics of Regulating Ethnic Relations in Singapore" (paper presented at the Canadian Political Science Association conference, University of Victoria, Victoria, British Columbia, June 4, 2013), 3.

14. Kenneth Paul Tan, "Ethnic Representation on Singapore Film and Television," in *Beyond Rituals and Riots: Ethnic Pluralism and Social Cohesion in Singapore*, ed. Ah Eng Lai (Singapore: Eastern Universities Press, 2004), 289–315; 301.

15. Nathan F. Bullock, "Spaces of Citizenship in Contemporary Singaporean Theatre: Stating the 2011 General Election," *Asian Theatre Journal* 36.2 (2019): 472–89; Eng-Beng Lim, "Glocalqueering in New Asia: The Politics of Performing Gay in Singapore," *Theatre Journal* 57.3 (2005): 383–405; William Peterson, *Theatre and the Politics of Culture in Contemporary Singapore* (Middletown, CT: Wesleyan University Press, 2001).

16. Yvonne Ng, "Singapore Cinema in Search of Identity," *Kinema: A Journal for Film and Audiovisual Media* (2001): 1–4.

17. Tessa Wong, "Unease in Singapore over Filipino Workers," *BBC News*, December 29, 2014, www.bbc.com/news/world-asia-28,953,147, accessed October 10, 2019.

18. Joel S. Fetzer, "Election Strategy and Ethnic Politics in Singapore," *Taiwan Journal of Democracy* 4.1 (2008): 135–53.

19. The Proclamation of Singapore, drafted by E. W. Barker and signed by then–Prime Minister of Singapore Lee Kuan Yew on August 9, 1965; www.nas.gov.sg/archivesonline/photographs/record-details/72ffcf37-b8b1-11e3-927b-0050568939ad, accessed March 7, 2020.

20. Jothie Rajah, *Authoritarian Rule of Law: Legislation, Discourse, and Legitimacy in Singapore* (Cambridge: Cambridge University Press, 2012), 279.

21. John Lui, "Where Is the Audience for Local English Films?," *Straits Times*, January 1, 2014, www.straitstimes.com/singapore/where-is-the-audience-for-local-english-films, accessed October 11, 2019; Ng, "Singapore Cinema in Search of Identity," 3.

22. Ng, "Singapore Cinema in Search of Identity," 1.

23. Tan, "Ethnic Representation on Singapore Film and Television," 289.

24. Ong Keng Sen, "*Lear*: Linking Night and Day," in *Lear* (program) (Tokyo: Japan Foundation Asia Center, 1997), 5.

25. Judith Buchanan, *Shakespeare on Film* (Harlow, UK: Pearson, 2005), 10.

26. Peterson, *Theatre and the Politics of Culture in Contemporary Singapore*, 216.

27. Ong Keng Sen, "Encounters," *Drama Review* 45.3 (2001): 126–33; 128.

28. Mary Cowden Clarke, *The Girlhood of Shakespeare's Heroines in a Series of Tales*, 3 vols. (London: W. H. Smith, 1850–51).

29. Ong, "Encounters," 129.

30. Ong Keng Sen, *Search: Hamlet* (unpublished diary, n.d.), 4. Manuscript.

31. Ong, "Encounters," 132.

32. "Interview with Gayatri Chakravorty Spivak," in Mark Sanders, *Gayatri Chakravorty Spivak: Live Theory* (London: Continuum, 2006), 104–24; 121.

33. Quoted in Alison McAlpine, "Robert Lepage," in *In Contact with the Gods? Directors Talk Theatre*, ed. Maria M. Delgado and Paul Heritage (Manchester: Manchester University Press, 1996), 151.

34. "'[T]radaptation' is Garneau's own term for his creative interaction with Shakespeare." Margaret Jane Kidnie and Jane Freeman, "Robert Lepage," in *Hall, Brook, Ninagawa, Lepage*, Great Shakespeareans 18, ed. Peter Holland (London: Bloomsbury Arden, 2103), 113–47; 129.

35. Ong, "Encounters," 132.

36. "*Othello* aus weiblicher Sicht," *Hamburger Abendblatt*, July 15, 2000.

37. Ong, "Encounters," 129.

38. Mari Boyd, "Kishida Rio," *The Columbia Encyclopedia of Modern Drama*, ed. Gabrielle H. Cody and Evert Sprinchorn (New York: Columbia University Press, 2007), 769–70; Rio Kishida, *Thread Hell*, trans. Carol Fisher Sorgenfrei and Tonooka Naomi, in *Half a Century of Japanese Theater*, ed. Japan Playwrights Association (Tokyo: Kinokuniya, 2002), 4:161–221.

39. Ong Keng Sen, *Search: Hamlet* (program notes) (Elsinore, Denmark: Hamlet Sommer, 2002), 45.

40. Ong, *Search: Hamlet* (program notes), 18.

41. Ong, *Search: Hamlet* (program notes), 8.

42. Ong, *Search: Hamlet* (program notes), 20.

43. Avi Erlich, *Hamlet's Absent Father* (Princeton, NJ: Princeton University Press, 1977), 212.

44. Peter S. Donaldson, "*Hamlet*, the *Heike* and the Fall of Troy," *Shakespeare* 9.3 (2013): 291–303; 301, 300. Margreta de Grazia, *Hamlet without Hamlet* (Cambridge: Cambridge University Press, 2007).

45. Japan Foundation Asia Center, *The Japan Foundation Asia Center: Towards Mutual Understanding in Asia in the Twenty-First Century* (Tokyo: Japan Foundation Asia Center, n.d.), 2.

46. David Tse Ka-shing, "It's Time to Put British East Asian Theatre in the Spotlight," *Guardian*, November 6, 2008, www.theguardian.com/stage/theatreblog/2008/nov/06/british-east-asian-theatre, accessed October 19, 2019.

47. *Chicken Rice War*, *Straits Times* Razor TV, July 25, 2013, www.youtube.com/watch?v=A66vXeZEMag, accessed October 10, 2019. SPH Razor is the digital arm of Singapore Press Holdings.

48. Walter Law, *Chicken Rice War*, SMK Batu Lintang Drama Club, May 3, 2018, www.youtube.com/watch?v=nutYy1HboZ4, accessed October 10, 2019. SMK is an abbreviation for Sekolah Menengah Kebangsaan (national secondary school).

49. Quoted in Mark Fisher, "*Diaspora* with TheatreWorks and the Singapore Chinese Orchestra," July 13, 2009, *Edinburgh Festival Guide 2009*, http://edinburghfestival.list.co.uk/article/18721-diaspora-with-theatreworks-and-the-singapore-chinese-orchestra/, accessed February 1, 2012.

50. Ong, "Encounters," 132.

51. Leow Bee Geok, *Census of Population 2000, Statistical Release 1: Demographics Characteristics* (Singapore: Department of Statistics, Ministry of Trade and Industry, Republic of Singapore, 2001), 10.

52. Elizabeth A. Kalden, "All the World's a Stage Now," *Straits Times*, April 21, 1998, 2.

53. "A Talk with Director Ong Keng Sen" (interview by Mok Wai Yin), in *Descendants of the Eunuch Admiral—A Meditation* (program) (Singapore: Victoria Theatre, 1995), 2.

54. Philip Smith, *Shakespeare in Singapore: Performance, Education, and Culture* (New York: Routledge, 2020), 157.

55. Yong Li Lan, "Ong Keng Sen's *Desdemona*, Ugliness, and the Intercultural Performative," *Theatre Journal* 56.2 (2004): 251–73; 263.

56. Gilles Deleuze and Félix Guattari developed the concepts of *deterritorialization* and *reterritorialization* to analyze processes that decontextualize sets of fixed relations. See Gilles Deleuze and Félix Guattari's two-volume *Capitalism and Schizophrenia: Anti-Oedipus* [vol. 1, 1972], trans. Robert Hurley, Mark Seem, and Helen R. Lane (London: Continuum, 2004), and *A Thousand Plateaus* [vol. 2, 1980], trans. Brian Massumi (Minneapolis: University of Minnesota Press, 1987), 61–63.

57. Carol Chillington Rutter, "Maverick Shakespeare," *A Companion to Shakespeare and Performance*, ed. Barbara Hodgdon and W. B. Worthen (Malden, MA: Blackwell, 2005), 335–58; 353.

58. Smith, *Shakespeare in Singapore*, 186.

59. Shilpa S. Davé, *Indian Accents: Brown Voice and Racial Performance in American Television and Film* (Urbana: University of Illinois Press, 2013), 2.

60. Sonia Massai, *Shakespeare's Accents: Voicing Identity in Performance* (Cambridge: Cambridge University Press, 2020), 3. See also Chapter 1.

61. "Han'guk-ui [*Hamlet*] segyemudae-sodo t'ong-handa," *Dong-A Ilbo*, October 8, 1996, review title quoted in Street Theatre Troupe, *Hamlet*, Theater Series 6 (Seoul: Guerilla, 2003), 154.

62. Marvin Carlson, "Brook and Mnouchkine: Passages to India?," *The Intercultural Performance Reader*, ed. Patrice Pavis (London: Routledge, 1996), 79–92; 91.

63. Rey Chow, *Not Like a Native Speaker: On Languaging as a Postcolonial Experience* (New York: Columbia University Press, 2014), 75–76.

EPILOGUE

1. Jacques Derrida, *Monolingualism of the Other; or, The Prosthesis of Origin*, trans. Patrick Mensah (Stanford: Stanford University Press, 1998), 14–15, 39, 34, 41.
2. Judith Buchanan, *Shakespeare on Film* (Harlow, UK: Pearson, 2005), 71.
3. Roger Manvell, *Shakespeare and the Film* (London: Dent, 1971), 136–43; Birkett, quoted on 137.
4. Buchanan, *Shakespeare on Film*, 71.
5. Kenneth S. Rothwell, *A History of Shakespeare on Screen: A Century of Film and Television*, 2nd ed. (Cambridge: Cambridge University Press, 2004), 160.
6. The term *translingualism* was seemingly coined by Steven G. Kellman, "J. M. Coetzee and Samuel Beckett: The Translingual Link," *Comparative Literature Studies* 33.2 (1996): 161–72; see also Steven G. Kellman, ed., *Switching Languages: Translingual Writers Reflect on Their Craft* (Lincoln: University of Nebraska Press, 2003). Using the concept of "translingual practice," Lydia H. Liu analyzes cultural exchange among China, Japan, and the west in *Translingual Practice: Literature, National Culture, and Translated Modernity—China, 1900–1937* (Stanford: Stanford University Press, 1995).
7. Richard Wollheim, *Painting as an Art*, A. W. Mellon Lectures in the Fine Arts 31 (Princeton, NJ: Princeton University Press, 1987), 4.
8. W. B. Worthen, *Shakespeare and the Force of Modern Performance* (Cambridge: Cambridge University Press, 2003), 3. J.L. Austen, *How to Do Things with Words* (Oxford: Oxford University Press, 1962), 5.
9. On Zaslove, see Wayne Johnson, "Wild West Comes to *Macbeth*," *Seattle Times*, May 15, 1990, https://archive.seattletimes.com/archive/?date=19,900,515&slug=1,071,896, accessed March 13, 2020. Bully: "Reworking of Macbeth Opens July 12," *Kingston* (Jamaica) *Gleaner*, July 10, 1997, https://newspaperarchive.com/kingston-gleaner-jul-10-1997-p-11/, accessed March 13, 2020. For more information on Chapelle's film, see www.imdb.com/title/tt2747688/?ref_=adv_li_tt, accessed April 2, 2020.
10. Suzuki: Ian Carruthers and Takahashi Yasunari, *The Theatre of Suzuki Tadashi* (Cambridge: Cambridge University Press, 2004), 210–46; "Chronology of the Productions," www.scot-suzukicompany.com/en/pro file.php, accessed March 13, 2020. Sato: Leonard Pronko, "Approaching Shakespeare through Kabuki," *Shakespeare East and West*, ed. Minoru Fujita and Leonard Pronko (London: Routledge, 1996), 23–40; 29.

Fee: Roy Berko, review of *Macbeth* (Great Lakes Theater Festival), September 28, 2008, http://royberkinfo.blogspot.com/2008/09/, accessed March 13, 2020. Chong: Marty Hughey, "Oregon Shakespeare Festival Brings Throne of Blood Back to Its Stage Roots," interview with Ping Chong, www.oregonlive.com/performance/2010/07/oregon_shakespeare_festival_br.html, and Charles Isherwood "Sprawling Cinema, Tamed to a Stage," *New York Times*, November 11, 2010, www.nytimes.com/2010/11/12/theater/reviews/12throne.html, both accessed March 13, 2020.

11. Wai Chee Dimock, *Through Other Continents: American Literature across Deep Time* (Princeton, NJ: Princeton University Press, 2006), 3.

12. Adele Seeff, *South Africa's Shakespeare and the Drama of Language and Identity*, Global Shakespeares (New York: Palgrave Macmillan, 2018), 1.

13. Amartya Sen, "How to Judge Globalism," *American Prospect*, January 5, 2002, https://prospect.org/features/judge-globalism/, accessed September 30, 2019.

Rosalind ponders in the epilogue of *As You Like It* that "If it be true that good wine needs no bush, 'tis true that a good play needs no epilogue." Yet, acknowledgements in books do not cajole readers into applauding so much as they demystify intellectual genealogies, networks of collaboration, and sources of research funding. The idea for this book emerged from my arrival on a new shore after a difficult period in life. In addition to being my emotional anchor, Basile Joubin accompanied me to an untold number of live productions, festivals, and screenings of films and videotaped perform-ances. He served as my sounding board for new ideas. In highlighting my intellectual and emotional debt to those who have nurtured me, I hope to show paths that others may follow or reinvent in the future.

For supporting my project, I am grateful to the series editors Stanley Wells, Peter Holland, and Lena Cowen Orlin. At Oxford University Press, Eleanor Collins shepherded the book to fruition. The two anonymous readers as well as Douglas Lanier, Erika T. Lin, Mark Thornton Burnett, and Ema Vyrou-balová set aside precious time they never really had and provided invaluable feedback during various stages of this project. I am deeply indebted to Michael Gnat, Kate Babbitt, and Irene Pavitt for their editorial acumen. It is a blessing to have attentive and patient readers and editors.

The late Christy Desmet, who took me under her wing, had been my guide and comfort in a harsh world when I was most vulnerable. Along with Desmet, Sujata Iyengar published the first peer-reviewed article in my career and has been an unfailing ally and mentor. At MIT, Peter S. Donaldson and Belinda Yung have played a pivotal role as collaborators and friends in the founding of *MIT Global Shakespeares*, an open-access digital video archive. It has been an honor and joy to work with Michael Best, Janelle Jenstad, Eric Rasmussen, James Mardock, and Kevin Quarmby on the *Internet Shakespeare Editions* as its General Performance Editor and, later, a board member, at the University of Victoria, Canada. Both digital humanities projects compelled me to ask new questions about deep connections among performances across cultures.

The opportunity to give a TEDx Fulbright Talk helped to shape my argument about Shakespeare and social justice, which developed more fully when Christopher Thurman and Sandra Young kindly invited me to the 2019 Shakespeare Society of South Africa conference in Cape Town. My research on Yukio Ninagawa took a new direction when Andrew C. Elsesser invited me to speak at a landmark revival of the *Ningawa Macbeth* during Lincoln

Center's Mostly Mozart Festival in New York. My theory of reparative adaptation was inspired by Lanier's pioneering work and developed further when Rachael Jolley, editor of the *Index on Censorship* magazine, invited me to speak at the PEN America World Voices Festival in New York, during a British Council "Shakespeare Lives" event at the British Embassy in Washington, DC, and on a panel with Simon Callow on arts and censorship at the Hay Festival in Wales. The idea of reparative adaptation as a place-based myth came to me during an MLA panel on the commemorations of Tang Xianzu and Shakespeare as national poets that I coorganized with Liana Chen. Esther Kim Lee, then editor of *Theatre Survey*, initiated my research on South Korean theatre. Ryuta Minami and Hyon-u Lee have been indispensable in assisting with primary literature and setting me on the right path in my writing on Akira Kurosawa and Yang Jung-ung. I have also learned a great deal on Kurosawa's unique aesthetics from Judith Buchanan and Mark Thornton Burnett.

Conversations with Simone Chess have expanded my horizon on transgender theory in Chapter 3, while Rossella Ferrari showed me new terrains of transnational Chinese theatres. My visit to Japan would not have been as productive without Minami who took me to Kabuki-za and Takarazuka theatres in Tokyo and Ninagawa's Saitama Arts Theatre. My Korean teacher Yunkyoung Kang, a specialist on spatial concepts in Korean semantics, and Japanese teacher Yasuko Matsumoto deserve special thanks. In our weekly tutorial sessions, Léandra Cormier and Saida Erradi showed me the beauty of the French language, enabling me to appreciate the intellectual gymnastics of French critical theories. Nely Keinänen's research drew my attention to the reception history of a Finnish film inspired by *Romeo and Juliet*. I am fortunate to receive the intellectual generosity of collegial interlocutors on global Shakespeare, including Zoltan Markus, Sheila Cavanagh, William N. West, Ray Siemens, Geoffrey Way, Vanessa Corredera, Elizabeth Rivlin, Richard Vela, Thomas Leitch, Katherine Schaap Williams, Ronan Paterson, Michael Saenger, Nathalie Vienne-Guerrin, Sarah Hatchuel, Yan Brailowsky, Susan Frye, Elizabeth Pentland, Peter Kirwan, Paul Edmondson, Valerie Wayne, Jonathan Hsy, Jyotsna Singh, Thea Buckley, Michelle Dowd, Julia Reinhard Lupton, Andrew Dickson, Calvin Hui, Ronan Hatfull, David Der-wei Wang, Liam Semler, John Gillies, James C. Bulman, Anna Stegh Camati, Niamh O'Leary, Michael Dobson, Angela Pao, Tom Bishop, Mercedes de la Torre and Carlos Drocchi of the Fundación Shakespeare Argentina, Farisa Khalid, Daniel Atherton, Lisa S. Starks, Valerie Traub, Gretchen York, Charles Laughlin and the University of Virginia Asian Cosmopolitanisms group and Institute of the Humanities and Global Cultures, and numerous others whose exemplary works appear in the notes and Further Readings.

The curiosity and probing questions from my undergraduate and graduate students at George Washington University and Middlebury College Bread Loaf School of English have motivated me to keep writing through the night. Emily C. Bartels has been a beacon of light at Middlebury. I would also like to thank Miseong Woo for inviting me to teach an intensive graduate seminar at Yonsei University in Seoul, South Korea, where my idea of polyphonic adaptations took shape.

Various parts of this project were sponsored by the American Council of Learned Societies Frederick Burkhardt Fellowship at the Folger Library; Fulbright Distinguished Chair Award in Global Shakespeare Studies at Queen Mary University of London and University of Warwick, UK, where I am indebted to Victor Fan's and Bridget Escolme's warm hospitality and intellectual generosity; and the International Visiting Fellowship at the University of Essex (UK), where Mary Mazzilli served as a gracious host. At George Washington University, I gratefully acknowledge support from the Office of the Vice President for Research, Confucius Institute, School of Business, Elliott School of International Affairs, Columbian College of Arts and Sciences, and Sigur Center for Asian Studies.

Olivia Curran (University Honors Program Research Assistant) has been indispensable in the preparation of the index.

ableism Social prejudice and practices that discriminate against, or in some instances create positive but problematic stereotypes about, people with physical, intellectual, or psychiatric disabilities. The ideology operates in favor of able-bodied people. As a trope in performance and film culture, ableism permeates discourses of difference.

Buddhism, Mahāyāna Along with Theravada (Sanskrit "Lesser Vehicle"), Mahāyāna ("Great Vehicle") is one of two main branches of Buddhism. Mahāyāna is well known for its complex rituals, universal ethics, and its Lotus Sutra—scriptural instruction in the use of "expedient means," any effective technique that aids awakening. One of Mahāyāna Buddhism's central tenets is the idea that anyone can achieve awakening (enlightenment) and become a bodhisattva, one who seeks to become a Buddha. Enlightenment is the result of understanding the true nature of reality. The Buddhism practiced in East Asia, especially Japan, is largely derived from Mahāyāna Buddhism.

Buddhism, Shinto First recorded in the eighth century, Shinto ("Way of God") practices focus on diligent rituals connecting the human world and ancestors, and modern Japan with its past. At the center of the belief is the realm of spirits, also known as essences, giving rise to festivals, ancestral worship, and war memorials. A polytheistic religion, Shinto Buddhism believes that the *kami* ("spirits") inhabit all things.

Bunraku A form of traditional, early seventeenth-century Japanese puppet theatre, involving puppeteers, musicians, and chanters. It was proclaimed by UNESCO as an Intangible Cultural Heritage of Humanity.

color-blind casting A theatrical practice, also known as nontraditional or multiethnic casting, that casts characters regardless of racial characteristics so as to increase diversity onstage. The practice may highlight social dynamics based on racial dynamics in conjunction with the plot, regardless of dramaturgical intentions. The term is sometimes considered **ableist**, and the merit of such practice has been debated.

Confucianism A worldview and political ideology based on the teaching of Confucius (551–479 BC) that formed a shared philosophical foundation among East Asian cultures. Confucianism focuses on *rén* (altruistic virtue, evidenced in interpersonal relationships), the fellowship of *junzi* (exemplary persons), and family ethics and family-centered nomenclature, notably *xiào* (filial piety).

diaspora The forced or voluntary movement across geopolitical borders either to seek better social opportunities or to escape undesirable ideologies, as the case may be. The term also refers to the involuntary dispersion of Jews beyond Israel.

discourse A way of arguing or writing existence into being. An organized structure through which a society discusses particular issues. The structure may or may not always be visible.

hayagawari A technique in Kabuki theatre known as "rapid changes of roles." An actor would remove his disguise or transform into a new character by quickly pulling off a layer of clothing to reveal new costumes underneath. To facilitate rapid transformations, sometimes a mask suitable for male and female characters is worn. A popular form of *hayagawari* is "seven changes" (*nanabake*) in which one actor takes on seven roles within a single performance.

heteroglossia The coexistence of different words and discourses that describe the same things (in the same language), which, according to Mikhail Bakhtin, is the source of social conflict. In his study of novels, tensions between canonical and marginal uses of the same national language lead to the differences between the narrator's voice and the voices of the characters.

huaju, **or spoken drama** Post-1907 western-influenced spoken drama theatre without singing or dancing. It is a form of dialogue-based realist theatre that was introduced to China through intellectuals who studied in Japan in the early twentieth century. Unlike stylized Chinese opera (*xiqu*), *huaju* performances do not involve singing and dancing. At first emulating post-Victorian western-style realist theatre, Sinophone *huaju* theatre, like the Korean *shingŭk* and

Japanese *shingeki*, initially focused on adaptations of Anglo-European drama, such as Lin Shu's adaptation of Harriet Beecher Stowe's *Uncle Tom's Cabin* in 1901 as *Heinu yütian lu*. This was followed by new plays written for the genre. Tian Han, Cao Yu, and Hong Shen were considered some of the most successful early *huaju* playwrights. *Huaju* was seen as a political tool and a vehicle for propaganda during the War of Resistance against Japan (1937–45). It was used again later to spread ideas supporting the Chinese Communist Party. Over time, the genre developed variants in Hong Kong, Taiwan, Singapore, and throughout the **Sinophone** world in Mandarin, Cantonese, Taiwanese, and other dialects.

hybridity A cross between two or more cultures, races, plants, or languages. As a notion critiquing cultural imperialism, hybridity is a concept closely related to theories proposed by Homi K. Bhabha, Stuart Hall, Gayatri Spivak, and Paul Gilroy.

intercultural performance Performance that incorporates elements of disparate cultural traditions and/or playtexts from other cultures to achieve artistic innovations. Intercultural performance by artists from more dominant cultures, such as the Anglophone circle, has sometimes been criticized for its forceful and disrespectful appropriation of cultures that are traditionally seen as vulnerable, such as those from the Global South. However, intercultural performance *originating from* the Global South, for example, has been seen as an act of empowerment.

Jidai-geki Period drama, a genre of Japanese film, television drama, theatre, and video game. Usually set in Edo Japan between the seventeenth and nineteenth centuries, these works feature samurai warriors, merchants, craftsmen, and bureaucrats.

jingju, or **Beijing opera** A type of traditional, stylized Chinese operatic theatre in the Beijing dialect that combines song, dance, combat, lavish facial makeup, headpieces, costumes, and acrobatics to perform dramatic narratives. Music, performed live by a small band at the side of the stage, emphasizes percussion beats. There are four main role types, including *sheng* (main male role), *dan* (female role), *jing* (painted-face "mighty" male role), and *chou* (clown). There are several subcategories under each role type. This genre is also known as *guoju* (national theatre) in Taiwan.

Kabuki A Japanese all-male stylized theatre of songs and dance dating back to the early seventeenth century. *Ka* denotes song, and *bu* means dance; *ki* signifies skill. Kabuki was proclaimed by UNESCO as an Intangible Cultural Heritage of Humanity. Central to the Kabuki stage is a walkway through the audience called the *hanamichi* (flower path). Actors enter and exit through this elevated walkway.

kkonminam A distinct phenomenon ("flower boys") in post-1990s Korean pop culture in conjunction with the rise of "soft" masculinity of male K-pop groups and under the influence of Japanese *bishōnen* (beautiful youth) manga. Though present in premodern East Asian cultures, *kkonminam* rose to prominence in the twenty-first century with their makeup, smooth skin, and mannerisms that are considered socially to be feminine. While *kkonminam* have a large female fan base, gender and sexuality do not define the category of identity onstage and off.

kung fu An umbrella term for Chinese martial arts. In film studies, *kung fu* films emphasize the hero's fist-fighting skills, whereas *wuxia* films often depict the adventures of sword-wielding knights-errant in pursuit of justice.

Kyōgen A form of traditional, stylized, masked, all-male Japanese performance that provides comic relief during intermission between more solemn Noh theatre acts. It usually has a small cast of two or three actors. With minimalistic props, Kyōgen performances feature slapstick and satire in exaggerated mannerism. Musical instruments include flute, drums, and gongs. It has developed into a stand-alone, full-fledged performance genre detached from Noh theatre. One of the most renowned modern-day Kyōgen players is Nomura Mansai, who has also directed several productions, including *Merry Wives of Windsor* in 1991 and *Richard III* which he codirected for the Suzuki Company of Toga in 2007.

locality The geopolitical cultural location of an artist, work, or audience. Locality signals the rootedness and positionality of the cultural horizons of artists and audiences, whose relationship to an artwork is always influenced by their location-based cultural experience.

Lu Xun The penname of Zhou Shuren (1881–1936), a leading figure and "father of modern Chinese literature" who wrote in both vernacular and classical Chinese and combined nineteenth-century European and classical Chinese literary conventions. Maintaining both sympathetic engagement with and ironic detachment to the follies of their characters, Lu Xun's short stories, such as *The True Story of Ah Q*, are simultaneously incisive social satires and compassionate portrayals of marginalized figures.

namsadang nori All-male vagabond clown theatre (*nam* means men, *sadang* acrobat, and *nori* performance), a folk street performance tradition in Korea. It consists of percussion music of gongs and drums, a mask dance depicting comic scenes, an acrobatic tightrope walking act with witty exchanges, and puppet plays. The performance primarily entertains rural audiences in outdoors settings. The mask dance is satiric in nature and critiques class- and gender-based oppressions by reenacting women's stories in a male-dominated society. The theatre has been designated by the UNESCO as an Intangible Cultural Heritage of Humanity.

Noh Traditional Japanese stylized musical drama of up to five characters, each of whom carries a fan. The Shite, or main character, wears a mask. The Waki acts as the antagonist to the Shite, while the Hayishi (musician) plays the transverse flute, hip drum, shoulder drum, and stick drum. There are a number of moods or narrative types: the Kami mono (or *waki no*), a mythic story of a shrine, featuring the human in the first act and a deity in the second; the Shura mono (or *ashura no*), a warrior play with the Shite as a ghost in the first act and a warrior reenacting his death in the second; the Katsura mono (or *onna mono*), stories of women, featuring refined song and dance; a miscellaneous category comprising plays dealing with madness (*Kyōran mono*), vengeful ghosts (*Onryō mono*)—both common themes—or those set in the present (*Genzai mono*); and the Kiri no (or *ono mono*), stories of demons, goblins, or monsters featuring bright colors and fast-paced, tense finales. One of the most famous Noh Shakespeare productions is the Ryutopia Noh Theatre's *Hamlet* in Niigata (dir. Yoshihiro Kurita, 2007).

onnagata Male actors who specialize in female roles in the all-male Kabuki theatre, which is distinct from the western concept of cross-dressing. It represents a masculine, stylized construct of women that is not based on verisimilitude. Renowned *onnagata* actor Bandō Tamasaburō says, in the documentary film *Das geschriebene Gesicht (The Written Face*, dir. Daniel Schmid, Euro Space, Switzerland, 1995), that he acts a woman "with the eyes and feelings of a man, like a man painting the portrait of a woman." As his "masculine instinct evolves, . . . patterns of womanliness take shape" in his stage representations of women.

p'ansori A form of Korean opera or narrative song. It is performed by a singer with a fan in hand and a drummer with a double-headed barrel drum. *P'an* refers to open space, and *sori* refers to singing. There is a great deal of improvised interaction between the singer and the drummer. It was originally performed in marketplaces, public squares, and open-air venues.

polyphony Multiple, equally valid, voices in an artwork that are not subordinated to the singular voice of the author. A plurality of unmerged consciousness and voices, polyphony is one of the key concepts of structuralism and in Mikhail Bakhtin's criticism of Fyodor Dostoevsky's novels.

post-gender casting The practice of casting without emphasizing the performer's gender in regard to the character as written. Distinct from cross-gender casting or transgender performance, which emphasizes the dissonance between performer and the character, post-gender casting considers a character beyond the constraints of biology or social convention.

reparative criticism A mode of literary criticism that is invested in the remedial and reparative function of literary works, with the assumption that literature has a moral and social function to make its reader more ethical and improve its reader's social circumstances.

samurai films A Japanese period film genre with violent characters who often engage in sword-fighting sequences. These epics are often set in the Tokugawa era (1603–1868; aka Edo period). Akira Kurosawa's films are well known for their portrayals of psychologically scarred warriors, with stylized action and death scenes.

Sengoku jidai The Warring States period, 1467–1600, in Japan, and the setting of Akira Kurosawa's film adaptation of *Macbeth*, *The Throne of Blood*. The period is marked by militarism, civil wars, and the rise of powerful *shōguns* who are the hereditary commanders-in-chief. Marginalized to a ceremonial figure, the Japanese Emperor delegated power to the *shōguns* during this time.

shamanism, Korean A folk religion that thrives in twenty-first-century urban and rural Korea. Mostly female, *mudang*s or shamans in Korean folklore and religious practice serve as intercessors between the world of the living and the spirits through prayers, rituals, or a technique of ecstasy. An important distinction is that shamans, being intermediaries, do not use sorcery and thus are not direct parallels to western witches. Korean shamanism combines elements from **Buddhism** and Taoism.

shinbutsu shūgō The primary organized religion until the Meiji era in Japan and an amalgamation of the native *kami* (spirits) worship and Buddhist rituals. As a result of the fusion, Buddhist temples are often attached to local Shinto shrines.

shingeki A modern form of Japanese theatre developed by Kabuki actors and in opposition to the stylized, all-male **Kabuki** theatre. It has a close relationship with the development of China's *huaju* theatre. The first *shingeki* plays were adaptations of Shakespeare, followed by new Japanese works. Drawing on European naturalism and symbolism, *shingeki* played a key role in revitalizing the theatre scene in Japan after World War II. Ninagawa Yukio, a major Shakespearean director, is one of the key figures of *shingeki*.

shingŭk A term that was coined in the 1910s for a modern form of theatre in South Korea. It typically refers to modern Korean-language plays written under the influence of Beckett, Shaw, Ibsen, and other Western European models. It also refers to classical western plays in Korean translation performed as "high theatre" based on theatrical naturalism or Stanislavskian psychological realism on a proscenium stage. Like the birth of *huaju* in China and *shingeki* in Japan, *shingŭk* in South Korea is tied to modernity, nationalism, and the appropriation of western values such as democracy and individualism.

shinpa The shortened version of *shinpageki*, or new school drama. The typically melodramatic, "modernized" plays fuse flamboyant **Kabuki** styles with realistic dialogues in the vernacular. *Shinpa* plays dramatize contemporary domestic life and are often based on adaptations of western classics such as Shakespeare.

Sinophone Pertaining to the polyphonic cultural sphere of Sino-Tibetan languages and cultures. As opposed to the term "Chinese-speaking," the Sinophone realm refers to cultures that are in dialogue with one another beyond nationalist contexts and sometimes circumvent the idea of a Chinese homeland altogether. The Sinophone world includes communities that are connected to or are resisting various forms of dominant Sinocentric ideologies through cultural production in Cantonese, Tibetan, Hakka, and Southern Min in China, Singapore, Hong Kong, Taiwan, Tibet, and elsewhere.

structuralism A method of literary and cultural criticism that focuses on charting nonapparent conventions and rules governing how particular systems function synchronically. It views human languages, cultures, literary works, and cultural products as systems, and the methodology concerns itself with examining the relationships within and between systems.

t'alch'um Korean mask dance drama focusing on ritual dances, exorcism, parody of social ills, and critique of class privilege. *T'alch'um* satirizes apostate Buddhist monks, decadent officials, and corrupt shamans. The genre includes visually striking creatures such as birds with lions' heads (*juji*) and water spirits with seaweed over their bodies (*jangjamari*).

transsexuality A state of gender with a self-identification that is distinct from prevailing cultural norms for one's sex assigned at birth. As a capacious term, transsexuality can denote a transitory state, a final destination for medical transition, or any number of combinations of identities along the trans spectrum. Each individual identifies differently, ranging from binary to fluid.

wuxia Martial knight-errant epic period films. *Wu* denotes martial arts, and *xia* refers to sword-wielding knights. This genre is distinct from *kung fu* films, which emphasize the hero's fist-fighting skills. *Wuxia* films often harbor nationalist sentiments.

xiqu A stylized Chinese theatre form that often includes operatic elements of dance, songs, acrobatics, and metonymy. More than 360 regional variations of this genre exist in many dialects ranging from Mandarin, Cantonese, and Southern Min to Suzhou dialect and Shanghainese.

Further Reading

Twenty-first-century scholarship is the focus here. Some of the best places to start to explore global Shakespeares are digital archives, book series, and journals dedicated to the subject, including the *MIT Global Shakespeares* (ed. Peter S. Donaldson and Alexa Alice Joubin), an open-access video and performance archive (globalshakespeares.mit.edu/) with study modules on individual plays in global contexts (globalshakespeares.mit.edu/study-modules/), peer-reviewed essays, interviews, scripts, and more; the British Black and Asian Shakespeare database which does not contain performance videos (University of Warwick, bbashakespeare.warwick.ac.uk/); *Borrowers and Lenders: The Journal of Shakespeare and Appropriation* (ed. Sujata Iyengar, Matt Kozusko, and Louise Geddes, University of Georgia), such as the special issue on "Global Shakespeares in World Markets and Archives" (ed. Alexa Alice Joubin), 11.1 (2017, www.borrowers.uga.edu/7167/toc); *The Shakespearean International Yearbook* (ed. Tom Bishop and Alexa Alice Joubin, Routledge); *Multicultural Shakespeare* (ed. Yoshiko Kawachi and Krystyna Kujawinska Courtney, University of Łódź); Bloomsbury series on Global Shakespeare Inverted (ed. Silvia Bigliazzi, David Schalkwyk, and Bi-qi Beatrice Lei); and the Palgrave Macmillan series on Global Shakespeares (ed. Alexa Alice Joubin). Useful digital textual resources include the *Palgrave Encyclopedia of Global Shakespeare* (ed. Alexa Alice Joubin, Ema Vyroubalová, and Elizabeth A. Pentland, meteor.springer.com/globalshakespeare) and the *World Shakespeare Bibliography* (ed. Laura Estill and Heidi Craig, www.worldshakesbib.org/), which is a digital record of Shakespeare scholarship and theatre productions worldwide from 1960 to the present.

In terms of comparative studies of Shakespeare and the region of East Asia, the following essays and edited books are helpful readings: a special issue on "Asian Shakespeares on Screen: Two Films in Perspective," *Borrowers and Lenders: The Journal of Shakespeare and Appropriation* 4.2 (2009, ed. Alexa Alice Joubin, www.borrowers.uga.edu/7158/toc); "Intercultural Theatre and Shakespeare Productions in Asia," coauthored by Shormishtha Panja, Suematsu Michiko, Alexa Alice Joubin, and Yong Li Lan, in *Routledge Handbook of Asian Theatre* (ed. Siyuan Liu, Routledge, 2016), 504–26; *Shakespeare in Asia: Contemporary Performance* (ed. Dennis Kennedy and Yong Li Lan, Cambridge University Press, 2010); *Re-playing Shakespeare in Asia* (ed. Poonam Trivedi and Minaim Ryuta, Routledge, 2010); and chapters 10–12 of *Shakespeare and Asia* (ed. Jonathan Locke Hart, Routledge, 2019). Examining the cultural exchange between Britain, China, and Japan primarily in the early modern period, Adele Lee's *The English Renaissance and the Far East* (Fairleigh Dickinson University Press, 2018) offers one chapter each on Chinese and Japanese appropriations of Shakespeare (chapters 4 and 5). On a related topic is *Shakespeare in East Asian Education* (ed. Sarah Olive, Uchimaru Kohei, Adele Lee, and Rosalind Fielding, forthcoming from Palgrave), the Global Shakespeares series ed. Alexa Alice Joubin. The bulk of scholarship on this topic exists in the form of essays.

A number of digital video archives are useful for research and classroom use, including *Shakespeare Performance in Asia* (ed. Peter S. Donaldson and Alexa Alice Joubin), which is part of the MIT Global Shakespeares archive (web.mit. edu/shakespeare/asia/); and Asian Shakespeare Intercultural Archive (ed. Yong Li Lan, Suematsu Michiko, Kobayashi Kaori, and Lee Hyon-u), a-s-i-a-web.org/.

For an Irish director's perspective on Ninagawa, see Conor Nanratty's *Shakespeare in the Theatre: Yukio Ninagawa* (Arden Bloomsbury, 2020). Recent English-language publications on Shakespeare and Japanese film and theatre include the wide-ranging collection edited by Ryuta Minami, Ian Carruthers, and John Gillies, *Performing Shakespeare in Japan* (Cambridge University Press, 2001); Tetsuo Kishi and Graham Bradshaw, *Shakespeare in Japan* (Continuum, 2005); Michiko Suematsu, "Verbal and Visual Representations in Modern Japanese Shakespeare Productions," *The Oxford Handbook of Shakespeare and Performance* (ed. James C. Bulman, Oxford University Press, 2017), 584–98; Robert Tierney, "*Othello* in Tokyo: Performing Race and Empire in 1903 Japan," *Shakespeare Quarterly* 62.4 (2011): 514–40; Shoichiro Kawai, "Kabuki *Twelfth Night* and *Kyogen Richard III*: Shakespeare as a Cultural Catalyst," *Shakespeare Survey 64*, ed. Peter Holland (Cambridge University Press, 2011); Mark Thornton Burnett, "Akira Kurosawa," in *Welles, Kozintsev, Kurosawa, Zeffirelli*, Great Shakespeareans 17 (Bloomsbury, 2015), 54–91; James Brandon, "Some Shakespeare(s) in Some Asia(s)," *Asian Studies Review* 20 (1997): 1–26; Kawachi Yoshiko, "Shakespeare's Long Journey to Japan," *Shakespeare's Asian Journeys* (ed. Bi-qi Beatrice Lei, Judy Celine Ick, and Poonam Trivedi, Routledge, 2017), 37–55; and Daniel Gallimore, *Sounding Like Shakespeare: A Study of Prosody in Four Japanese Translations of* A Midsummer Night's Dream (Kwansei Gakuin University Press, 2012). One of the key studies of Kurosawa as a filmmaker is Stephen Prince's *The Warrior's Camera: The Cinema of Akira Kurosawa*, rev. and exp. ed. (Princeton University Press, 1999). In terms of theatre, Jonah Salz provides a comprehensive survey in his edited volume, *A History of Japanese Theatre* (Cambridge University Press, 2018). For a more focused account of modern Japanese theatre, see *Modern Japanese Theatre and Performance*, ed.

David Jortner, Keiko I. McDonald, and Kevin J. Wetmore, Jr. (Lexington, 2006). A good read on film history is Yomota Inuhiko's *What Is Japanese Cinema? A History* (Columbia University Press, 2019), which has been translated by Philip Kaffen, and a good reference book is *The Oxford Handbook of Japanese Cinema* (ed. Daisuke Miyao, Oxford University Press, 2014).

Local and touring South Korean theatre productions are the focus of *Glocalizing Shakespeare in Korea and Beyond* (ed. Lee Hyon-u, Dongin Publishing, 2009). Adele Lee examines a key South Korean film in "The Player King and Kingly Players: Inverting *Hamlet* in Lee Joon-ik's *King and the Clown* (2005)," *Borrowers and Lenders: The Journal of Shakespeare and Appropriation* 12.1 (2018, www.borrowers.uga.edu/784121/show); and the following essays touch on various aspects of Korean stage productions: Daeyeong (Dan) Kim, "Shakespeare and Korea: Mutual Remappings," *Textual Distortion* (ed. Elaine Treharne and Greg Walker, Boydell and Brewer, 2017), 72–84; Hyunjung Lee, "Conceptualizing Korean Shakespeare in the Era of Globalization," *Performing the Nation in Global Korea: Transnational Theatre* (Palgrave, 2015), 93–126; and Kim Moran, "The Stages 'Occupied by Shakespeare': Intercultural Performances and the Search for 'Korean-ness' in Postcolonial Korea," in *Re-playing Shakespeare in Asia* (ed. Poonam Trivedi and Ryuta Minami, Routledge, 2010), 200–20. A number of useful references for Korean film studies are *Rediscovering Korean Cinema* (ed. Sangjoon Lee, University of Michigan Press, 2019); Kyung Hyun Kim, *Virtual Hallyu: Korean Cinema of the Global Era* (Duke University Press, 2011), a study of South Korean cinema since the late 1990s; and *The Remasculinization of Korean Cinema*, also by Kim (Duke University Press, 2004). *Modern Korean Drama*, an anthology edited by Richard Nichols (Columbia University Press, 2009), samples fantastical and realistic works by key playwrights including Oh Tae-suk (whose Shakespeare adaptations are discussed in Chapter 3 of this book).

The latest engagement with Shakespeare and China and the Sinophone world is the special issue on "Tang Xianzu and William Shakespeare, Quatercentenary Celebration," edited by Alexa Alice Joubin for the *Asian Theatre Journal* 36.2 (2019): 275–348, which contains four essays on the cultural politics of commemorating Tang and Shakespeare in Britain, China, Hong Kong, and Taiwan. Joubin deconstructs the myth of Sinophone Shakespeare in "2011, June 26: Encountering Shakespeare's Plays in the Sinophone World," *A New Literary History of Modern China* (ed. David Der-wei Wang, Harvard University Press, 2017), 924–30. Wei Feng's *Intercultural Aesthetics in Traditional Chinese Theatre: From 1978 to the Present* (Palgrave, 2020) considers *xiqu* adaptations of Shakespeare, Brecht, and Beckett, and Iris H. Tuan's *Translocal Performance in Asian Theatre and Film* (Palgrave, 2018) has a chapter on Wu Hsing-kuo's *A Midsummer Night's Dream* and

Ninagawa's *Hamlet* in Taiwan. Shakespeare on stage and in the educational system of Hong Kong is the focus of *Shakespeare Global/Local: The Hong Kong Imaginary in Transcultural Production* (ed. Kwok-kan Tam, Andrew Parkin, and Terry Siu-han Yip, Frankfurt/Main: Peter Lang, 2002). Li Ruru offers an updated account of Shakespeare in the People's Republic of China (excluding Hong Kong, Tibet, and Taiwan) in "'There Is a World Elsewhere': Shakespeare on the Chinese Stage," *The Oxford Handbook of Shakespeare and Performance* (ed. James C. Bulman, Oxford University Press, 2017), 599–618, and Adele Lee critiques cinematic adaptations of Shakespeare in Hong Kong in "'Chop-Socky Shakespeare'?! The Bard Onscreen in Hong Kong," *Shakespeare Bulletin* 28.4 (2010): 459–79. A useful resource is the online study module, designed by Alexa Alice Joubin and Peter S. Donaldson, with a full performance video of Wu Hsing-kuo's solo Beijing opera *Lear Is Here*, which is part of the *MIT Global Shakespeares*, globalshakespeares.mit.edu/modules/module/lear-is-here/. Another resource is the *Taiwan Shakespeare Database*, which is based at the National Taiwan University, shakespeare.digital.ntu.edu.tw/shakespeare/. Last, but not least, here are two of the latest books on transnational Sinophone theatre and cinemas: Rossella Ferrari's *Transnational Chinese Theatres: Intercultural Performance Networks in East Asia* (Palgrave, 2020) and *The Oxford Handbook of Chinese Cinemas* (ed. Carlos Rojas and Eileen Chow, Oxford University Press, 2019).

One of the key readings on Singaporean theatre is William Peterson's *Theatre and the Politics of Culture in Contemporary Singapore* (Wesleyan University Press, 2001), and a good place to start to learn more about the city-state's film culture is *Singapore Cinema: New Perspectives* (ed. Kai Khiun Liew and Stephen Teo, Routledge, 2017). Philip Smith's *Shakespeare in Singapore: Performance, Education, and Culture* (Routledge, 2020) considers primarily Shakespeare in education, with brief analyses of select performances and the film *Chicken Rice War*. Marcus Tan uses Ong Keng Sen's adaptations of Shakespeare as part of the case studies in *Acoustic Interculturalism: Listening to Performance* (Palgrave, 2012). Yong Li Lan examines Ong's adaptation of *Othello* in "Ong Keng Sen's *Desdemona*, Ugliness, and the Intercultural Performative," *Theatre Journal* 56.2 (2004): 251–73.

The following essays, monographs, and collections address broader methodological questions: Mark Thornton Burnett, "Introduction," Hamlet *and World Cinema* (Cambridge University Press, 2019), 1–22; Atom Egoyan and Ian Balfour, eds., *Subtitles: On the Foreignness of Film* (MIT Press, 2004); *The Routledge Handbook of Shakespeare and Global Appropriation* (ed. Christy Desmet, Sujata Iyengar, and Miriam Jacobson, Routledge, 2020), including the coeditors' introduction (1–12) and the chapter on "Others Within: Ethics in the Age of Global Shakespeare" by Alexa Alice Joubin (25–36); *The Oxford*

Handbook of Shakespeare and Performance (ed. James C. Bulman, Oxford University Press, 2017), especially the essays in part 4, "Global Shakespeare," by Dennis Kennedy ("Global Shakespeare and Globalized Performance"), Sonia Massai ("Shakespeare with and without Its Language"), and Alexa Alice Joubin ("Global Shakespeare Criticism beyond the Nation State"); Alexa Alice Joubin, "Boomerang Shakespeare: Foreign Shakespeare in Britain," *The Cambridge Guide to the Worlds of Shakespeare Vol. 2: The World's Shakespeare, 1660–Present* (ed. Bruce Smith, Cambridge University Press, 2016), 1094–1101; *Race* by Alexa Alice Joubin and Martin Orkin, New Critical Idiom series (Routledge, 2019); *Local and Global Myths in Shakespearean Performance* (ed. Alexa Alice Joubin and Aneta Manncewicz, Palgrave, 2018); *Shakespeare and the Ethics of Appropriation* (ed. Alexa Alice Joubin and Elizabeth Rivlin, Palgrave, 2014); Rustom Bharucha, "Foreign Asia/Foreign Shakespeare: Dissenting Notes on New Asian Interculturality, Postcoloniality and Re-colonization," *Shakespeare in Asia* (ed. Kennedy and Yong), 253–82; *World-Wide Shakespeares: Local Appropriations in Film and Performance* (ed. Sonia Massai, Routledge, 2006); Linda Hutcheon, *A Theory of Adaptation* (Routledge, 2006); and Martin Orkin, *Local Shakespeares: Proximations and Power* (Routlegde, 2005).

A Chronology of Shakespeare and East Asia

Year	Historical events	Shakespeare on stage and screen
1609	Dutch East India Company imports first tea from China	
1616	Death of William Shakespeare, Tang Xianzu, and Miguel de Cervantes	
1619		*Hamlet* reportedly performed by employees of the Dutch East Indies Company in Jayakerta, Indonesia
1624	Taiwan colonized by the Dutch, 1624–1662	The Curtain Theatre in Shoreditch, London, closes
1807	The Slave Trade Act abolishes the slave trade in most of the British Empire.	Charles and Mary Lamb's *Tales from Shakespeare*
1824	The Anglo-Dutch treaty cedes Malaya and Singapore to Britain	
1839	Opium Wars begin (1839–1842)	First mention of Shakespeare in Chinese by Lin Zexu in *Annals of the Four Continents*, who attempts to stop the opium trade
1842	China cedes Hong Kong to Britain for 150 years (Treaty of Tianjin)	First mention of Shakespeare in Japanese (1841 translation of a Dutch translation of an English grammar book)
1859		Birth of Tsubouchi Shoyo, pioneer of Shakespeare studies and translation in Japan
1868	Meiji Restoration begins Japan's era of modernization, westernization, linguistic and cultural reform	Public reading of excerpts from *A Midsummer Night's Dream* and *Romeo and Juliet* in Yokohama, in 1866 and 1869
1877		First Japanese translation of the Lambs' *Tales from Shakespeare* Shakespeare introduced into university curriculum in China
1879		Guo Songtao, China's first Minister to England, attends Henry Irving's *Hamlet* Scenes from *The Taming of the Shrew* performed in English in the Gaiety Theatre in Yokohama

Continued

Year	Historical events	Shakespeare on stage and screen
1882		Shakespeare introduced into Hong Kong's school curriculum
1895	China cedes Taiwan and Penghu to Japan for 50 years	
1898	Britain granted a ninety-nine-year lease of the New Territories (Hong Kong)	
1903		Kawakami Otojiro's *Othello* recasts Taiwan as the outpost of the colonial Japanese empire; adapted by Lu Jingruo as *Spring Dreams* in 1915
1904		Lin Shu and Wei Yi, trans. the Lambs' *Tales from Shakespeare* into Chinese
1905	Japan–Korea Treaty. Korea became the protectorate of Imperial Japan	
1909		Kawakami Otojiro's *Hamlet* performed in Korea by a Japanese *shinpa* theatre company
1910	The Japan–Korea Treaty starts the annexation of the Korean Empire by Imperial Japan	
1913		First Chinese-language *huaju* performance of Shakespeare: Shanghai Eastern Girls' High School's *Woman Lawyer* (adapted from *The Merchant of Venice* by Bao Tianxiao) Hong Kong Mummers stages *Twelfth Night*
1914		First Chinese opera performance of Shakespeare: Ya'an *Chuanju* Theatre's *Hamlet*
1919	Declaration of Korean Independence May Fourth movement begins in China	*The Tempest* from the Lambs' *Tales from Shakespeare* translated into Korean
1925		First Korean-language production of Shakespeare (*Julius Caesar*, by Kyungsong vocational school)
1927	Chinese civil war begins	First Chinese cinematic Shakespeare: *The Woman Lawyer* (*Merchant of Venice*), dir. Qiu Yixiang, silent film

1928		Tsubouchi Shōyō completes his Japanese translation of the *Complete Works*
1931	Japan invades Manchuria	Bu Wancang's silent film adaptation of *The Two Gentlemen from Verona* (*A Spray of Plum Blossom*, Lianhua Film Co., Shanghai)
1941	Holocaust begins Pearl Harbor raid Japanese occupation of Hong Kong begins	Novelist Dazai Osamu's anti-militarist rewriting of *Hamlet* (*Shin Hamuretto*)
1942	The British surrenders and the Japanese Occupation of Singapore begins	*Hamlet*, dir. Jiao Juyin, is staged in a Confucian Temple in Jiang'an, China
1945	End of Japanese colonization of Taiwan End of Japanese occupation of Hong Kong Korean peninsula divided between Soviet and American occupation forces at the 38th parallel	*The Hero of a Tumultuous Time* (*Macbeth*), dir. Huang Zuolin, Shanghai
1949	The People's Republic of China founded The nationalists, led by Chiang Kai-shek, retreat to Taiwan	Sol Jun-Sik publishes the first Korean translation of *Hamlet* directly from the English text First Mandarin performance of Shakespeare in Taiwan: *Clouds of Doubt* (*Othello*) staged by the Experimental Theatre of Taipei
1954	Mutual defense treaty between the USA and Taiwan	Shakespeare festival in Hong Kong, April 23
1957	Sir William Goode appointed as the Governor of the Singapore	*Throne of Blood* (film adaptation of *Macbeth*), dir. Akira Kurosawa, Japan *West Side Story* (*Romeo and Juliet*), dir. Jerome Robbins, original Broadway production
1958	Mao Zedong launches the Great Leap Forward	Laurence Olivier's *Hamlet* screened in China
1960		*The Bad Sleeps Well* (film adaptation of *Hamlet*), dir. Akira Kurosawa, Japan
1961	Showa Genroku—period of rapid economic growth in Japan	Shakespeare Society of Japan established
1962	Singapore merged with Malaysia	
1963		The Shakespeare Association of Korea established

Continued

Year	Historical events	Shakespeare on stage and screen
1964	The Olympics held in Tokyo	Shakespeare Theatre Festival, Seoul
1965	The Malaysian Parliament votes to expel Singapore from the Federation; Singapore becomes independent	*Crocodile River* (*Ngoh yu ho*, dir. Lo Wei, 1965), a Hong Kong film shot in Bangkok (spin-off of *Romeo and Juliet*)
1970		Royal Shakespeare Company tours to Tokyo for the first time with *The Merry Wives of Windsor* and *The Winter's Tale*
1971	The United Nations General Assembly voted to admit the People's Republic of China and to expel Taiwan	
1974		Ninagawa Yukio's debut Shakespeare production, *Romeo and Juliet*
1978	Deng Xiaoping announces the open door policy	*Young Lovers*, dir. Michihiko Obimori, Shaw Brothers, Hong Kong (*Romeo and Juliet*)
1980	Gwangju massacre; martial law declared in South Korea Japan became the biggest motor-vehicle-producing country in the world	Premiere of Ninagawa's "cherry blossom" *Macbeth* in Tokyo (tours throughout the world in the following decades)
1983	Arthur Miller visits China	*Othello*, dir. Ma Yong'an, performed in black face by Ma, Beijing Experimental *Jingju* Theatre Mandarin–English bilingual *A Midsummer Night's Dream*, dir. Tisa Chang, Pan Asian Repertory Theater, New York
1984	Sino–British Joint Declaration, Hong Kong	Shakespeare festival in Hong Kong Shakespeare Society of China founded
1985	International Exposition, Tsukuba, Japan	*Ran* (film adaptation of *King Lear*), dir. Kurosawa, Japan John R. Briggs's Asian-American production *Shogun Macbeth*, New York Ong Keng Sen founds TheatreWorks in Singapore
1986	Nuclear disaster at Chernobyl	Wu Hsing-kuo and his wife Lin Hsiu-wei found the Contemporary Legend Theatre in Taiwan and stage *Kingdom of Desire*, a Beijing opera adaptation of *Macbeth* First Shakespeare festival in China (Beijing and Shanghai, April 10–23)

1987	Taiwan's martial law is lifted First free and fair direct presidential election in South Korean history	*Kunju Macbeth* (*Story of Bloody Hands*), dir. Huang Zuolin for Shanghai Kunqu Theatre, tours Edinburgh, London, and other European cities
1988	The Olympics held in Seoul	*One Husband Too Many* (*Romeo and Juliet*), dir. Anthony Chan (film, Hong Kong) Sergei Yutkevich's *Othello* (USSR, 1956) screened in China
1989	Tiananmen Square massacre Fall of the Berlin Wall	*Hamlet*, dir. Lin Zhaohua, Beijing People's Art Theatre
1991	Collapse of the Communist bloc in Europe North Korea (DPRK) and South Korea (ROK) join the United Nations (UN)	The Fifth World Shakespeare Congress held in Tokyo
1992	Chris Patten becomes last British governor of Hong Kong, overseeing the colony's handover to China	*King Lear*, dir. Suzuki Tadashi (SCOT) *Shamlet*, dir. Lee Kuo-hsiu, Pingfeng Acting Workshop, Taipei (a parody of *Hamlet*); revived in 1995, tours Shanghai in 1994 and Toronto in 1996; re-staged in Taipei in 2000, 2006, 2007; Beijing in 2008
1993		*The Comedy of Errors*, dir. Ian Judge, Royal Shakespeare Company, Taipei International Drama Festival
1994	Anti-Harassment March in Taipei, with feminist activist Ho Chun-rui's slogan "Yes to orgasm, no to sexual harassment"	Second Shakespeare festival in Shanghai, China *A Midsummer Night's Dream*, dir. Ninagawa Yukio, Tokyo
1997	Britain returns Hong Kong to Chinese jurisdiction Globe Theatre opens in London	*Kiss Me Nana*, dir. Liang Chi-min, Godot Theatre, Taipei; revived in 1999 Pan-Asian multilingual *Lear*, dir. Ong Keng Sen (Singapore, Hong Kong, Tokyo)
1999	Shakespeare voted Writer of the Millennium, BBC News	*King Lear*, dir. Ninagawa Yukio, Tokyo, London, Stratford
2000	Chinese-French playwright, painter, and novelist Gao Xingjian awarded the Nobel Prize of Literature	Hong Kong Experimental Shakespeare festival *Chicken Rice War* [*Jiyuan qiaohe*], dir. Cheah Chee Kong (Singaporean film) *Hamlet*, dir. Michael Almereyda,

Continued

Year	Historical events	Shakespeare on stage and screen
		double A Films, with references to Buddhism and Tibetan culture *Desdemona*, dir. Ong Keng Sen (TheatreWorks, Singapore)
2001	"9/11" attacks	*Richard III*, dir. Lin Zhaohua (Beijing People's Art Theatre), Berlin Asia Pacific Cultural Festival *Romeo and Juliet*, dir. Oh Tae-suk, Bremen, Germany *King Uru* by Myunggon Kim (*King Lear*), Korean National Theatre
2002	Massive demonstration in Hong Kong against the legislation of the Hong Kong Basic Law Article 23 which erodes the freedom of speech FIFA World Cup jointly held by South Korea and Japan	*Search: Hamlet*, dir. Ong Keng Sen, Kronborg Castle, Denmark *A Dream in Hanoi*, dir. Tom Weidlinger, documentary film
2003	SARS outbreak	Shakespeare in Taipei Festival
2005	Beijing's National Grand Theatre of China opens (designed by Paul Andreu) Opening of Hong Kong Disneyland	*The King and the Clown*, dir. by Lee Joon-ik (South Korea) Shanghai *Jingju* Company's *Hamlet* performed at Denmark's Hamlet Sommer festival
2006	China surpasses the United States in carbon dioxide emissions	*As You Like It*, Japanesque film dir. Kenneth Branagh *The Banquet* (*Hamlet*), dir. Feng Xiaogang (feature film in Mandarin) *Prince of the Himalayas* (*Hamlet*), dir. Hu Xuehua (feature film in Tibetan) *Romeo and Juliet*, dir. Oh Tae-suk, Mokhwa Repertory Company (Korea) tours to London Chinese-English bilingual *King Lear* (dir. David Tse), Stratford-upon-Avon
2007	Taiwan applied for membership in the United Nations and is rejected by the General Assembly	Wu Hsing-kuo's *Lear Is Here* staged at the Lincoln Center Festival in New York and in San Jose, California
2008	The Olympic Games held in Beijing The first direct China-Taiwan flights after nearly 60 years	*Frivolous Wife* (*Nallari Jongbujeon*, dir. Lim Won-kook, Lotte Entertainment, South Korea), based on *The Taming of the Shrew*

2009	The former Taiwanese president Chen Shui-Bian and his wife convicted in Taiwan for bribery, embezzlement and money laundering.	Taiwan *Yu* Opera's *The Bond* (based on *The Merchant of Venice*) tours to the Fourth British Shakespeare Association (BSA) conference in London. Co-written by Perng Ching-hsi and Chen Fang.
2010	G-20 Summit held in Seoul, South Korea	*Throne of Blood*, dir. Ping Chong, Oregon Shakespeare Festival *Zhuliye [Juliet]*, film directed by Chen Yu-Hsun, Hou Chi-jan, and Shen Ko-shang (Zeus International Production), Taiwan
2011	Tōhoku earthquake and tsunami, followed by the Fukushima Daiichi nuclear disaster	Oh Tae-suk's *The Tempest* and Wu Hsing-kuo's *Lear Is Here* tour to Edinburgh International Festival
2012	World Shakespeare Festival and Summer Olympics held in London Shakespeare's works featured prominently in the opening and closing ceremonies of the London Olympics	*Titus 2.0* in Cantonese (dir. Tang Shu-wing, Hong Kong), Chiten Company's *Coriolanus* in Japanese, *A Midsummer Night's Dream*, dir. Yang Jung-ung, Yohangza Theatre Company (South Korea), and *Richard III*, dir. Wang Xiaoying, National Theatre of China tour to the Globe Theatre in London Taiwan Shakespeare Association founded
2013	PRC launches the "One Belt, One Road" initiative	*Stoker*, dir. Chan-wook Park (Fox Searchlight) Asian Shakespeare Association founded in Tokyo
2014	Umbrella Revolution in Hong Kong Sunflower Student Movement in Taiwan China overtakes Japan to become the world's second-largest economy	World-wide celebrations of the 450th anniversary of Shakespeare's birthday Asian Shakespeare Association's inaugural conference held in Taipei Royal Shakespeare Company announcesd a £1.5m government-backed initiative to commission a new Mandarin translation of the *Complete Works* Dominic Dromgoole's Globe production of *Hamlet* tour to more than 200 countries and territories (2014–2016)
2015	Oregon Shakespeare Festival commissions projects to translate the plays into modern English	*The Treacherous* (*Gansin*, dir. Min Kyu-dong, Lotte Entertainment, South Korea) alludes to *Hamlet* The British Council, National

Continued

Year	Historical events	Shakespeare on stage and screen
		Museum of Taiwan Literature, and The Shakespeare Birthplace Trust present "All the World's a Stage: Shakespeare in Taiwan Exhibition" in Taipei, 2015–2016
2016	South Korean President Park Geun-hye impeached	Worldwide commemoration of the 400th anniversary of Shakespeare's and Tang Xianzu's deaths Ninagawa passes away Desdemona Chiang's Asian-American *Winter's Tale*, Oregon Shakespeare Festival
2017	Halimah Yacob elected as the first female president of Singapore	
2018	Tourist boom in Japan: 31.19 million in this year	Revival of Ninagawa's "cherry blossom" *Macbeth* at Lincoln Center, New York
2019	Protests in Hong Kong against a proposed law allowing extraditions to China in Hong Kong Emperor Akihito abdicated; the first Japanese emperor to do so since 1817	*Parasite*, dir. Bong Joon Ho (Barunson E&A), wins four Oscars in 2020 for directing, screenplay, Best Picture, and Best International Feature Film Replica of Shakespeare's birthplace built in China; a "peony pavilion" erected in Stratford-upon-Avon
2020	In an attempt to curb the outbreak of the pandemic of COVID-19, the Chinese government orders a lockdown of Wuhan, a city of 11 million, two days before Chinese New Year, on January 23, 2020. The World Health Organization declares the outbreak a pandemic in March	Performance venues and film and theatre festivals shut down, along with any large gatherings, across the world; global travels disrupted Due to "cast indisposition," *The Taming of the Shrew* (dir. Maria Gaitanidi) at the London Globe cancelled on March 3. Later that month, all performances in the Globe Theatre and Sam Wanamaker Playhouse cancelled due to the coronavirus.

Index